BALANCHINE'S APPRENTICE

UNIVERSITY PRESS OF FLORIDA

Florida A&M University, Tallahassee
Florida Atlantic University, Boca Raton
Florida Gulf Coast University, Ft. Myers
Florida International University, Miami
Florida State University, Tallahassee
New College of Florida, Sarasota
University of Central Florida, Orlando
University of Florida, Gainesville
University of North Florida, Jacksonville
University of South Florida, Tampa
University of West Florida, Pensacola

BALANCHINE'S
Apprentice

≧≡≤

From Hollywood to New York and Back

JOHN CLIFFORD

University Press of Florida

GAINESVILLE · TALLAHASSEE · TAMPA · BOCA RATON

PENSACOLA · ORLANDO · MIAMI · JACKSONVILLE · FT. MYERS · SARASOTA

26 25 24 23 22 21   6 5 4 3 2 1

ISBN 978-0-8130-6900-5
Library of Congress Control Number: 2021930643

The University Press of Florida is the scholarly publishing agency for the State University System
of Florida, comprising Florida A&M University, Florida Atlantic University, Florida Gulf Coast
University, Florida International University, Florida State University, New College of Florida,
University of Central Florida, University of Florida, University of North Florida, University of
South Florida, and University of West Florida.

University Press of Florida
2046 NE Waldo Road
Suite 2100
Gainesville, FL 32609
http://upress.ufl.edu

As Twyla Tharp so succinctly put it,
GEORGE BALANCHINE IS GOD.

CONTENTS

PREFACE

George Balanchine died on April 30, 1983. Even writing this today, thirty-seven years later, I still feel a great sadness and loss. He had entered Roosevelt Hospital in November 1982, after months of seriously declining health, so we knew that his end was near. For some time he had been losing his balance and eyesight, displaying a loss of memory, and was uncharacteristically short-tempered. These problems were first thought to be complications from his heart attack and coronary bypass surgery in 1980, various eye operations, and the medication he took for his angina, but according to the autopsy report by his doctors in the *New York Times* (May 8, 1984, a year after his death), these were symptoms of the Creutzfeldt-Jakob brain disease that manifested as early as 1978 and finally took him from us.

I wrote this book to honor him and to tell why he was so important to me personally, as well as to recount the story of my life. Balanchine was not just my teacher and choreographer, not just my mentor. He was much more to me, as you shall see.

This memoir was begun in September 1985, at the suggestion of my Los Angeles Ballet music director and good friend Dr. Clyde Allen. He's a history buff, so he suggested I write down my memories, not only of my time with "Mr. B" (as all who worked for Balanchine called him) but also of my early years in show business with its truly eclectic mix of personalities.

My Los Angeles company that I founded in 1974, the Los Angeles Ballet, and its affiliate school, were forced to close their doors in 1984 because of external pressures from the Los Angeles Music Center that my board of directors could not overcome. My thirty-six dancers and over three hundred and fifty students were on their own, and so was I. It seemed a good time to start writing things down.

In the beginning, I just wanted to take the reader back in time to when I was a happy-go-lucky teenager. Later of course, with age and experience, came some reflection and understanding of my mistakes, but rather than hide I prefer to be up-front about my missteps.

Between the ages of nineteen and twenty-six, I was a dancer and choreographer with the New York City Ballet (1966–1974), and I returned several times as a guest artist until 1980. This was unusual as it was not Balanchine's habit to have guest dancers, especially men. The only exceptions I'm aware of are when he invited the Paris Opera "Étoile," Ghislaine Thesmar, for a few seasons, and Rudolph Nureyev, when he choreographed *Le Bourgeois Gentilhomme* for him in 1979, but that was for the New York City Opera and not the New York City Ballet itself. During my years at NYCB, I choreographed eight ballets for the company, danced principal and soloist roles in forty-six others, and had new ballets created on me by Balanchine, Jerome Robbins, John Taras, Jacques d'Amboise, Todd Bolender, and others. Why did this happen to me? Why was I so fortunate? There were many great male dancers in the company, many I considered to be much more talented than me. Also, why did Balanchine decide to give me carte blanche of his company and school to choreograph on? Why me?

There have been four major chapters in my career so far. The first was from my youth to the age of nineteen, when I acted and danced on television and first met George Balanchine. The second was my years with the New York City Ballet, which were great years for the company, and of course, for myself. During those seven and a half years, the New York City Ballet toured the Soviet Union, Peter Martins joined the company and Suzanne Farrell left, Jerome Robbins returned in triumph, Gelsey Kirkland shot to fame, and the 1972 Stravinsky Festival was presented, and I was part of it all.

This is considered to be a historic period for the New York City Ballet and dance in America. Balanchine had gone through a major depression after Farrell left and Robbins had returned to great acclaim (both these events happened in 1969), and many critics publicly said Balanchine should retire. He came back, however, with an incredible burst of energy and creativity, especially for the 1972 Stravinsky Festival. I was very fortunate to have been a part of that, not only as a dancer but also as a choreographer. The third chapter of my life was in some ways the most challenging. It began with my decision to leave New York City Ballet and return to my home in Los Angeles to develop a local company. This third chapter of my career ended as I began to write this book. At that time, I didn't know what would happen. It was the first time in twenty years that I did not have a clear option. I am currently in phase four as a freelance choreographer, ballet master for The George Balanchine Trust, and artistic director for another attempt at a resident company for Los Angeles, the Los Angeles Dance Theater.

I have always considered life itself as an adventure. The great ballerina of the Bolshoi Ballet, Maya Plisetskaya, once told me, "Dance is not Life. All Life is a Dance!" Looking back, I wish I had done certain things differently, but for those people who are interested in classical ballet or what it was like to work for a true genius, I hope this volume will shed light on Mr. Balanchine's humor, humanity, and work as a great teacher as well as a choreographer. I will, however, endeavor to entertain, first and foremost, because that is fundamentally what I am, and always will be—an entertainer.

PART I

1

Meeting "Mr. B."

I wasn't exactly born in a trunk, but pretty close, and being raised in Hollywood certainly had its advantages. I was born on June 12, 1947, at the Queen of Angels Hospital in Los Angeles. My parents were Robert Clifford and Betty Louise Cadwell, and they met while performing in the *Earl Carroll Vanities,* one of the last bastions of vaudeville. My father was the top half of a two-man adagio acrobatic act called "Park and Clifford," and my mother sang light opera and pop songs, like a latter-day Deanna Durbin. She was the "class act," as it was then known. It wasn't until I was thirty-two that I found out Clifford was a stage name. My family name is something completely different, Povailitis, which is the Greek spelling of a Lithuanian name. I came to understand this many years later when Vangelis, the Greek composer of the musical score for the film *Chariots of Fire,* told me that Povailitis was a common name in Greece. When I told Balanchine my real name, and that Clifford was only my father's stage name, and that I was really Greek-Lithuanian, he said, "You know, dear, I always knew!" He never missed a beat.

When they weren't touring, my parents performed at the former Moulin Rouge Theater on Sunset Boulevard, near Vine Street in Hollywood. I appeared on that stage for the first time when I was around three years old, and one of my earliest memories is seeing the audience—upside down. This was due to the fact that I was doing a headstand on my father's hand. He would often bring me out at the end of his act, throw me up into the air, and I'd land either on my two feet, being supported by one of his hands, or in a headstand. The audience always loved it, and I loved the applause. My mother had a beautiful lyric soprano voice; actually for years I thought I would be a singer instead of a dancer. With my background, I don't see how I could have been anything but a "ham." Luckily, Balanchine didn't mind it when

Top right: My mother, circa 1947. Courtesy of the author.

My father and me, circa 1950–1951. Courtesy of the author.

My birthday party at five years old with the cast of *Minsky's Follies,* circa 1952.
Courtesy of the author.

I was being a little too extroverted. He understood that it was in my
genes. I once heard him say to a dancer who was criticizing my over-
the-top performing style, "He can't help it. He's from Hollywood."

I also have early memories of touring across the United States with
my parents when I was about four. My crib was a dresser drawer in the
various hotels. Between being tossed about in my dad's act and touring
the country at that young age, it becomes obvious why I can't ever be
still. From as far back as I can remember, there was this strange thing
about me: I could not stop moving! I suppose if I were a child today,
I'd be medicated. "Hyperactive" I think covers it.

So, I expended that energy by dancing. Because I was brought up in
a basically vaudevillian environment and was always around dancers, it
seemed totally natural to me. I still remember standing in the orchestra
pit watching the show girls, and to this day I'll never forget those fishnet stockings and high heels. I saw show business as a perfectly normal
way of life and, besides, I knew no other.

My mother and father divorced when I was six years old, which I
think explains my sense of independence. I've had five different fathers
in the course of my life (maybe six, but I lost count) and, looking back,

I think the lack of a strong father figure explains part of my intense devotion to Balanchine. He became the male role model I never had as a kid. I was also lucky that at such a young age I got to see different lifestyles and religions. I was baptized Roman Catholic, my third father was Jewish, my fourth father was . . . I forget. Once, when I was around five and my parents were on tour, I was boarded with a family of Nazarenes, an evangelical Christian sect. Talk about confusing! After all these fathers and experiences with different religions, I decided that everything was subjective. No person or religion was totally right or wrong, good or bad. I suppose you'd call me an agnostic at heart. I believe in "spirit," not "religion." I also spent two years in the first and second grades in a Catholic military boarding school. The discipline I received there proved very useful to me as a professional dancer. I learned at a very young age how to take orders.

I have somehow managed to put my priorities first. This meant a daily class and not falling into the trap of so many of my contemporaries from the 1960s, namely drugs. I reserved all my excesses for my work. Adhering to form and discipline saved me from myself on more than one occasion. Don't get me wrong. I'm no saint. I tried pot a

Me in military school at six years old. Courtesy of the author.

couple of times, but that was it, never pills or anything stronger. However, considering that I came of age in the wild and open 1960s, when "free love" and recreational drugs were everywhere, it's worth noting that I never became part of that world, nor was I particularly interested. I didn't need hallucinogens. I was high enough on life.

I was around nine years old when it became clear that my dancing around the house was not a childish phase. My mother quite reluctantly went shopping for a ballet teacher (she said she wanted me to be a lawyer because I liked to argue). We were living in Hollywood at the time, and Kathryn Etienne's ballet school was quite popular and convenient. Mme. Etienne ("Ketty") was from the famous Charisse Ballet Troupe, a family of eleven dancing children who toured all over Europe in the 1930s. Before that, they were the opening act for Anna Pavlova at New York's Hippodrome. As a matter of fact, that's how Cyd Charisse got her name. Her first husband was one of Ketty's brothers, Nico Charisse. He was first her teacher, then later her husband. How very Balanchine.

I studied not only classical ballet with Mme. Etienne but also a form of Flamenco, and I even learned how to play the castanets. I loved all types of dance even then. Her students regularly performed at various ladies' clubs, and that got me onstage very early as a "ballet dancer." My first appearance was approximately two months after I started studying. I was usually a Pierrot. I was also the only boy. My regular partner was Suzanne Cupito, now known as Morgan Brittany, who was an actress on the series *Dallas* and "Baby June" in the film of *Gypsy*; she was quite a beauty even at ten years old.

During those years (late 1950s), one of the most respected and successful TV dance-makers was Tony Charmoli, and he was also the choreographer of Dinah Shore's weekly variety show. Once a year she would present child performers, singers, tap dancers, acrobats, jugglers, and more, and in 1957, just after I turned ten, she decided to present a ballet. After an open audition Suzie and I were chosen to dance the Waltz from Act I of *Swan Lake,* choreographed by Mr. Charmoli. About a year later she was doing another children's program, and Tony remembered us, so we were invited back, but what was even more important, that year was my first introduction to George Balanchine.

In the 1950s the New York City Ballet performed annual summer seasons at the Greek Theater, a 4,600-seat amphitheater in Los Angeles,

Suzanne Cupito and me at ten years old with students of Kathryn Etienne's school of ballet. Courtesy of the author.

and in 1958 they presented Balanchine's production of *The Nutcracker*. This was the same year it was shown on national television and started the *Nutcracker* Christmas tradition in America. The first full-length *Nutcracker* in the United States was produced by the San Francisco Ballet, but the Balanchine version on national television brought it to a huge audience. Having the *Nutcracker* play during the summer was a very novel idea, and the whole town was buzzing about it.

The audition for the local children was held in the downstairs rehearsal room of the Greek Theater, and there were at least three hundred of us all lined up with our mothers. I must say this for my mom: she always stayed in the background. For those *Nutcracker* auditions, she just dropped me off. I sometimes wished she would have been more supportive and involved, but her non-involvement did make me stand on my own two feet, as it were, so I suppose that was good in the long run.

I still remember the ballet combination given by the company's ultra-perky ballet mistress, who had been a former star with the company, Janet Reed. She had us all do an *échappé-passé* combination from the Polichinelles *divertissement* for children and a giant Mother Ginger in Act II. I suppose I did it all right because she separated me from the rest of the dancers and told me to wait. After she dismissed most of the children, she kept a few of us boys and started teaching us the Prince's pantomime monologue from the second act. The Prince's pantomime in the Balanchine version of *The Nutcracker* is the same as in the original 1892 Imperial Russian Ballet production, which was choreographed by Lev Ivanov to the plan of Marius Petipa. It is very

Me and Dianne Reese in a production of *George Balanchine's The Nutcracker®* at the Greek Theater (1958). Courtesy of the author. Choreography by George Balanchine © The George Balanchine Trust.

musical, relatively complicated, and tells the story of how the Nutcracker battles the Mouse King to save little Marie and bring her to the Kingdom of Sweets. After that audition, I was chosen to play the triple role of Drosselmeyer's Nephew/Nutcracker/Prince. The same boy plays all three roles.

The final stage rehearsals, when the children first worked directly with Balanchine, were surprisingly quite fun and totally without tension; I later learned this was the norm for him. I remember he smiled a lot and told a lot of jokes and seemed extremely relaxed. It was clear, though, that he was in complete control and that his dancers loved and respected him. That was obvious even to me, a child.

There was one rehearsal I will never forget. As the Nutcracker I had to have a sword fight with the Mouse King and, at one point, jump on his back. Exuberant as I was, and having a chance to show off for the "Boss," I jumped right over the Mouse King's back, grabbing the poor guy by his neck, and we both went tumbling. Balanchine stopped the rehearsal, everybody was laughing, and I was mortified. Balanchine said, in his nasally Russian-tinged English, "You know, dear, you don't have to jump so high." (He called his dancers "dear" a lot.) Don't get me wrong: I loved that he noticed me, but I was really embarrassed by that tumble. At another point, right before the Prince's Pantomime, there is a gesture to stage right and then stage left. Evidently I was doing this too far upstage and turning my back to the audience. Balanchine stopped the rehearsal and said, "You know, dear, I know that girl up there is very pretty, but you have to show the *audience* what you're doing." I think I blushed. Even all these years later I remember his gentle critique. It was so easy working for Balanchine, even at that age. He'd tell a dancer clearly and precisely what to do, and he showed a confidence that they could do whatever he wanted. If you couldn't do something correctly the first time, he would say, "No dear, do it a little more like this." There was never a sense of disappointment or frustration on his part. Being supportive seemed to be in his nature.

The actual performances were a revelation for me. The sound of a full orchestra, a huge opera house stage, all those dancers in such sumptuous costumes, that magical growing Christmas tree, and the brilliance of the lead dancers filled me with tremendous joy and excitement. My earlier times onstage in my father's act and those school shows just couldn't compete with this!

Violette Verdy in the Dewdrop role in *George Balanchine's The Nutcracker*® (late 1950s). Photographer unknown. Choreography by George Balanchine © The George Balanchine Trust.

I remember sitting on the little throne during the second act and watching a wonderfully alive, flirtatious dancer as the Dewdrop. She was the twenty-five-year-old Violette Verdy, who to my eyes looked and acted much younger because she always seemed to be giggling.

Balanchine would cast me with her in the Grand Pas de Deux exactly ten years later. Happily she became one of my closest personal friends and my most regular partner.

The Sugar Plum Fairy and her Cavalier in that production were the original dancers of these roles, the imperious Maria Tallchief and the dashingly handsome Nicholas Magallanes, but I was mostly taken with the young ballerina whose dancing was so flawless, ethereal, and in a way mysterious (as if she were always hiding a secret) that she didn't seem quite real. Even her name was unforgettable: Allegra Kent. She danced the Dewdrop in some performances, and the Sugar Plum Fairy in others, and in both she was absolute perfection. After the Prince's

Me and Allegra Kent in Bal-
anchine's *Nutcracker Pas de
Deux* (1973). Courtesy of the
author. Choreography by
George Balanchine © The
George Balanchine Trust.

Pantomime, the Sugar Plum Fairy comes to the little Prince, takes him
by the hand, and leads him to the throne. Whenever Allegra took my
hand, I would look up at her and see she had a slight drop of per-
spiration on her forehead. However, she was still perfectly calm and
cool, almost as if she were a geisha. I think she was nervous (she had
just turned twenty-one), but she was always incandescent. I later also
danced that *pas de deux* with her, and which was a dream come true.

Back then I developed a major crush on her, and even after working
with her, choreographing for her, and dancing with her for many years,
I still have it.

After *The Nutcracker* I spent the next few years basically doing
what any young student dancer did. I studied, studied, studied, and it
seemed with every teacher in Los Angeles. In those days, my city had
a veritable goldmine of wonderful teachers. After two years exclusively
with Mme. Etienne and private lessons with her sister Maria Charisse, I
began taking classes with David Lichine, the choreographer of *Gradua-
tion Ball* and a celebrated dancer with the Col. de Basil-Rene Blum Ballets Russes de Monte Carlo. David was inspiring, very temperamental,
and my first male teacher.

Boys need a male teacher, I've found, and I really learned a great deal
from him. More than anything specific, I learned to just *dance*. Tatiana

Riabouchinska was his wife, and I later learned that she was one of the three "baby ballerinas" hired at age fourteen by Balanchine for the new de Basil Ballets Russes de Monte Carlo. The other two were Tamara Toumanova, age twelve, and Irina Baronova, also twelve.

Another wonderful teacher was Maria Bekefi. She taught very intense and more-focused classes than Lichine's, which I sorely needed. One day, an extremely young-looking pregnant girl came in for class wearing large thick glasses. She looked very familiar but I had never seen her in Bekefi's class before. She also looked as if she would give birth any second. Underneath her rounded belly were the two most beautiful legs and delicate feet I'd ever seen. At the barre we were all terrified she would hurt herself because she continued to stretch and stretch, doing a *développé* to her ear, an arabesque *penchée* into an over-split, etc. It wasn't until years later that I found out it was Allegra, who was pregnant with her first child. I hadn't seen her since *The Nutcracker* and she looked very different pregnant and in those glasses.

I was also fortunate to take classes from the legendary Carmelita Maracci. I was fourteen years old when I started with her, but unfortunately, like Bekefi, she was quite elderly. In her case this was a pity because she could barely walk, and although she was known for having had a prodigious technique in her youth, any demonstration was way beyond her by then. Her classes, though, didn't seem as much about ballet technique as they were about music and philosophy. She would sometimes lecture for hours on Beethoven or other composers, and she would have us do what, to me, seemed odd things at the barre, like letting go of it during *frappés* and, using the hand we held on to the barre with for dear life, instead snap our fingers in a syncopated rhythm to the music (she was a trained Flamenco dancer, too); or she'd ask us to balance with our eyes closed. That seemed crazy at the time, but it did get us to feel our "centers." Many other dancers also claim to have learned a great deal from Maracci. Allegra studied with her often, as did American Ballet Theatre's Cynthia Gregory. Irina Kosmovska, who became a most influential teacher in Los Angeles, also studied and danced for her when she had a small touring company. I would say Maracci was truly a genius level teacher.

Up to that point, I did not think my career was going to be exclusively as a ballet dancer. I loved ballet, but I was also studying tap with Willy Covan (Eleanor Powell's teacher) and was appearing on many

Publicity photo of *Death Valley Days,* circa 1958. Courtesy of the author.

television shows as an actor—for example, *The Donna Reed Show, Day in Court, Death Valley Days,* and some others.

I just wanted to be an entertainer, and I did not consider myself solely a dancer. I also sang in school productions and was actually being encouraged to consider an operatic career by Bernice Hutchinson, the choral director at Hollywood High. I guess I inherited my strong tenor voice from my mother and my athletic ability from my father, but by around fifteen I just couldn't get enough of dancing. I was obsessed, intoxicated, and addicted to the sheer joy of movement. Dancing was like flying to me. It was totally freeing.

When I was still fifteen, a musical theater group for teenagers was started by director Gerald Gordon, called Los Angeles Youth Theater. It produced a short summer season of two productions in its first year. One was the Lane-Harburg *Finian's Rainbow* and the other was the Bernstein-Sondheim *West Side Story,* where, naturally, I tried out for the part of Baby John.

For the audition I performed a solo I had choreographed to the Mambo section of the score. Mr. Gordon asked, "Who choreographed that?" I told him I did, and he asked if I'd like to choreograph the whole show. I thought, *Sure. Why not?* I hadn't yet choreographed much, let alone for large groups (that production used around thirty-six teenagers). I've never had a fear of tackling new projects, so I said yes. The performances were a success, and I personally received wonderful reviews in the *Los Angeles Times*, which were my first professional reviews. I had just turned sixteen when the show premiered, and as such a young choreographer, I obviously caught their attention. After that experience I knew that being a choreographer was definitely in my future. Coincidentally, the young conductor for that show was the nineteen-year-old Leonard Slatkin, now one of America's most respected conductors.

2

Eugene Loring's American School of Dance

At this time in Hollywood, the preeminent dance school was the one owned and run by the American ballet and film choreographer Eugene Loring. Loring was a well-respected American choreographer (he had choreographed *Billy the Kid,* with music by Aaron Copland, for example), but he had not done anything significant in the ballet world for some years. He said his school was founded to train dancers for commercial work and not just for classical ballet. The students who received scholarships took classes in ballet, jazz, and modern dance, plus pantomime, choreography, and Kineseography, which was Loring's system of dance notation. I do think all these diverse classes were beneficial, but there seemed to be a determined effort there not to allow a dancer to develop too far in any one discipline. Certainly, having classes in the Martha Graham technique, taught by former Graham soloist Deborah Zall, helped me as a dancer and choreographer, as did studying pantomime with a dancer from Marcel Marceau's company and learning the Louis Horst approach to teaching choreography. We also studied musical forms, and how to employ the A-B-A musical technique in our choreography. I remember Loring asked us to use Renaissance music exclusively for these classes in choreography. Many actors studied there too in those years. It was normal to find Jane Fonda, Mary Tyler Moore, Toni Basil, or Yvette Mimieux in class, and even Cyd Charisse was there for private lessons with Loring. He was her choreographer of choice for several of her films, such as *Silk Stockings, Meet Me in Las Vegas,* and others. She was around forty-five in those years but her body looked fantastic. She'd wear only a leotard and tights, no skirt, or anything that would take away from those still fabulous legs.

I loved all the teachers, especially Carlton Johnson and George Jacks for jazz. The ballet teachers, too, were all excellent. Eleanora Marra, from Diaghilev's Ballets Russes, who was one of the original Sisters in Balanchine's *Prodigal Son,* was wonderfully spirited. Her classes were always great fun.

June Morris, a dancer formerly with American Ballet Theatre and who later became a personal friend, was another fine teacher. Her specialty was pirouettes at the speed of light. She could help a dancer over the fear of any turn very quickly. She also danced in Jerome Robbins's early ballets at American Ballet Theatre, and she told me many stories about his first ballets and what his personality was like before he became famous and a legendarily "difficult" choreographer (much more about Robbins later).

Loring would sometimes teach too, but he didn't seem to enjoy it. He was totally dry and humorless when teaching. When I first auditioned for him to see if I'd be accepted into his school, he asked me to demonstrate a few simple steps. He didn't give me any corrections and seemed rather distant. I knew I was a good enough dancer to get scholarships to all the other ballet schools, but Loring didn't seem impressed at all. After the audition he called us into his office (my mother was with me this time). He said, "Your son has a knack. We'll give him a half scholarship." At this time my mother was not married and we had very little money. A "half" scholarship meant that I would have to pay for half of the classes or work at the studio. Well, we couldn't afford to pay, and I didn't mind working, so . . .

My first job was to clean all the toilets and mirrors, and mop the floors. I was given the biggest workload of any of the scholarship students and I think Loring was trying to break my (to him) annoyingly optimistic spirit. For instance, while I was doing my chores, I used to sing to make the time go by. The acoustics in the bathrooms were great, and the school was usually empty. If Loring was at the school he would invariably come in, look at me coolly, raise an eyebrow, and say, "Must you?" The more I learned about him, and I was at his school for about three years, the more I discovered that he was a very bitter man. He was not at all pleased with his artistic lot in life. He once let it slip that he never felt respected as a choreographer or teacher, and he literally hated every other choreographer, especially Balanchine! When the New York

City Ballet had its annual summer seasons at the Greek Theater, he would harangue us, for two hours straight, during his Saturday afternoon scholarship class, on the evils of Balanchine and the errors of the Balanchine style. "Balanchine is *not* classical," he would say over and over. It started to sound pathological, even to me, a young teenager.

3

Balanchine's Ballet of Los Angeles and *The Danny Kaye Show*

Balanchine had spent quite a lot of time in Hollywood when he was married to Vera Zorina and choreographed *The Goldwyn Follies* and other Hollywood films for her, and he always thought Los Angeles should have its own ballet company. So, with the help of local impresario James A. Doolittle, the director of the Greek Theater and then the preeminent presenter of ballet and opera in Los Angeles, Balanchine started to lay the foundation for a professional Los Angeles ballet company. He came up with a very clever ploy to launch this new endeavor. He scheduled a performance of his *Serenade* for the 1964 summer season of his company at the Greek Theater, to be danced by local Los Angeles students chosen at an open audition. Much to Loring's annoyance, no dancers from his school were cast because their pointe work wasn't up to the standards of the other schools that focused more on classical ballet. He nonetheless allowed studio space to be rented at his school for these rehearsals. That was when we students saw the high level of classical technique these other dancers had, compared to what we'd been learning at his school. The difference was like night and day. All those beautifully trained girls looked like thoroughbreds compared to us. No wonder Loring was angry. I saw the Greek Theater performance and thought all the local dancers looked just wonderful. After that show Balanchine and Doolittle made plans for a full-time local professional ballet, with Balanchine as the artistic adviser and Doolittle as the president of the future board of directors. A performance was scheduled to take place within a year at the Dorothy Chandler Pavilion, the major theater of the brand-new Los Angeles Music Center. At that point, the name of the ensemble was the Ballet of Los Angeles.

I did not go to the auditions for that new company because I had heard from various dancers that I was too short and that the male dancers had to be at least five feet ten, or more.

I was five feet eight. I also thought I wasn't good enough to get in anyway. An important lesson to learn is: always, always, go to an audition!

The Music Center performances consisted of Balanchine's *Pas de Dix,* his one-act *Swan Lake,* and his *Firebird.* Allegra Kent and Maria Tallchief (both of whom had grown up and been trained in their youth in Los Angeles) were the guest artists in *Swan Lake* and *Firebird.* Karel Shimoff, a Los Angeles native who had just joined the New York City Ballet (NYCB), and of whom Balanchine thought very highly, led the *Pas de Dix* with Jacques d'Amboise. According to all reports, Los Angeles finally had a real classical ballet company.

I don't remember why I didn't go to these performances. Possibly I just couldn't afford the tickets, and I was of course depressed that I was too "short" to be in it. Besides, as mentioned, at that time I didn't want to be a full-time ballet dancer. That came a year later.

After these performances Balanchine asked Irina Kosmovska to be the ballet mistress and principal teacher for this new company, and he returned to New York. Irina immediately began teaching a demanding two-and-a-half-hour daily class to keep the dancers in shape while the new board was being formed. A dancer I knew introduced me to her during this period, and she invited me to take these classes. The company's organizational future was left in the hands of its new board of directors. Their first responsibility was to find a permanent artistic director, but the understanding was that they could call on Balanchine whenever they needed help, ballets, or advice.

What they did then was the worst thing possible. Eugene Loring, of all people, was hired to be the artistic director of a company founded by Balanchine. What a colossal mistake.

By creating the Ballet of Los Angeles, Balanchine had envisioned a purely classical ballet along the lines of the New York City Ballet, which itself was an American continuation of the former Imperial Ballet of St. Petersburg. This was the polar opposite of what Loring wanted "his" company to be. Loring wanted an *American* company along the lines of American Ballet Theatre, and dancing his and more "American"-styled contemporary ballets, not ballets based on the Russian classical style of

Marius Petipa. For instance, at Loring's school we never had any ballet variations classes drawn from any classics such as *Swan Lake*, *The Sleeping Beauty*, or *Giselle*.

Loring wrote a curt note to Balanchine thanking him for his help, but noting that now, under Loring's direction, Balanchine's input and advice were no longer needed. In other words, "Thanks, but no thanks." This was told to me years later by Betty Cage, NYCB's general manager. Consequently, Kosmovska found herself relegated to teaching just one class a week, and Loring proceeded to run the company much as he ran his school, and to bring in many other teachers from Los Angeles.

Now making up the roster along with Kosmovska were Yvonne Mounsey, a former NYCB principal and a Jerome Robbins favorite, who was already running her own successful school; Tommy Rall, who was a dancer from American Ballet Theatre and who had performed in movies such as *Kiss Me Kate*; June Morris from Loring's school; and choreographer and teacher Bella Lewitzky, the Lester Horton prodigy. All this would have been fine had there been a real ballet company being developed, but there wasn't.

In those days there were many weekly television variety shows in Los Angeles, and there was quite a lot of work for dancers. Red Skelton, Dinah Shore, and Danny Kaye all had their own shows and gave many dancers steady employment. Their choreographers each had what amounted to their own individual little troupe of dancers with an average of twelve to fourteen in each ensemble. Luckily, Tony Charmoli was now the choreographer for *The Danny Kaye Show* on CBS, and I had just finished high school and needed to work, so I auditioned for him and he accepted me. I looked at what was going on in local ballet, and was not really interested in working again with Loring, so I took the full-time job on the Kaye show.

During those years, when the ballet scene in Los Angeles was in turmoil, I was appearing weekly on television. Not bad for an eighteen-year-old, and it was a great learning experience for me. We would usually do an opening number where we would back up the guest star, and later we would have our own separate dance number, plus the salary was great. At the time I was completely satisfied.

One week our guest was Broadway's superstar Gwen Verdon. Unfortunately, on the day of the first rehearsal, I had an accident with my small Honda motor scooter when its wheel got caught in a trolley track. (Santa Monica Boulevard still had those old trolley tracks.) I was only banged up a bit, but I did need prescription painkillers and had bandages all over my right leg. When I arrived at rehearsal I could barely stand up, but I convinced everyone I'd be all right in four days when the filming took place. When Kaye saw my bandaged leg (I was wearing shorts), and that I was a bit unsteady because of those painkillers, he let out quite a few four-letter words (that man could really swear). At least he didn't fire me! When Gwen came to rehearsals a few days later (she wasn't there for the first couple of days), she looked at me and said, "Oh My God! I can't dance with him! He's young enough to be my son!" So they quite rightly hid me in the back. I must admit that I did look much younger than my eighteen years. In any case, she was a great joy to work with and a consummate pro.

Two years later, when I was dancing with NYCB, I was at a club called Arthur, which at that time was the trendiest nightclub in the city. Liza Minnelli was there often with her then-husband, Peter Allen, and so was her mother Judy Garland. I was there one night with my best friend in those years, Marnee Morris, and felt a tap on my shoulder. It was Gwen Verdon! She said she had just been at a performance of our company and had recognized me from the Kaye show. She graciously said I had danced very well. It's so interesting how truly talented people are always generous with their compliments. Gwen Verdon was really the queen of her profession, and I was so fortunate to watch her up close in rehearsals and to work with her, if only for that one brief time.

The end of my television chorus boy career came during Carol Channing's first TV special. She was touring the country with her hit Broadway show *Hello, Dolly!* As fate would have it her TV special would be aired at the same time as the Los Angeles live shows. Hermes Pan was the choreographer for the TV special, and he wanted thirty-six male dancers for the show. At the audition I was *not* chosen as one of the guys. I was devastated but hoped it was because I looked too young.

As I was picking up my dance bag to leave, an assistant came in and whispered something into Pan's ear. Pan then said, "Okay, all the Charmoli dancers, sit on the right side of the room." Well, I *was* a "Charmoli dancer," so I moved to that side of the room and kept my mouth shut. It turned out that a dancer was automatically hired if he was a Charmoli dancer. I definitely got that job by default!

On the first day of rehearsal there were plans for a huge opening number in which we thirty-six dancers had to sing and dance to the song, "Hello, Dolly!" However, Gower Champion, the director-choreographer of the original Broadway production and the upcoming national tour, was not pleased when he heard about Pan's bigger TV version. He got a court order to stop that number, claiming it was unfairly competing with his production.

We dancers then spent ten days just standing and singing "Hello, Dolly!" Later we stood on a revolving turntable for the finale. We didn't dance one step. I read three books that week and a half and decided that my days on TV were over. I started studying much more earnestly with Kosmovska, and I pushed myself as hard as I could. My idea still was that my career was going to be that of a Broadway singer-dancer and/or I would go to New York, join a smaller ballet company like the Joffrey Ballet for a year or two for the experience, and then try to get into a Broadway show.

Looking back on my TV experiences, I think my ability to learn new roles very quickly is a direct result of learning new dances on a weekly basis. For the Kaye show and for all the television shows of that time, the dancers would learn their dances over a four-day period, perform the show live on the fifth day, and start all over again the following week. There was no wasted time. When I got to Balanchine, I just brought this discipline with me, and it sure did come in handy.

4

School of American Ballet (Part 1)

My First Trip to New York

In early January 1966 I took my TV savings and went to New York City and started looking around for ballet schools. I took a class daily at the American Ballet Theatre School from Valentina Pereyaslavec, who was quite fun, a cross between Lichine and Kosmovska. Loud (she literally barked out her commands) and temperamental, she gave a very disciplined class that was an excellent workout. I also studied at the Joffrey School with Hector Zaraspe, an elegant man and a very precise teacher, although his classes really weren't quite demanding enough for my liking. And I studied at Balanchine's School of American Ballet (SAB). Now, that school was *very* different. At SAB they really meant business.

I had had no contact with Balanchine since performing in *The Nutcracker* seven years earlier, and he did not come around the school a lot in those days, or at least the students didn't see much of him. When he did appear, it was usually with Suzanne Farrell on his arm. They seemed to be inseparable. They would peek their heads into a class, whisper together for a minute, and then leave. I was not in much awe of him then, as so many of the other dancers were. I had not been brought up at his school, and I had been a professional dancer, earning my own living, for over a year. I respected Balanchine, of course, but I was not in the least bit intimidated by him. In all honesty, I felt I was one of the better students my age at the American Ballet Theatre School, and I also felt I did well in the classes at the Joffrey School, where I also took classes for a few months. But at SAB I was definitely out of my league in the area of a refined ballet technique. The other boys there my age were technically so much better. Paul Mejia was one, John Prinz was another, and so was Robert "Ricky" Weiss. Mejia and Prinz had just joined the company before I came, though they still took many classes at the school, but Ricky was the first boy who befriended me, and I will always thank him for that.

Ricky, in those years, had a very lively and quirky personality, and one day before class he said, "So, you're from Hollywood?" I said "Yes." He then asked, "Why don't you study here?" I said I did, but he said, "No. I mean all the time? This is the *best* school in the city!" By then I knew he was right. I realized I still had a lot to learn, and clearly the best place to do it was at SAB. The two things I had for sure were my unstoppable energy and my ambition, but my technique really needed help. I believed all I needed to do was work, work, work, and that was no problem for me. I thrived on work. I trusted that with enough work my technique would improve enough to put me on a par with these other boys. They had had the advantage of growing up at that school, but I had to play catch-up, and fast!

Diana Adams was then the school's director. She had been one of Balanchine's fabled muses (rumor had it that he had once been madly in love with her) and was still quite a formidable presence. She reminded me of one of the nuns from my Catholic school days because she was tall, intimidating, and always dressed in black. When my savings were starting to run out I finally worked up the nerve to ask her for a scholarship. She looked down at me with a bemused expression and said, "Well, we wondered when you would ask. You've got one if you want it." I was quite understandably overjoyed.

I was now really looking forward to taking two and sometimes three classes a day at "the *best* school in the city."

In those days the School of American Ballet was on Broadway between 81st and 82nd streets. There were two nice big studios and one smaller one, all with well-worn wooden floors. The classes were excellent (I describe them and the teachers in more detail later), but sadly, after about two months at the school, I found I couldn't live on the seventy-five dollars of monthly scholarship money alone. I had gone through all my TV savings and New York City was, even then, a very expensive place to live. I was staying in a cheap hotel—well, cheap by New York

City standards—and I couldn't afford that any longer. I decided I'd better go back to Los Angeles and back into television. I was still not interested in being exclusively a ballet dancer and I still didn't think I was good enough to have a big career in classical ballet. But all that soon changed.

5

Back to Los Angeles

Sir Anton Dolin—"Western Ballet"—
Maya Plisetskaya and the Bolshoi Ballet

Back in Los Angeles, the Ballet of Los Angeles had gone through many changes. Even the name was changed. It was now the Western Ballet Association. Best of all, Eugene Loring was no longer the artistic director. A ballet master from the Warsaw Opera, Stefan Wenta, was named "Chef de Ballet" and a well-meaning but woefully under-qualified board member Maggie Louis (wife of fashion designer Jean Louis), assumed virtually all the responsibilities of the executive director, artistic director, and board president combined. There was a de facto general manager of sorts, but Maggie called all the shots. Karel Shimoff, the dancer who had led the *Pas de Dix* in the first performances of the Ballet of Los Angeles, had decided to leave the New York City Ballet and assume the full-time position as their leading ballerina. Kosmovska was once again the ballet mistress and teaching the majority of classes, along with Wenta, who was a pretty good teacher. The board had also repaired their damaged relationship with Balanchine. A season was planned for the Scottish Rite Auditorium, which wasn't an ideal theater for dance because there was no orchestra pit, but at least it had a spacious stage.

When I returned to Los Angeles that spring of 1966, I resumed studying with Kosmovska and was invited to join the Western Ballet Association as a soloist. After a few weeks I asked Maggie if I could maybe use a few dancers and start choreographing something small. (I had been dabbling with choreography since my first experience with the LA Youth Theater and *West Side Story*, and during my scholarship days at Loring's school there was a choreography workshop and I had made a few small ballets for that, but nothing serious.) Maggie said yes, and the results were a *pas de trois* to the "Hoedown" section of Aaron Copeland's *Rodeo,* a ballet set to Shostakovich's Piano Concerto No. 1, and the *Sylvia Pas de Deux.* I was still eighteen.

The repertory for the début performances was *Giselle Act II, The Sleeping Beauty Act III, Les Sylphides, Le Pas de Quatre, Pas de Dix, Serenade,* my *Sylvia Pas de Deux,* and my new Shostakovich ballet, *The Class.* For this I used four girls and myself in a classroom setting. Wenta's ballets were the *Jupiter Symphony* to Mozart and a modern ballet to Hindemith's Kammermusik No. 2. This was a pretty large repertory for a brand-new company.

I was cast as the lead in *Pas de Dix* and *Jupiter Symphony.* (I was a faun in the third movement, with a lot of girls). I also danced as the Bluebird in *The Sleeping Beauty Act III* and cast myself in my own two ballets, *The Class* and *Sylvia Pas de Deux.*

As fate would have it, Balanchine returned to oversee the final rehearsals of *Serenade.* He took one look at the ambitious programming, and, in no uncertain terms, albeit politely (but in front of the whole company), told Maggie where they were going wrong. He asked why a novice company, with very young dancers, most of them inexperienced, put on programs that consisted mainly of the standard classical repertory? At that time, the Bolshoi Ballet, The Royal Ballet, American Ballet Theatre, and NYCB were still having yearly seasons in LA. Even the Royal Danish Ballet was a semi-regular visitor. He suggested that the "Western Ballet" scale down their plans and do new and less "exposing" ballets (his words).

He watched rehearsals of my two ballets and Wenta's and said, "Do more ballets like Clifford's (he pronounced it *Cleeeford*) or Wenta's. New ballets that other people aren't doing." He also said later, as the company grew, that we could do whatever we wanted, but, in the beginning, it was just foolish to try to compete with the major companies. I suppose doing the classics made the board feel they would draw a bigger audience, but it didn't. I thought what he had to say was very sensible.

Barbara Horgan, who was then Balanchine's secretary and later became the executive director of the Balanchine Trust, spoke to me after the run-throughs of my ballets and said, "Johnny, when you were at our school why didn't you tell us you choreographed?" I wasn't aware that she or Balanchine had even known I was there. "Nobody asked me," I said. It never occurred to me to tell anybody that I was interested in choreography. Barbara said Balanchine liked my ballets and wanted me to come back to New York in September when the school started up its fall term. I was very flattered but told her that I couldn't possibly live on the seventy-five-dollar monthly stipend. "Don't worry. We will work something out," she said. Well, with the haphazard way the LA company was going, and no really strong artistic leadership, I knew this would be the only season I would perform with them, and I was more than thrilled by Mr. B.'s offer. I told her I'd be happy to come back.

However, before I went back to New York I had half a summer to fill, and I had quite an adventure and life-changing event about to happen, thanks to Sir Anton Dolin.

Dolin was in LA to stage his *Le Pas de Quatre* for the Western Ballet. June Morris, knowing that his exuberant personality and mine would probably click, introduced us. Dolin's real name was Sidney Francis Patrick Chippendall Healy-Kay, but all his friends called him "Pat." His name was changed to "Anton Dolin" by Diaghilev when he was a member of Diaghilev's Ballets Russes (he was one of the two original Friends in Balanchine's *Prodigal Son*). Dolin soon became a close personal friend and a great mentor. He was also quite interested in me sexually, but I was *faster* than he was, and he took my rejection of his advances in relatively good humor. Even though he never "had his way with me," he still taught me private classes for the four weeks he was in LA. It usually was a class in pure Cecchetti technique (the most acclaimed international ballet teacher of the first three decades of the twentieth century, and the teacher of Diaghilev's Ballets Russes), and sometimes there were classes in the method of Nikolai Legat (a legendary dancer and teacher with the Russian Imperial Ballet).

Dolin also taught me all the standard classical male variations, most notably his version of Albrecht from *Giselle*. He worked me very, very hard, and I learned a great deal. He even gave me a surprise birthday party when I turned nineteen, and he invited the celebrated ballerina Tamara Toumanova. It was fascinating to meet her and hear her stories. Also present were Nana Gollner (an original American Ballet Theatre ballerina) and Paul Petroff. It was quite a group. I loved listening to these people reminisce about the old Ballet Russe de Monte Carlo and the early days of American Ballet Theatre. Whenever dancers get together they gossip incessantly. It was very educational.

During that same busy summer, the Bolshoi Ballet came to town and Dolin arranged for me to take their company classes. But before that, he took me to see a movie called *Plisetskaya Dances,* and that film quite literally changed my life.

I had never seen Maya Plisetskaya dance at that point, nor even heard of her, but her dancing in that movie simply astonished me. It was incredible to watch a dancer with that much life and energy. I had never thought that ballet, "classical" ballet, could be that exciting. I had seen Nureyev dance with the Royal Ballet when I was fifteen, but I did not get the same rush as when I saw her. She took incredible chances and was like some unstoppable force of nature. Watching her absolute joy and freedom in that one film showed me what seemingly limitless possibilities there were in classical ballet. This was an epiphany for me and it truly changed the direction of my career.

The Bolshoi had two hour-long company classes a day, one at 11:00 and the other at 12:00. The first was usually taught by ballet master Alexander Leveshev and the second by Plisetskaya herself. She also took her own class. Dolin arranged for me to take both daily classes, and again, I don't know why I was so fortunate, but Plisetskaya started taking an interest in me. She began giving me a lot of personal corrections after class, details I remember and pass along in my own teaching today. I started to believe that perhaps I too could become a classical dancer. At SAB, when I was there the first time, I wasn't so sure (my feet were never great, and I have a very funny Balanchine story to share later), but surrounded by all these wild exuberant Russians and with Plisetskaya's encouragement, I felt right at home. Thanks to Dolin, I didn't miss a single show for six weeks. I was either given the impresario Sol Hurok's front-of-house seats or I was allowed to watch from the wings.

I was also lucky to be invited to some of their private parties in the dancers' hotel rooms at the Roosevelt Hotel on Hollywood Boulevard, and I would go swimming with them at the hotel pool. Back then I just had a huge crush on Maya. (My second ballerina crush. Allegra was the first). I would bring her flowers after performances and she would often invite me to sit in her dressing room during intermissions.

One day Shirley MacLaine and her brother Warren Beatty showed up to watch a class. Afterward she came over to me and started to try to speak to me in Russian. I said, "Sorry Miss MacLaine, but I don't speak Russian." She looked at me, shocked, and said, "Why, you're an American?" I said yes, and she laughed and said, "Oh, I thought you were in the company." I remember thinking, "Wow, what a wonderful compliment." It was very flattering to be mistaken for a Bolshoi Ballet company dancer just when I was thinking maybe I could be a classical dancer after all. I said, "No, I'm just a local boy." She laughed again and said, "Really? Well, keep it up."

I found out later that during this tour, Plisetskaya was having a torrid affair with Beatty. I guess that was why he came to watch classes and rehearsals so often. They would dash off together after rehearsals and performances, much to the consternation of her KGB handlers who would go racing after them. It was like watching a silent slapstick comedy. She was such a big star at that point that there was not much they could do. She never defected as other Russian ballet dancers had, so I suppose she had an "understanding" with her government.

I remember sitting next to Beatty one night and watching his face light up when she gave a dazzling performance of Kitri in *Don Quixote*. We walked backstage together and he kept gushing, "Wasn't she great! Just fantastic! I've never seen anything like her." He sounded like a love-struck teenager. There were lots of ballet students I knew at the stage door, and the looks on their faces when they saw me walking in with *the* Warren Beatty were priceless. After all these years, she is still the best Kitri I have ever seen, and she certainly set the standard for this role. Films don't do her justice at all. I am very fortunate that I happened to be in the right place at the right time.

While on the subject of Plisetskaya, I should describe what it felt like for me to watch her dance. It had been a big surprise for me to see a ballet dancer be that flamboyant. She was so full of life that even sitting in a restaurant people couldn't take their eyes off her. Seriously. Some people just seem to carry their own spotlights with them. We are very lucky that we have good films of her in her prime, and my favorite, of course, is *Plisetskaya Dances,* which shows her in a variety of her roles. Even so, that's not the same as seeing her live. In that film one can see her incredible jumps and supernaturally expressive *port de bras,* but what I noticed when watching her up close in class, and from the wings, was that she didn't actually jump that much higher than the other girls. It was her softness of landing (due to a very deep *plié*) and the care she took with the way she looked in the air, that made her appear to fly. It was effortless. She jumped for the illusion, not for the actual height. She was not a great turner, and yet she could spin like the wind for her *pique* turns and *chaînés*. She had very high extensions for the standards of the day, and she was one of the first, along with Allegra Kent, Suzanne Farrell, Moira Shearer, Leslie Caron, and Mimi Paul, to really get into a full (180-degree) arabesque *penchée* split. Now, a split *penchée* (it's sometimes called a "six-o'clock") is the norm, even for men, but back in the 1960s it was still highly unusual. Plus Plisetskaya had an incredibly limber back, and consequently her arabesque lines were some of the most beautiful in ballet. Maya was also one of the most musical dancers I've ever seen, playing with the music, in much the same way Violette Verdy did. She also took a lot more chances than most dancers do even today. Her first *Swan Lake* I saw I still remember in great detail. I had seen her dance other ballets a few times by then and I expected her Black Swan to be the most striking, but oddly it was her Act II White Swan that was more unusual. I remember sitting in my seat during the intermission after that act, debating whether I should stay to see anything else. I wanted to leave the theater with just that beautiful memory. It's simply that as the White Swan, she continued a seamless legato movement throughout the entire *pas de deux*. I thought it so disciplined that a dancer as fiery as she was could be that subdued and demure. She did not have the delicate long legs that are now in vogue, but when she was actually dancing you didn't see any flaws. All you saw was her total effect.

Since the White Swan presented an unceasing legato movement, it came as a bit of a shock when it ended. In the Soviet version, this finishes in an arabesque *penchée,* not in the dip (swoon), which is more or less traditional. When Maya posed in that arabesque, it was almost like a jolt. It was as if you were sitting in a speeding car and had gotten used to going at a certain speed and then hit the brakes. In other words, you were watching this completely hypnotic movement, but when she stopped, with no flick of the wrist, nothing obvious, and just simply froze, the whole audience sort of lurched forward in their seats. It was as if a statue had come to life for a few minutes and then returned to being a statue.

Much of her success in this was of course due to her partner, Nikolai Fadeyachev. As I learned more about partnering, I realized that she hadn't been creating all that magic on her own. Fadeyachev had been

Maya Plisetskaya, circa 1966. Photographer unknown.

in total control as to where her weight should be, to put her in the positions she wanted, and then he had become practically invisible, which is exactly what a good partner should do. Every partner needs to be this self-effacing. Nothing is worse than the affectations Nureyev inspired for a while. Rudi was always posing in fifth position or in a *tendu*. The man can actually upstage the ballerina by doing that, especially if the man has great pointed feet. If you see films of Fadeyachev or Conrad Ludlow, New York City Ballet's greatest partner, you can really see what the art of fine partnering is all about.

When Maya ended this adagio, the audience went wild, but she didn't budge. Then Fadeyachev let go of her in the arabesque *penchée* and she stayed perfectly on balance. She then pulled herself up to a normal arabesque without him even touching her, and the audience went nuts, but she didn't acknowledge their applause or break the mood. Then Fadeyachev moved in to steady her, but she was so on balance that I think it surprised even him. She stayed in this arabesque for only a second and then ran off with him chasing after. It was a truly spectacular moment.

Her White Swan was perfect, but her Black Swan went a bit over the top. This character, Odile, was almost too natural for her personality. She had so much energy and she was so violent that at times she would blow the endings of certain combinations. She had so much velocity on one series of *chainé* turns that when she struck the final pose, she literally could not stop her momentum. She just sort of careened offstage into the wings. It was actually rather funny.

There was another incident that came during the step at the end of the coda (the Russian version), where Odile does a *pas de chat* to tendu front, followed by a quick brush, or *développé* back, to arabesque. She was moving so fast that when she got to the end, instead of doing an arabesque she crashed into a backbend attitude *en pointe*, and her foot ended up way past her head, and she balanced in that amazing position. I mean she really balanced. Magic time.

It was always such a great adventure to watch her. She was never the same twice.

Among the men of the Bolshoi, the one who impressed me the most was Vladimir Vasiliev.

He was not as perfect technically as Baryshnikov or others of today, nor as sensual as Nureyev, but to me Vasiliev was something else entirely. He had a generous, almost boyish, passion. When he danced, he seemed totally without any ego at all. He really became the character. He was only twenty-six years old and in his prime when I first saw him. On a physical level he seemed superhuman. His jumps were higher than anyone's, including Nureyev's, and his power in pirouettes was supernatural. Ten or eleven pirouettes were his norm (Nureyev usually did only four). But it wasn't the number of his turns that got me—it was their sheer force. I once saw him do four *en dedans* attitude turns, then do four more turns in a *passé* position and continue turning to four more in a back attitude! All without any *relevés* in between. Unbelievable.

However, as I've gotten older, I must agree with Balanchine that Fred Astaire was the greatest male dancer who has ever lived. Balanchine always told us this in his company classes, and as usual he was right. Astaire's grace, technical ability, and musicality cannot be topped. Even though Astaire was not from the ballet world, it didn't matter. Years later, I met this legend and told him of Balanchine's respect and admiration. I thought he would already have heard of this, but he seemed utterly surprised when I told him Balanchine said he was the best dancer ever. He said, "Balanchine said this about me?" I was so glad to let him know of Balanchine's feelings, and he seemed to be very humbled and appreciative.

6

Guatemala—*Variations for Four*—London

That same busy summer in the year of my return to Los Angeles, Dolin had some engagements to fulfill in Guatemala, Central America. He was asked to stage his *Variations for Four* (which is a male version of his *Le Pas de Quatre*) and his version of *The Nutcracker,* plus *Giselle,* for the Ballet of Guatemala. He asked if I'd like to accompany him and dance the John Gilpin (of the London Festival Ballet) role in *Variations for Four.* This solo was unusual because it is a very controlled male adagio with lots of balances in arabesque and slow turns. It's almost like a girl's variation because it's not based on big jumps and fast turns but rather on line and a lyrical quality. I've always been interested in being a well-rounded dancer, not just a jumper or turner, so this part intrigued me. Unfortunately I was not blessed with a perfect body or feet, but I did have a good arabesque line and higher than normal extensions for a male, so perhaps I could pull off this most elegant and classical role.

I also got my first taste of choreographing for a professional company. Dolin asked if I would like to choreograph "The Waltz of the Flowers" in his *Nutcracker.* I said, "Yes, absolutely." I used a solo couple and a large corps of girls, much as I did in the subsequent version I made for my Los Angeles Ballet in 1978. Even then I really loved working with a large corps. All the shows went well enough, but for the life of me I cannot remember one step of my choreography, but Dolin seemed happy, so I guess it was okay.

Our return to Los Angeles provides an interesting anecdote about Dolin's personality. While we were coming through customs, the agent decided to open Dolin's briefcase, which was filled with gold rings, watches, and trinkets. I guess he had gone on a shopping spree, but he hadn't declared anything on the customs form. The agent said, "You can't come in without declaring this." Dolin said, "No, no, these are my rings and things. I didn't purchase anything. This is what I normally

Anton Dolin's *Variations for Four* (1966) Guatemala cast. *From left to right:* Richard Devaux, René Lejeune, John Clifford, and Bernard Horseau. Courtesy of the author.

take with me when I travel." The agent told him to try a ring on, and of course it didn't fit. Dolin then just began to snow job the poor man. "You must know who I am! I am *Sir* Anton Dolin." (As a point of fact he wouldn't actually be knighted until fifteen years later). He showed the customs agent his publicity photographs (which he always carried with him) and was becoming quite loud and drawing attention. He continued his theatrics in his best Tallulah Bankhead imitation (he knew her and did a great imitation): "These are my things and I really can't be bothered with all this nonsense right now. I have a car waiting!" He could be heard all over the airport, and I thought we'd be arrested any second. He was really holding up the line. They finally just let him take his loot. Stuffing it into his briefcase, we made a quick exit. I was worried for a few minutes and thought, *Good God, maybe Dolin really is smuggling!*

Back in Los Angeles, the box-office receipts for the Western Ballet had turned out to be a disaster. They had charged twenty-five dollars per ticket, and that was a lot in 1966.

The performances were danced well enough and the reviews were quite good, but the audiences were very, very small. When I told Maggie I was going to New York to take Balanchine up on his offer, she was furious and called me "a very ungrateful little boy." I didn't see what being "ungrateful" had to do with it; I simply wanted to leave for a more professional atmosphere. She had assumed I would sign up for another season, but there wasn't even a season planned at that point. The real reason I decided to go back to the School of American Ballet and become a professional ballet dancer (and maybe even a choreographer because of Balanchine's interest) was because of Maya Plisetskaya. She had forever changed my life.

However, Dolin was not done with me yet. Before I could make plans to go back to SAB and take Balanchine up on his offer, Dolin called to say he had gotten an invitation for me to take classes with the Kirov Ballet (now Mariinsky) while they were performing in London for a few weeks. Dolin had returned to London, and he insisted I fly there immediately. He told me he had arranged my tickets with a local travel agent, and I should pick them up that day! Since I did have a couple of weeks before the SAB fall term started, I thought: why not?

The very next day I was off to London and what I thought would be an amazing opportunity. I arrived around six in the morning and went to Dolin's flat as arranged. He opened the door rather groggy and exclaimed, "What are *you* doing here?" He then calmed himself, made some tea, and said he had totally forgotten to call me the day before to tell me the whole thing was off.

He said Doreen Wells and David Wall (according to Dolin the two of the brightest young lights of the Royal Ballet) had wanted to take the Kirov's classes too but for some reason were not allowed in, so instead of accepting me, an unknown American, while refusing two established English ballet stars, the Russians had decided that no outsiders could take their classes. Dolin said I could stay and study at White Lodge, the school for the Royal Ballet, but I didn't see the advantage in that as I was really more interested in choreography, and Balanchine's offer was just too good to pass up.

So New York it would be. Again!

PART II

1

School of American Ballet (Part 2)

Choreography and Teachers Stanley Williams, André Eglevsky, and Pierre Vladimiroff

I arrived back in New York mid-September of 1966. My scholarship was renewed with a $250 monthly living allowance, and I was told I could begin choreographing whatever I wanted and on whomever I chose. A student at the school, Bojan "Bo" Spassoff, needed a roommate for his one-room studio apartment, so that solved the living situation, and the money was just enough to get by.

My first ballets at the school were choreographed only for Balanchine's viewing, and this was how it worked. I was allowed to squeeze in any rehearsal time I could find and I would simply post on the bulletin board a list of the dancers I wanted to use. I knew the students were all eager to work with me because they knew being in one of my ballets would bring them to Balanchine's attention. So obviously I had my pick. I was also beginning to be a bit tongue-tied and nervous around Balanchine; not afraid, I was just beginning to realize how important he was. Remember, I had been a professional dancer for years, unlike the other young students, and I had worked with other famous choreographers, such as Anton Dolin, Hermes Pan and Eugene Loring, plus I had taken classes with the Bolshoi. All this added up to a distinct advantage and a certain confidence. But choreographing for Balanchine's personal approval was quite something else. I believed in that old saying, "Success is where preparation and opportunity meet." Well, I was prepared, and now I had the opportunity.

My first ballet was to Malcolm Arnold's *Scottish Dances,* a neo-classic four-movement suite of about twelve minutes in length. The music was very danceable and a bit like the four dance episodes from Aaron

Copland's *Rodeo.* The student dancers I chose for the leads were Lynn Bryson and my roommate Bo, with a corps of sixteen girls. Lynn was a beautiful Southern California dancer from Natalia Clare's ballet school. Clare was a very well-respected teacher who had a wonderful group of young dancers in a student company called Ballet la Jeunesse. She taught mainly girls, but I also studied with her for a year when I lived close by in the Los Angeles suburb of Encino.

After two weeks my *Scottish Dances* was completed, and I invited Balanchine to view it. It went quite well and he seemed pleased. He said, "Not bad, dear." (I later learned that "Not bad" was his usual comment when he approved of something.) He continued, "Is this something you did in Los Angeles?" I said, "No, I made it here." He seemed surprised at this and said, "But you've only been here two weeks!" I said, "Well, yes," and that really got his attention. "You mean you choreographed this whole ballet in two weeks?" I said, "Yes," but again didn't understand why he seemed so surprised. (Mr. B. often expressed his surprise by opening his eyes very wide.) He said, "Well, do something else. Do something else right away." The following week Lynn was taken into the company, which was a surprise, because in those days Mr. B. usually took dancers in after they were apprentices in *The Nutcracker,* not during a repertory rehearsal period.

I had previously choreographed a piece in LA to Morton Gould's *Spirituals for String Choir and Orchestra,* which had not been publicly performed, but had been presented in a private showing for the elegant 1940s Hollywood movie star Greer Garson, who was a close friend of Dolin's. She was quite effusive in her praise, so I staged that ballet next for the school. The Gould score is extremely jazzy, with blues and gospel overtones, and I thought the contrast with the more classical Malcolm Arnold ballet would be a good idea. No one had ever asked these students to move in such a jazzy style before, and the school had no classes in jazz technique at that time. I put in some modern dance movements with a lot of Martha Graham–style floor work, which was also new for the students. It seemed to create quite an impression with the SAB faculty, who at that time were mostly older Russians. I think I was developing a reputation as a choreographer within the company too. Some of the company's dancers—Jacques d'Amboise, Patricia

Neary, and others—would often poke their heads in the door to watch my rehearsals. The principal dancers for *Spirituals* were Renee Estopinal, who had danced it in the Western Ballet, and Starr Danias, who did the adagio with me. Starr later became a principal with the Joffrey Ballet and was featured in the film *The Turning Point*. (Her role in that was as the flirtatious dancer who successfully seduces Baryshnikov.)

Mr. B. seemed to like *Spirituals* even better than *Scottish Dances,* and the very next day Renee was taken into the company. I remember it was a Saturday afternoon immediately after a class, and I was with her when Diana Adams told her the good news. She was in shock because she hadn't been at the school more than two months. I felt so happy for her, because it was my ballet that had brought her to Balanchine's attention, but I was also beginning to feel a little left out as a dancer. True, I had only been at the school a month; Renee and Lynn had been there for two summer courses, and they would surely have gotten into the company sooner or later. I knew I wasn't a great dancer by SAB standards, but we were a group, Southern Californians all, and alumni of the ill-fated Western Ballet Association, so I was a bit down. Perhaps my dancing just wasn't up to par.

In truth, Renee was just eighteen, tall (five feet eight) strikingly beautiful—weren't they all?—with gorgeous long, long, legs and sky-high extensions equal to those of Sylvie Guillem (the latter-day French ballerina known for impossibly high *développés*), and she was yet another alumna of Kosmovska's. Later she became one of Balanchine's favorites and was destined for a stellar career; sadly, injuries plagued her, which curtailed her ascent. This was a real loss because those who saw her dance all agreed she was a star in the making.

Mr. B. then wanted me to start work on a third ballet. This time I chose music from the *L'Arlésienne Suites* by Georges Bizet. I had taken the neoclassic approach for *Scottish Dances,* and *Spirituals* had been jazzy and used all that floor work, so now I wanted to do something ultra-classical. I chose Kevyn O'Rourke as my lead, and like Renee, Lynn, and me, she was from Los Angeles and the Western Ballet. She had danced in my Shostakovich ballet there, and had been the "Waltz" girl in *Serenade* at the Greek Theater performance when Balanchine had launched the Ballet of Los Angeles. She was very reserved and elegant, with an almost Margot Fonteyn–like kind of class, and had a much different quality than that of Renee and Lynn.

Now, let me get to the men's teachers.

SAB's advanced men's classes were then taught by André Eglevsky (age fifty), Pierre Vladimiroff (seventy-four), and Stanley Williams (forty-two). There were two classes a week each given by Eglevsky, Vladimiroff, and Williams, for a total of six a week. It was a wonderful combination of excellent training. Also included in our schedule were two *pas de deux* classes each week, one by Williams and one by Eglevsky. In addition there were three evening mixed (girls and boys) technique classes. These were on Monday, Wednesday, and Friday and were called the "late-C" classes. They were optional for the boys, but I always took them anyway. There was also an afternoon level-C class on Saturday, right after the men's class, and we had the option of taking both classes, one right after the other, which I usually did. The teachers for the late-C classes were Antonina Tumkovsky, whom I considered just about the best teacher in the school (and very much like Kosmovska); Muriel Stuart, a former soloist with Anna Pavlova's company; and Alexandra Danilova, the great ballerina of Diaghilev's Ballets Russes. She later became a very close friend of mine and staged *Coppélia* for my Los Angeles Ballet in 1981. André Eglevsky never taught the evening classes because he lived on Long Island and took the train home, and I presume Vladimiroff was just too old for that heavy a workload.

I could not really figure out Pierre Vladimiroff at first. He had a very gentle persona, but he also carried an air of extreme sadness about him. Because of his age (he seemed much older than seventy-four), he sometimes lost his balance and concentration, and would stand for minutes on end between exercises, almost as if he were in a trance. He'd then recover just as he was about to fall over. This brought him back to his senses and he would invariably say, "Now we dance *my* waltz!" On more than one occasion he told a New York City Ballet soloist or principal dancer that he was "very good" and one day might even dance for Balanchine. Vladimiroff was a sweetheart, but we never took him very seriously. After I began taking Balanchine's class, though, I was amazed at the similarity to Vladimiroff's. The speed of the barre was almost identical.

Balanchine later told me that before he left Russia, Vladimiroff had been a celebrated principal dancer at the Mariinsky Ballet and later became Pavlova's partner in her own company after Diaghilev's death. Balanchine said Vladimiroff had suffered a nervous breakdown with the dissolution of that company on Diaghilev's death and was forced to dance in nightclubs to make a living. In his delicate mental state he just couldn't handle the stress, Mr. B. said. Vladimiroff was the husband of Felia Doubrovska, who also taught at the school; but she never taught the men, only the girls. While Balanchine was choreographing for Diaghilev, he created the role of the Siren in his *Prodigal Son* for her, and she was his original Polyhymnia in his *Apollon Musagètes*. These two, along with Danilova, formed a unique three-pronged direct link to the Imperial Russian Ballet and to Diaghilev.

The first time I had been at SAB, in early 1966, Eglevsky did not like me at all. He would come in with his cane and prod and poke me, and he would use his knuckles to knock us on the top of our heads for corrections, which I hated. It was the same way the boys were reprimanded in my military school (except that the commandant there wore a ring), so that brought back some unpleasant memories. Eglevsky really couldn't be bothered with me during my first phase at SAB, although things seemed to change the second time around. After it became clear that Balanchine was interested in me, Eglevsky started to pay me more attention and taught me a great deal. He later became an advocate of mine, and I ended up adoring him.

I loved Stanley Williams's classes from the very first day I was at the school. Stanley in those years taught a thoroughly Danish (Bournonville) technique, and he had charm to spare. (He subsequently changed his classes quite a bit, as I describe later.) His class accentuated a very light *ballon*, a precise elegant line, a *batterie* as clean as possible, and boundless energy. His classes were very exciting for another reason. The professional dancers then in them were a veritable "Who's Who" of the ballet world: Erik Bruhn, Rudolph Nureyev, and most of the company's male dancers showed up regularly—especially Edward Villella. They came to take his class but never Eglevsky's, which made Eglevsky a lot less popular than Stanley among the students. Eglevsky was hurt by this, but his classes were a bit heavier on the legs and not as much fun as Stanley's. Professional dancers wanted, and sometimes needed, a lighter class. His classes were consistently good, but his personality as a teacher was also lacking something. He often seemed bored, and disinterested, and I thought he was, but I was wrong.

Years later I came across him watching the men's-class films from the Vaganova school at Lincoln Center's Library for the Performing Arts. The Vaganova is what was formerly called the Imperial School, where Balanchine was trained, as were Pavlova, Nijinsky, and Danilova; in the USSR the school became the Vaganova Choreographic Institute, and Nureyev, Baryshnikov, Makarova, and others were trained there. Eglevsky would regularly give these same very difficult exercises to his students, but he never told us where they came from. None of us knew how conscientious he had been about his teaching. Who knew that those seemingly impossible combinations he gave came straight from the Vaganova school? It was a pity that he wasn't more popular, but I could see how important a teacher's personality was in drawing out the best from students.

8

School of American Ballet (Part 3)

New York City Ballet and Its Ballerinas

I don't know the actual turning point or direct event to pinpoint when I became a Balanchine fanatic. I am normally pretty stubborn and independent, so I fought against the sense of awe and hero worship surrounding Balanchine at his school. Nonetheless, from late September to early November I really started to fall under his spell. I had already sampled a few Broadway shows on my first trip to New York six months earlier and I thought classical ballet would be too restrictive, even choreographically; but after seeing more musicals I decided it would be too boring to do the same thing night after night. I loved *Sweet Charity* and *Hello, Dolly!*, among others, but doing the same show every night? Not for me. Plus, Plisetskaya had lit a big fire under me for classical ballet.

During that fall I began to think that life in Balanchine's world would actually be more fulfilling than Broadway, and I realized I had so much to learn! I knew I wasn't a good dancer by New York City Ballet standards, but I could try. I also started to understand that I knew absolutely nothing about the "Art" of choreography. I needed to choreograph, as I needed air to breathe, and I wanted to do it well, so I decided working for Balanchine would be the best possible thing.

On a whole other level, I couldn't have hit a better time to be living in New York City. Gwen Verdon and Ethel Merman were still performing on Broadway, as was Melba Moore; I saw her in *Purlie* many times. Leontyne Price, Joan Sutherland, and Birgit Nilsson were singing regularly at the Metropolitan Opera (because of my mother I loved the opera), so that was also heaven. Lots of theater all over the place, and the city's manic energy was a perfect match for mine.

Yet the best thing for me was that Balanchine was coming more frequently to watch my ballets. He never just showed up without being invited, of course, which I thought was very polite. I didn't think he was interested in me as a dancer, though, because as far as I knew he hadn't watched me in the school's classes. Later Jacques d'Amboise told me Balanchine was very aware of my dancing. Also, some company dancers started talking to me when they came to the school, asking me what I was working on, etc., and everyone was being very friendly, especially Jacques. He seemed to have fun watching me working on my triple *tours en l'air* in class (yes, I was doing triples—not cleanly I'm sure, but they were there), and he would correct me often and laugh good-naturedly at my puppy dog eagerness. He became something like my big brother or uncle.

Even the company's senior ballerina Melissa Hayden asked me to be her partner when she took the *pas de deux* classes. In those days, it was quite common for some of the company dancers to take that class alongside the students. It was such a thrill for the girls, I'm sure, when Jacques, Tony Blum, or Conrad Ludlow would show up to be their partner. All the teachers became friendlier to me too, and that seemed to be because Balanchine was clearly showing an interest. Alexandra Danilova showed me how to sew on my shoe elastics and would often take me to dinner at the Carnegie Tavern, her favorite restaurant in those years. She talked incessantly about Balanchine and gave me many insights into his character that others would not have known.

They had left Russia together in 1924 and lived together as lovers during the late 1920s and early '30s. Mr. B. always respected her, his original Terpsichore, and although Alicia Nikitina danced the premiere of *Apollon Musagètes*, Mr. B. told me he had choreographed that role for Danilova, "Choura" (her nickname). She quickly became one of my closest friends and allies, and this lasted until her death in 1997. She became like my mother in so many ways and she always gave me the best advice. I used to watch her girls' variation classes just to learn how those old ballets should be danced. The tempi were much faster than today, and the style has been quite changed. It's a real pity her classes weren't filmed.

In late November the company's season was about to begin, and Barbara Horgan, who had nudged me to return to New York, now told me Balanchine wanted me to see all the performances. She said to go to the stage door and there'd be a ticket waiting in my name. She said Mr. B. wanted me to "watch and learn." I was not told I was a member of the company, or anything like that, only that I should go to every performance—in those years eight per week. My seat usually was in the viewing booth in the back of the orchestra section, but sometimes I got prime orchestra or first balcony seats. So of course I went to every show, and watched, and boy, did I learn.

My favorite choreographer up until that time had been Jerome Robbins. I saw the movie version of *West Side Story* twenty-three times, but I had never actually seen any of his ballets live, with the exception of one performance of *Fanfare* when I was fifteen, danced by the Royal Danish Ballet at the Greek Theater. NYCB was then doing his nightmare version of *Giselle*, Act II, *The Cage*, which I absolutely flipped over, and his *Afternoon of a Faun*, which initially I didn't get. That ballet seemed a bit underwhelming the first time I saw it. Later, I got it.

After watching the company for a few weeks, I began feeling a tad guilty that I didn't like some of Balanchine's ballets more. *Monumentum pro Gesualdo* and *Movements for Piano and Orchestra* left me absolutely cold. The first time I saw *Apollo* I thought: *Why are they walking around on their heels?* It seemed that there were a lot of odd choreographic effects in *Apollo* that were just there to make it look different. Why did they walk on their damned heels? I didn't like that. I also wasn't crazy for *Concerto Barocco* at first. I didn't understand all that walking in the adagio movement, making what I considered "daisy chains." I started feeling confused because I knew very well by then how important Balanchine was and that he was considered a genius. His company clearly had the best dancers, and his school the best teachers, the orchestra was great, and they were in the opulent New York State Theater. What was I missing about some of his ballets? What wasn't I getting?

It certainly wasn't his ballerinas. I thought they were all outrageously beautiful and also discovered that some stories I'd heard were untrue. There was gossip at other schools, and some critics even wrote that Balanchine didn't like "personalities," that his choreography was without "soul," and that his whole approach was too "cold." Even though I didn't understand *Apollo, Monumentum,* and *Movements,* it was obvious that Balanchine not liking personalities was nonsense. The ballerinas and premier male dancers who were in the company then were Melissa Hayden, Violette Verdy, Suzanne Farrell, Mimi Paul, and Patricia McBride. (The extraordinary Allegra Kent was on maternity leave when I first started watching nightly.) The male principals were André Prokovsky, Edward Villella, Anthony Blum, Jacques d'Amboise, Conrad Ludlow, Francisco Moncion, Nicholas Magallanes, and Arthur Mitchell. It was truly a company filled with personalities.

People said Balanchine liked everyone to be the same. But there you had Hayden, a true "Prima Ballerina Assoluta," according to critic Clive Barnes, and Verdy, effervescence itself. Champagne had less sparkle. I was lucky I got to partner Violette relatively soon after joining the company. She just bubbled whenever she came onstage. You also had the very young Patricia McBride, with a most spectacularly beautiful face, similar to Audrey Hepburn's, and a totally unique and unaffected style. The regal Mimi Paul looked like a Royal Ballet ballerina because she was always so classy. She had it all—face, neck, arms, and incredibly high extensions. The important thing, and what was very clear, was that all these dancers were true artists. No matter their chronological age, each carried a real maturity. They weren't "boys and girls." They were men and women. I later found this all came from Balanchine's class and what he expected from his dancers. It wasn't just all about the technique. Far from it.

There were also those amazing soloists.

Gloria Govrin is not like anybody else in ballet and was one of the first dancers in the company who really knocked me out. She was like Plisetskaya in that she seemed larger than life and she had so much fun onstage. I just loved watching her. There was Patricia Neary, again not your typical ballet dancer, so forceful, and with what seemed the longest legs in the world. The delicate and elfin-faced Kay Mazzo, the uber-technician Marnee Morris, Sara Leland with the sexiest legs (quite like a ballet version of Ginger Rogers or a blond Rita Hayworth), Teena McConnell, Bettijane Sills, and the petite Suki Schorer—all were as different from each other as anyone could want. The male soloists included Kent Stowell, Frank Ohman, William "Billy" Weslow, Deni Lamont, Earle Sieveling, Paul Mejia, Shaun O'Brien, and the extraordinary John Prinz. Prinz was clearly Balanchine's favorite young male of that time and it was so obvious why. He was very flamboyant and almost arrogant in a Nureyev kind of way. He was a daredevil who had an enormous jump, great legs and feet, especially wonderful hands and *port de bras,* and he really commanded the stage. He was overtly masculine but also very sexy in a feline way. Balanchine was beginning to choreograph new ballets for him, such as *La Source* with Violette Verdy, and to put him into some Villella roles like *Tarantella.* Prinz was definitely a big star on the rise.

All the dancers certainly had a "look." But each was also an individual. As Violette so succinctly put it, "It was a company full of Borzois, and I felt like a little French poodle." Violette could always turn a phrase. Even those with the more traditional ballerina body types, like hers, Allegra Kent's, and others, all danced with a sleekness, articulation, and speed unique to Balanchine.

The mold-breaker, though, was Suzanne Farrell.

In those days Farrell seemed to be omnipresent and, looking back, why not? She was only twenty-one when I returned to New York and she was clearly Balanchine's favorite, and for very good reasons. She was tall, long-limbed, and strikingly beautiful, with an elegant long neck and a Botticelli face. She had a strong, if unusual, technique, and was also highly musical, which was of utmost importance for Balanchine. She didn't have much of a jump, but she had a gorgeous line and was a spectacular turner, and she was daring. She took more chances on-stage even than Plisetskaya. She would dance at least one, if not two, of the principal ballerina roles in every single performance, and did so until she left the company in 1969. Even if you liked Suzanne, it was almost too much of a good thing in those days. It was always Suzanne, Suzanne, Suzanne! But for Mr. B that was just fine. I believe she was truly the last of Balanchine's many muses. Mr. B. and Pygmalion had so much in common. Both fell in love with their creation . . . and it always ended badly.

Sadly, but not surprisingly, there was a lot of jealousy from some of the other ballerinas Suzanne's age. A couple complained bitterly about the unfairness of Balanchine's obsession with her, and to anyone who would listen. I thought these dancers still had plenty to dance, but everyone wanted to be his "favorite." There could only be one primary muse for Balanchine at any given time, and now it was Suzanne's turn. True, he could choreograph fantastic roles for his other lesser muses, but from what I witnessed, Suzanne alone ruled his heart.

The irony is that in many circles, and among several critics, Mimi

Paul was preferred to Farrell at this time. Mimi was also a principal and danced most of the ballerina roles, but for Balanchine, on an emotional level, there was only Farrell. A dancer's career is short as it is, and Suzanne obviously lived to dance, and she clearly worshipped him, so Mr. B. wanted her onstage as much as possible.

A simple Balanchine formula might be: Young talented girl inspires Balanchine. He develops her technique as well as her artistry, and then he creates a new repertoire based on that dancer's special gifts, which he has developed. A very symbiotic relationship. Sounds simple, doesn't it? After that dancer becomes a mature personality, or "star," which sometimes happens with fame and age and can cause some dancers to put themselves before the choreography, Balanchine is in turn freed to be inspired by a different young ego-less dancer, for whom he creates a different repertoire. Each inspires the other, but built into this system, because of aging on the part of the ballerina, is that Balanchine would not stagnate but would be freed to find his next muse. This continuing process made it possible for Balanchine to be creative for such a long period, from which all dancers have benefitted. This happened with his men as well. Think of all those great ballets he choreographed for Edward Villella. People often forget that Balanchine created as many great roles for men as he did for women. *Apollo, Prodigal Son, Tarantella, Rubies,* and more are all great vehicles for men as well as for women. He eventually created a few for me too!

Even though I had seen his company in Los Angeles, I wasn't prepared for the impact the company dancing in their home theater would have on me. Here are a few quick first impressions of some of the ballets I saw in their proper surroundings.

Prodigal Son

When those nine boys in the corps de ballet made their first entrance, wearing those bald skull caps, to those bombastic musical chords by Prokofiev, in what can only be described as looking like a giant centipede, I thought my head would explode! I had never seen anything remotely like this onstage, or in films, for that matter. I was hypnotized from that point on. Villella, in the title role, was not merely a dancer. He was a world-class Olympic athlete who just happened to be dancing. He was also a great actor in this ballet. Farrell as the Siren was heartless, with ice in her veins and dripping evil from every pore, frightening in her glacial beauty. Now this was *drama* with a capital D.

Their totally erotic *pas de deux* actually shocked me, the boy who had grown up with strippers! When Eddie stuck his head between her thighs and lifted her onto his shoulders without using his hands—well, I couldn't believe the optical illusion Balanchine had created. At the end of this pas, when the Siren sits on his head in an act of total domination, I just couldn't believe Balanchine's choreographic daring as well as his psychological savvy. There were so many outrageous sexual references and innuendos all through this ballet (and as a healthy teenage male I loved these). I just couldn't wrap my brain around how I was sitting in a theater with 2,800 other people watching what could be considered almost pornographic in another setting. It wasn't, of course, but it was still very sexy stuff.

At the end of this ballet, when Villella crawls on his knees across the stage, with his hands locked behind his back, to beg forgiveness from his Father (the wonderful character dancer Shaun O'Brien), I thought my heart would break. My ambivalence about the ballets I didn't understand, like *Concerto Barocco* (which I now love) was no longer an issue. You don't need words when the actions are that clear and the acting that great.

The final moment, when the Father picks up his son and gently wraps his cloak around the boy in a gesture of forgiveness, is one of the greatest moments in all theater, not just in ballet. I stupidly left the company before I could dance this role, even though Balanchine told me I would. My only compensation for not dancing it is that I have now staged this great work for companies around the world, including the Paris Opera Ballet, the Ballet of La Scala, and others; but truthfully, I always regret that I never got to dance it.

Serenade

I first saw what many call Balanchine's greatest ballet when he staged it himself (or, rather, when his NYCB ballet mistress staged it, with him supervising) for the Ballet of Los Angeles. Seeing it in New York City, in Balanchine's home theater with its spectacular 1960s lighting, gave it a special sweep and authority. Melissa Hayden, as the "Waltz" girl, Violette Verdy as the "Russian" girl, and Mimi Paul as the "Dark Angel" was a cast to die for. Nicholas Magallanes in the Elegy movement and Conrad Ludlow in the Waltz both brought a deep meaning and gravity to these roles. I was beginning to realize that Balanchine's casting choices were as important as his choreography. I have never lost my awe and respect for this timeless art work of unquestionable genius. I love it more each time I stage it.

Brahms-Schoenberg Quartet

Only Balanchine could have pulled off this large-scale ballet to Arnold Schoenberg's orchestration of the Brahms Piano Quartet No. 1 in G Minor. Using a huge cast in four completely separate movements, he created a startlingly entertaining classical ballet without any obvious bravura technical tricks, like thirty-two *fouettés* or other such banal gimmicks.

In the first performance I saw, the first movement was led by Melissa Hayden, Anthony Blum (one of my favorite male dancers, whom I later used in nearly all my ballets), and the inimitable Gloria Govrin. Govrin looked as though she was jumping higher than the four soloist level boys behind her (including the high-flying John Prinz) and she had the plushest of *pliés*. Her voluptuous proportions—"Rubensesque," one critic called her—enabled her to look like a statue of a Greek goddess come miraculously to life.

She looked ten feet tall (she was actually five feet nine). "Big Glo's" first entrance was a huge step, a *temps levé* in arabesque followed by an enormous elongated *piqué* arabesque that stopped in a balance that looked impossible to hold. Her front arm reached up in a perfect high forty-five degrees, yet her arabesque leg also went up behind her in the opposite direction at another perfect high forty-five degrees. This "stretch" of that arabesque (both arms, legs, and even hands reaching out to infinity, unconfined by the mere proscenium of the stage) was what Balanchine taught daily in class and expected in every performance. Gloria commanded that extremely large stage with that one single entrance. Hayden and Blum were no less impressive. Melissa's daring attack of every step and Tony's always handsome and masculine presence (plus superb partnering) made them a perfect match.

The intimate second movement was basically a rhapsodic *pas de deux* for Patricia McBride ("Patty") and that incomparable partner, Conrad Ludlow ("Connie"). Patty looked as if she were in the air for most of this and Connie's impeccable partnering made every lift magical. She never showed strain, and there was no unnecessary posing or preening on his part; plus, he looked like a matinee idol from the movies of the 1940s, a lighter-haired Robert Taylor. The exit lift took my breath away; in my experience no dancers since have been able to equal that last swoop into the wings. (Actually, I think that last tricky lift was changed after Balanchine's death, for some unfathomable reason.) There was also always something so innocent and unaffected about Patty's dancing, no matter how sexy she could sometimes be. Think of "The Man I Love" *pas de deux* from *Who Cares?*

The third movement appeared to me to be an homage to Mikhail Fokine's *Les Sylphides*. A large corps of girls framed a couple who could have come straight out of a nineteenth-century ballet. The almost military flavor of the music for this section is sublime and Balanchine's choreography for the man's solo is spectacular. He choreographed this movement for Villella and Allegra Kent, but she was unfortunately out on maternity leave when I first saw it. Suki Schorer replaced her and did an excellent job, but I regret not seeing Allegra dance this. (Everything Balanchine choreographed for her never seemed quite the same when other dancers took on her roles. How could they be?)

Eddie Villella was magnificent and truly at the top of his form. His ability to hang in the air was unrivaled in those years, and even Nureyev couldn't top him in this. He also used his trademark macho attack to make what could look a bit old-fashioned appear completely contemporary. Balanchine used the *fortissimo* music for the man's variation, a march, which made it even more exciting. One lone man onstage dancing to that huge music played by the entire orchestra gives me chills even thinking about it. I still get goose bumps every time I hear it. Years later, Balanchine cast me in this virtuosic role, and my partners included Gelsey Kirkland, among other wonderful dancers such as Elise Flagg, who had a major success in it.

The Hungarian-flavored fourth movement was to me the biggest surprise and the most fun. Balanchine pulled out all the stops in this Gypsy-influenced music, which was very "show biz" with no apologies.

Led by an exuberant Jacques d'Amboise and a surprisingly sexy Suzanne Farrell, this movement was wild! I had only seen Farrell as a cool "ice princess" in her other roles, but here she was absolutely oozing sex appeal. I think it was d'Amboise who drew this out of her, along with the great choreography, of course.

Jacques was rather rough with his partnering in this, on purpose I think, just to push Farrell, but Suzanne gave as good as she got. The passion between the two of them just added to the heat. At the end it actually looked as though Jacques bit her breast in the last swoon. I think today's dancers and audiences would be shocked at how untamed this was—take-no-prisoners style ballet. I *loved* it! Balanchine "cold" and "too cerebral"? Absolutely not.

Stars and Stripes

The first cast I saw had Hayden and d'Amboise as the leads, with Gloria Govrin leading the Tall Girls' Regiment, Deni Lamont leading the Men's Regiment, and Carol Sumner leading the Small Girls' Regiment. *It was heaven.* In one performance I saw Govrin do nine pirouettes *en pointe* (!), and Lamont hamming it up in what can only be called Broadway style, and Sumner all delicacy and charm. Best of all was the great Melissa Hayden, in this ballet Balanchine created for her, showing the world what it meant to be a true "Prima Ballerina Assoluta." Her unique style and steely strong technique and authority are legendary. She was a wonderful role model for all the younger dancers in the company. Jacques was Mr. Personality, and this is not a putdown. I would learn from Balanchine in class (as I describe in detail later) how important the art of entertainment was to him. Certainly Jacques and Melissa had learned this lesson well.

When I got to dance this role, Balanchine cast me with Violette Verdy. Violette was equal to Melissa in strength and technique, but she brought a definite French charm and insouciance to the role. Was I lucky or what?

Western Symphony

Another of Balanchine's audience-friendly ballets was this good-natured but still fiendishly difficult semi-spoof on the American Wild

West and cowboys. A Russian using Western tunes and choreographing cowboys? It became obvious to me early on that Balanchine had a great sense of humor and really loved American culture.

Once again, the standout performer for me on that first viewing was Gloria Govrin. She, with the equally impressive Frank Ohman, led the fourth movement with so much brio, brass, and good-natured humor that it has been forever burned into my brain. I go to the ballet to have *fun*. Nothing was as much fun as watching this hysterical ballet, especially Govrin and Ohman going for broke in the finale. Glo's furiously fast *fouetté* turns with a double thrown in every so often (at Mr. B's suggestion, she later told me) and Frank's impossibly fast double *tours en l'air* to a double pirouette four times in a row seemed like a special effect. Both of them tore up that stage!

Tarantella and *Tchaikovsky Pas de Deux*

I first saw these in Los Angeles at the Greek Theater with Villella in both, partnering Verdy in *Tchaikovsky Pas de Deux* and McBride in *Tarantella*. Seeing these same dancers on the much larger State Theater stage further increased my respect for them.

Both ballets are physically demanding, and both need stylists as well as technicians. Many other dancers, both male and female, from many international companies, have danced both these *pas de deux* to great acclaim, and deservedly so. Balanchine left plenty of room in *Tchaikovsky Pas de Deux* for all types of dancers (less so in *Tarantella*, which needs smaller, fast technicians).

I've staged both these ballets for the Bolshoi Ballet and many other companies. In every case the dancers love the challenge of dancing them. It would have seemed impossible to this then-nineteen-year-old student that in less than four years he would be dancing these ballets with these same great ballerinas. I still cannot quite believe it.

The Four Temperaments

The last of the ballets that firmly cemented my loyalty to Balanchine was this incredible work. Not flashy, like many of the preceding ballets described in this chapter, *The Four Temperaments* made me grow up a little. I was mesmerized from the first movement, which was a simple *port de bras*. Such austerely beautiful music by Hindemith (music Balanchine later told me he had commissioned) and such an almost religious seriousness from the dancers really struck something deep inside me—at that time a rather callow California boy. It is difficult to describe why this ballet affected me so. It wasn't just the principal dancers. It was the ballet itself. Certainly Patricia Neary in "Choleric" was impressive, as were Melissa Hayden and Gloria Govrin, who were alternating in the "Sanguinic" section with Anthony Blum. Arthur Mitchell was still dancing the "Phlegmatic" role, and his otherworldly inherent nobility was something to cherish.

Slim and elegant (there's that word again), Richard Rapp was dancing "Melancholic," and then and there I knew I just had to dance that part someday.

After watching all these ballets there was no other life for me but to follow Balanchine. It was as simple as that. It was a vocation for me, as if I had discovered my true religion. No other companies or choreographers could hold a candle to what I saw in that theater.

It is not a stretch to say I had an epiphany. This was the life I wanted, that I *had* to have.

There was no other option.

9

My First Balanchine Class and Entry into the New York City Ballet

While I was going to performances every night, attending SAB, and choreographing for the workshops, I found time to do some guest performances with André Eglevsky's student company on Long Island. He obviously thought more of my dancing by this time, and he also asked for some of my choreography. The ballet I staged for him was *The Class,* which I had done for the Western Ballet. Three of the dancers were from the original LA cast: Renee Estopinal, Lynn Bryson, and Kevyn O'Rourke. Pamela Perry was new for the Long Island version. My first serious dance injury occurred during this engagement. We were in the middle of the finale when I sprained my ankle. I limped through the rest of the ballet, but it was a shock to have it happen in front of an audience. It underscored an important lesson though: the show *must* go on.

I then had the bright idea that if I couldn't take class because of my injury, perhaps Balanchine would allow me to watch his company class. I had never seen him teach, and I was very curious.

I asked Barbara, and she said simply, "Why don't you just ask him?" I had not really spoken to Balanchine much, except about my workshop ballets, and I had never asked for a favor. I didn't even know what he thought of me as a dancer. Barbara told me I could find him in the hall of the theater when he was walking to the studio, so I waylaid him there one morning, but I couldn't get any words out of my mouth.

I simply froze. He said, "What do you want, dear?" "Well, ah, ah, I hurt my ankle and I uh, uh, I can't take class." For once in my life, I was totally tongue-tied. He said, "Do you want something?" I think he was amused at my awkwardness. He was used to people being nervous in front of him, but I think he may also have been annoyed because he wanted to start the class and I was holding him up. Finally, I got it out:

"Mr. Balanchine, I sprained my ankle and can't take class at the school. Would it be all right if I watched your class?" He squinted, wrinkled up his nose (at the school in Russia his nickname was "Rat"), and said, "You just want to *watch* class?" I said, "Yes, if that's OK," and he said, "Of course, come in, dear," and with that he opened the door to my future.

In 1966 the company had around sixty-eight dancers, and it was a very tightly knit group. They knew they were the elite because they had all been selected by Balanchine. They worked for the best choreographer in the world (that was the opinion they all shared, at least those who regularly took his class), and they had the best theater ever built for dance. At first they appeared to be snooty and clique-ish. They even had their own language. "Hilda" meant something was really awful. "Pretty" was said with a sneer and translated as bad or mediocre. To "perch" meant to balance. To say, "It was never like that" meant that one had forgotten the step and changed it on the fly. Any new dancer in the company was called the "new German boy or girl" (I never did figure that one out). "Clear!" was called if someone was in the way and was about to be run over. Balanchine was definitely the "father," and the company was his "family." To this day I've never seen another company atmosphere quite like this.

As I got to know the dancers better, I found that there was a small anti-Balanchine contingent led by a couple of the men. This really had as much to do with their loyalty to their favorite teacher, Stanley Williams, as with their problems with Balanchine. Mr. B.'s classes were very demanding, and he sometimes seemed more interested in the women than the men, whereas Stanley's classes were definitely more oriented for the men. I now also believe the anti-Balanchine rebellion was a bit of macho posturing. Balanchine's well-known axiom, "Ballet is Woman," appeared to bruise some of these men's egos. However, it didn't seem to bother d'Amboise, Ludlow, Moncion, Mitchell, Blum, Magallanes, Stowell, Prinz, or Mejia.

Villella used to say that when he took Balanchine's class (before my time, as I never saw him in one), they were too hard on his legs. He did have rather short, heavily muscled legs, which he said cramped up in Mr. B's classes; but they did make it easier for him to move quickly, which Balanchine appreciated and used to great advantage. Perhaps he did need slower classes because he lost four years of training at a crucial time when he went to the Maritime College at his father's insistence. Even though he didn't take Balanchine's class, just think of all those wonderful ballets Balanchine created for him, like *Rubies* and *Tarantella*, and "Oberon" in *A Midsummer Night's Dream* (all roles I later danced). Clearly Mr. B. never held it against Eddie that he skipped his classes.

Peter Martins, when he first joined the company, rebelled at Balanchine's insistence on simple double pirouettes, quick preparations for all the turns, and very precise small simple steps like glissades. Peter had a super-clean technique, but in those early years he was quite stubborn. It took some time for him to adjust, as he admits in his autobiography, *Far from Denmark*.

Except by those two men and their acolytes, Balanchine was loved and revered. However, the company dancers were snobbish toward outsiders, so you can imagine the effect of Mr. B. walking into class followed by a young-looking boy (I was nineteen but looked much younger) in a cheap brown suit and tie. I thought I should dress up, and I wore this same suit to all the performances. Some but not all the dancers knew me from the school. Balanchine then said to the class, "We have a guest." He opened up a folding chair, put it in a front corner of the room, and said, "Now Cleeeford, you sit here, and you watch and learn." I felt as if I were under a microscope, but of course did as I was told.

At first I was surprised that his classes were so full of jokes. He had a rather serious, almost severe-looking face, and I thought he'd be a very strict teacher. Wrong. I realized immediately he had a wonderfully dry and quite naughty sense of humor. His class atmosphere was very relaxed and happy and not at all serious. He later confided in me he told his jokes because "It makes them forget they're working hard." So smart. Balanchine's classes were never pre-planned, but he would sometimes patiently emphasize one particular step a day, which in a way was like the classes Dolin had taught me the previous summer, drawing on how Cecchetti taught at the Ballets Russes. Since the dancers were dancing eight performances a week, Balanchine didn't feel the need to give a well-rounded class. If he saw a weakness in a particular step in the previous night's performance, he worked on it the next day. This caused a lot of concern among those few dancers who came to his class only sporadically, because they didn't get a well-rounded class for the day. I was just amazed that they didn't come every day and take advantage of his teaching.

After a few days of my attending these classes, several more dancers in the company started warming up to me. Mimi Paul went out of her way to be pleasant, as did Pat Neary, and so did a few of the younger dancers. Especially friendly was Robert "Ricky" Weiss, who'd already been nice to me at the school and who had just gotten into the company before I returned, and a couple of his friends, Johnna Kirkland and Giselle Roberge. We eventually became quite a tight little group.

After a couple weeks of my watching his class, Mr. B. asked me how my ankle was. When I told him it was better, he said I should take the class. I said I couldn't really do anything in the center yet, but maybe I could just do the barre section, and he said that was fine. His barre was much, much, harder than it looked, though. After that first barre my muscles absolutely felt as if they were on fire. I'd never felt such pain, but it was the good kind; and not an injury. After that day, I took every company barre, and after a couple of classes, that fire went away and I felt myself getting stronger. Gradually I started doing some center work, albeit standing as far back in the room as I could manage.

I was still going to all the performances and was still confused as to why I didn't care more for some of his ballets. I was used to more theatrical dances, like those of Jerome Robbins. Most of Balanchine's ballets had no plots and I didn't understand how he used the music. I was used to "copycatting" music.

I did begin to notice, though, that with Mr. B.'s ballets, the more I watched them, the more I saw in them, including the ones I didn't at first like. I found something new in them every time, and I was never ever bored. Robbins's steps and combinations were clever and I enjoyed their inherent drama and theatricality, but they did not have the same depth of Balanchine's works. I not only discovered different layers in Balanchine's ballets—I'd find whole new ballets.

Lincoln Kirstein started speaking with me more often by then, and one day he asked me how serious I was about choreographing. I told him making ballets was actually more important to me than performing. He said, "Really? Good. Make sure you come to all the performances.

You have to learn what George does, and how." A few days later Lincoln had a formal meeting with me about my future. I say "formal" because he asked to see me in his office instead of just speaking to me in a hall or classroom. I confessed to him that I felt slightly guilty about not really liking like some of Balanchine's ballets. He said, "Of course, not all of his ballets are good. You just decide which you like and which you don't. Give it time." I was unprepared for that. I thought he would have said all Balanchine's ballets were great. Lincoln also told me that day that Balanchine was very interested in me as a dancer as well as a choreographer. This really surprised me. I told him I thought Mr. B. was only interested in my choreography, not my dancing. But he said, "Oh, no, Johnny." (They all called me Johnny back then.) "You'd make a great Harlequin in *Harlequinade* and you'd make a good Oberon." He then began listing ballets he thought I should dance. Most of these were what Balanchine had made for Villella. I couldn't believe it. I had never presumed I was being groomed as a leading dancer too. I wasn't even in the company!

Ironically, watching Villella dance, I never assumed that I would ever do any of his parts. I loved the ballets he danced, but I saw no similarity in our styles. Also, although he had those incredible jumps, he wasn't a particularly great turner, and I had gotten up to twelve pirouettes on occasion, so I didn't dance the way he did at all. Eddie danced more like a boxer; indeed, he was a welter weight championship boxer in college. I danced, or tried to dance, like a male Plisetskaya, or a Vasiliev, or a Gene Kelly. As it turned out, I ended up dancing almost all of Villella's roles.

One day Carol Deschamps, the company's executive assistant who worked under the general manager, Betty Cage, told me she had heard that Balanchine wanted me to dance the lead in "Hoops" in *The Nutcracker*. "Hoops" is the Candy Canes dance to the Russian trepak music of the second act and, according to Danilova, is what Balanchine had danced himself in the Mariinsky's St. Petersburg production. It uses eight young girls and a solo boy whose basic job is to jump through his hoop at what seems the speed of light. My ankle was better by then, and I was very excited about the prospect of dancing "Hoops."

But just before *Nutcracker* rehearsals were to begin, Ms. Cage called me into her office and said, "Mr. B. would like you to dance Candy Canes but you can't do it this year." She told me it would have been very bad form in those days to allow a dancer who wasn't even in the company to dance a much-coveted solo role. I was disappointed, of course, but I understood the situation.

A few weeks later I headed back to the school when my ankle was completely healed, but on my first day back Diana Adams stopped me in the hall and asked me why I wasn't at the theater taking Balanchine's company class. I said, "Because my ankle is fine and I thought I should be back here." She said, "Johnny, you're supposed to take Mr. Balanchine's class when you're in the company. You should be in his class, not here." I said, "What do you mean? In the company?" She said, "Well you've been in for a couple of weeks now, didn't anyone tell you?" "Wait! What? I'm *in* the company? No, no one told me!" "We thought you knew," she said.

After that, I high-tailed it right back to the theater and signed the contract that had been sitting in Betty Cage's office the whole time! After my signing, she told me to see the company business manager, Zelda Dorfman, where my salary checks were waiting for me. Things were much more informal in those days. As you can imagine, I was ecstatic. I then started taking Balanchine's daily company class, plus the school's classes when I could find the time, and I started being taught the repertoire. Busy isn't the word! I had to discontinue choreographing for the school at that time (although I did many ballets for them again later), so the choreography to the *L'Arlesienne* music was never completed. My total time at SAB before getting into the company was about six weeks, not counting the three months earlier that winter.

The first thing I was cast in was the men's regiment in *Stars and Stripes.* Being short, I was put in the front row along with Paul Mejia, who was the same height, but I hardly had any rehearsal at all. Then I was put in the corps of the fourth movement of *Western Symphony.* I was also cast as Kastchei (the evil wizard in *Firebird*), which was a huge surprise because this was usually danced by soloist Deni Lamont or by Shaun O'Brien. I didn't know at the time that Balanchine himself had danced this in the original Fokine version when he was around my age. Later, Danilova told me this at one of our dinners. It was all happening so fast that I really didn't know what I was doing in any of these ballets! But at last I was onstage, and in the New York City Ballet. Watch out world.

10

New York City Ballet Corps—Piano Lessons—Paul and Suzanne

Balanchine was obviously interested in me as a choreographer, and now as a dancer, but all the same, my entrance into the company was unusually fast. Because of that, there was a lot of jealousy from the other male dancers. Unfortunately, I did not help matters much. Once, after a performance of *Stars and Stripes,* the assistant ballet mistress, Francia Russell (then under John Taras and Una Kai, the senior ballet masters), came backstage rather annoyed at me. During a crossing section in which all the boys had to do *grand jetés* diagonally across the stage, I evidently wasn't "with" everyone else. She said, "Johnny, you have to jump with the other boys." I didn't understand and asked if I had been out of line or off the music. She said, "No, you're just jumping too high." Hmmm. I never could adjust to a corps de ballet mentality, and I thought, *just get the other boys to jump higher.* I didn't say this out loud, of course.

My next assignments were in the corps of Mice and the Spanish dance in *The Nutcracker.* I also mimed the role of the Grandfather in the first act. That was when the ham in me really came out. I was still wearing retaining braces on my teeth and when I took them out, it looked as if I had no teeth. So, in the middle of the "Grandfather's Dance," I walked around miming that I had lost my teeth. I then "found" them (using my retainers) and stuck them in my mouth. I don't know how I got away with it. Balanchine was in the wings every single performance and never missed one. His favorite spot was in the downstage right wing, next to the stage manager's stand, so he saw everything that was going on. In the "Grandfather's Dance" all the Parents clap in time to the music while their children dance. Sometimes I would pretend I was deaf. After the music stopped, I would pretend that I thought the music was still going on, and I would continue to clap loudly in tempo to complete silence. This would crack up the audience and sometimes even the musicians, since I would also be stamping my foot and carrying on like a mad man right downstage near the orchestra pit. I would wait for the Father to tap me on the shoulder and pantomime, "No, the music's stopped now, Granddad."

There was also one section when I would be walking toward the orchestra pit and I would pretend to be about to fall in. I would warn the Grandmother (usually Johnna or Giselle), and she would grab me and pull me back just in the nick of time. I'd be right over the double basses and cellos, and they would all look up and start laughing. Ronald Bates, the stage manager, would tell me to tone it down, and I'd say, "Yes, you're right. Sorry." Then, a week later, I'd do it all again. I was incorrigible. The company performed *The Nutcracker* thirty-five to forty times every Christmas season, and I would be in every performance, so I did like to add these bits of business. Balanchine saw it all, of course. He was right there when I did all my shenanigans, but he never said a word to me. He just smiled when I did my shtick. I didn't know how far to push it, but I figured he must like it or he would have stopped me.

One time, during all this, I finally got Suzanne Farrell to laugh. Normally, she pouted disapprovingly when I was being tacky or trying to get a laugh. I succeeded, but it was only because she didn't recognize it was me. When I was still one of the Mouse King's army I had developed the habit, after the King was slain, of pulling out an enormous handkerchief and wailing into it, miming hysterical grief. Of course, the audience would break up. After I had milked this for all it was worth, I would pick up the shoe that Marie had thrown and, holding it aloft, would very classically *bourrée* offstage, sometimes *en pointe*. I could do the Georgian men's character-dancer technique of standing on my toes in soft ballet slippers. It hurt but was worth it. During one performance, I bourréed into the wings and found Suzanne standing there with Mr. B. She had obviously enjoyed my antics and laughingly, asked, "Who *is* that?" Happy at finally having caught her being amused, I pulled off the mouse head and said, "Oh, it's just me!" She instantly stopped smiling, but Balanchine seemed to find the whole episode rather entertaining. He laughed. She didn't. Ah, well . . .

Here I should add in my own defense that I made these "additions" only during pantomime sequences and never during choreographed dances. Unfortunately, even though I had been taken into the company, I didn't get cast in the Candy Cane lead that first year. I guess Mr. B. thought I had enough to handle—and I did!

Any free time started becoming very scarce. Understatement. What free time? Balanchine had now also sent me to take piano lessons from Madame Zoloty (I never learned her first name). I had not had any musical training other than singing in high school, and Mr. B. wanted me to study music more formally. I was excited about this and had every intention of seeing it through, except that, as it turned out, Paul Mejia was also studying with Madame Z. Although I never thought of myself as being insecure, I would go to those lessons as a total beginner and had to listen to her rave about Paul, who had been studying with her for years. "What a brilliant pianist he is. He should be a concert pianist. He's Balanchine's favorite, you know, and he wants him to become a choreographer too," she said over and over and definitely made me feel his inferior. I got so tired of hearing her continually praising Paul that after a couple of months, I just couldn't stand those damn piano lessons any longer. I really wanted to catch up and study as much as I could, but there was just not enough time to do everything; so I dropped those lessons.

When I told Gordon Boelzner (Balanchine's preferred company pianist) about this, and that I was worried Mr. B. might be upset I had stopped the piano lessons, Gordon said, "Don't worry. Balanchine told me, Cleeeford can *hear* everything." What a great compliment (and Mr. B. never brought up my studying music again).

I had now been in the company a few months and had resumed choreographing for the school, I was performing almost every night, and I was watching every single performance, which I did until the day I left the company. Also, by this time, Lincoln was taking me to plays and concerts. He told me how he had first met Balanchine in London when they were both in their twenties, and about the beginnings of SAB and the company. It was great hearing these stories first-hand from the man who had brought Balanchine to America, and it was obvious he was trying to educate me as Diaghilev had educated Balanchine. I was beginning to get the hint that both he and Balanchine had some sort of master plan for me.

Balanchine was about to start choreographing a special Juggler's solo for the first act of his full-length *Don Quixote,* which was about to open in two weeks, in mid-February 1967. When I joined the company, Paul Mejia, along with Prinz, was the male dancer in whom Balanchine was clearly most interested. Paul had a big jump, easy multiple pirouettes, and a soft, elegant style. We dancers all assumed this new solo would be for him since Prinz already had a solo role in this ballet. It came as a big surprise to everyone, especially Paul, when Mr. B. called me to understudy this from its first day of creation. This was most unusual for Balanchine, as he would typically not even have other dancers in the same room while he was choreographing. He said it "distracted" him. He wanted to focus only on the dancer he was working with. The next surprise was when he cast me in half the performances. Paul and I got six shows each. This was also most unusual for him. For a new dance he never had second casts or even understudies.

At the first onstage rehearsal, I did a rather bizarre thing that cemented in Balanchine's mind that I was a good turner. At the end of this solo, the dancer does turns "à la seconde" or what is commonly called a "grand pirouette" (turning hops on one leg, with the other leg stretched out to the dancer's side). After this step, the dancer pulls his leg into a *passé* position to do multiple pirouettes. That day Balanchine was standing right in front of me and no more than six feet from my face. When I pulled in for the turns, I was so freaked out by his being so close to me that I just kept turning! I was actually "spotting" his face. ("Spotting" is what it's called when you turn and snap your head back to the same spot to keep from getting dizzy.) Some of the dancers were watching and they said I did fourteen pirouettes. I didn't count them, of course, but I knew I must have done a lot because afterward Balanchine was looking at me with a shocked expression on his face. Even though he didn't allow a dancer to do more than two turns in his class, he certainly enjoyed a circus now and then, depending on the ballet. I had done up to twelve turns in other classes, when Ricky and I would have turning contests for fun (Ricky could do that many too), but I had never done this many in front of Balanchine. After that he always thought of me as a great turner. Of course, that day was a total fluke.

11

Balanchine at Work

Jewels—My First NYC Reviews—
More Classes and the Kiss

I was not yet dancing many solos, other than the Juggler in *Don Quixote* and Kastchei in *Firebird,* but I was dancing some featured corps parts. This was significant, because when a new dancer joined the company, Mr. B. could be clear early on by the kind of corps parts he first cast you in if he had his eye on you for bigger things. I was fortunate to get some good parts right away, those with an extra step or two. I certainly had no complaints.

In the spring of 1967 I had my first opportunity to be in a major Balanchine ballet from its very inception. A work titled *Jewels* was to be the new ballet for the spring season, and rumor had it that this would be the first three-act, plotless ballet ever choreographed. It had three sections or "acts," which were really complete ballets unto themselves: *Emeralds,* to music of Gabriel Fauré, would open, followed by *Rubies,* to the jazz influenced *Capriccio for Piano and Orchestra* by Igor Stravinsky, and finally *Diamonds,* to the final four movements of the five-movement Tchaikovsky Symphony No. 3. *Diamonds* was a large classical display piece, not only for its principal dancers, Suzanne Farrell and Jacques d'Amboise, but also for its huge corps de ballet of sixteen couples, four of whom were solo couples. My placement was in the next-to-last corps couple, fifteenth, out of the wings for the finale, a grand Polonaise.

Balanchine choreographed all three of these very different ballets simultaneously, going from studio to studio, sometimes with no break in between. He would also work on a finale before starting the first movement. Time was always used economically. This was an important lesson for me. As he always said, "The Muse works on union time." On April 13, 1967, the premiere of *Jewels* took place during the company's annual Spring Gala. With gorgeous sets by Peter Harvey, sumptuously elegant costumes by Barbara Karinska (she was Balanchine's favorite costume designer and she really outdid herself this time), and superb lighting by Ronald Bates, it was a spectacular success! Nothing like this had ever been attempted before. Tying it all together were the jewel motif and the genius of Balanchine.

Act I, *Emeralds,* was danced to perfection by Violette Verdy and Conrad Ludlow in the opening *pas de deux.* Following were solos for Violette and Mimi Paul, then a bravura *pas de trois* for Suki Schorer, Sara Leland, and John Prinz. After that came the "Walking" *pas de deux* for Mimi and the older, magisterial (no other adjective fits) Francisco Moncion. Then came a very upbeat finale. Years later Balanchine added another *pas de deux* for Verdy, and a somber but beautiful Epilogue. This totally changed the feeling of the whole ballet from an upbeat classical work to one of mystery and gravity.

The class and style that Verdy, Paul, and Moncion brought to these roles has never been equaled, in my humble opinion. Of course, when Mr. B. made a ballet for a particular dancer, he knew how to bring out the very essence of that person, so perhaps it's unfair to compare subsequent casts. Other dancers have admirably conquered the roles for the second and third sections, *Rubies* and *Diamonds,* but for *Emeralds,* I'm not so sure. Possibly, new dancers just need a little coaching for this most evocative of ballets. *Emeralds* was never just about technique. It needs a certain perfume and, dare I say, maturity, to make it really work.

Rubies followed, which was completely different from *Emeralds* in style, character, technique, and musicality. The music is Stravinsky's rhythm-driven *Capriccio for Piano and Orchestra.* If *Emeralds* was elegant, refined, nostalgic, even "French," *Rubies* was fast, sexy, brash, witty, and oh so American, but with a distinctly New York accent. McBride, Villella, and Neary as the "Tall Girl" soloist were the go-for-broke leads. Patty was on fire as I'd never seen her before, doing not just triple pirouettes, but quadruples, and Villella was, well . . . Villella! There had been no one like him before in ballet, or even in dance, for that matter.

In *Rubies* he was an uber-macho tough guy, yet very sexy, a Dead End Kid disguised as a ballet dancer. He jumped like a bolt of lightning, spun almost out of control, beat his legs ferociously, but all with a great likability and sense of humor. Truly, Eddie in his prime was unique.

And Pat Neary? She started the ballet off and also began the finale, and Balanchine caught every inflection of her personality and angular, long-legged aggressiveness. She was not so much the sexy show girl, as it is danced today. She was more like an Amazon Queen leading the troops. Actually my favorite in this role who most successfully combined the show girl sexiness with the Amazon approach was Renee Estopinal. During her brief period of being injury free she danced this fantastically well. After one show Balanchine said only one word: "Finally!"

To close came *Diamonds,* with the grandest of all grand classical *pas de deux* and the mother of all Grand Finales. If *Emeralds* was French, and *Rubies* American, then *Diamonds* evoked Imperial Russian ballet as it had been under the tsars. In this great display of classicism, choreographed in the style of Marius Petipa, Balanchine was paying homage to his history.

Suzanne Farrell and Jacques d'Amboise were the perfect original leads. She was only twenty-two and Jacques was thirty-four. Her persona in this was not some queen or prima ballerina. She was more a young princess still learning to grow into her crown. D'Amboise, on the other hand, seemed more her protector than her consort. Their *pas de deux* therefore had a subtext that has sadly been lost (Balanchine always had a meaning behind his most abstract ballets; he just didn't like to discuss this much). There was no tacked-on drama or overt romanticism, no "suffering"—only a pristine distillation of classical ballet at its most refined and elegant.

In the third movement Scherzo, where they both had bravura solos, and especially in the Polonaise finale, both these dancers totally went for it. This movement was quite fast, faster than today, and audiences seemed to be holding their breath until the final pose. The curtain descended and the ovations seemed endless, and so well-deserved. Since I didn't appear until the last movement Polonaise I had plenty of time to watch all of *Jewels* from the front and would just dash backstage at the end of the *Diamond*'s Scherzo. I'd have my costume and make-up already on, and I'd throw on a trench coat and sneak out front as the lights went down for the beginning of *Emeralds*. I nearly didn't make it backstage a few times, but it was worth it to see most of this great ballet from the audience's point of view.

I should explain how Mr. B. choreographed for the corps de ballet. His habit was to focus on whoever was picking up the steps the fastest and essentially choreograph on that one person. He'd usually start by demonstrating just a few steps. He would show these very quickly, improvising really, and everybody would try to pick them up. Whoever picked these up the fastest would become the person Balanchine then worked with. That person would then do the steps full out and we all copied them. Balanchine was incredibly agile and could still do pirouettes and even *tours en l'air*, but it was up to the dancers to translate what Mr. B. was showing. For classical ballets such as *Diamonds* he would use the proper ballet names of steps, but for more modern works he would just demonstrate the movements. That was another reason why Farrell had become Balanchine's favorite. One of her gifts was that she was faster than anyone else at picking up Balanchine's choreography. She instinctively caught every move and inflection he wanted. It was uncanny how she could do that, as if they shared the same brain. Consequently, it was actually easier for him to choreograph when he worked with her. He never had to repeat himself or explain what he wanted. She just instantly got it. To be fair, he also loved her natural movement style, so he instinctively gave her what he knew she'd look best doing. In that way it was also easier for her because all her ballets by Balanchine were, in a sense, "custom made." She didn't have a big jump, for instance, so Balanchine rarely choreographed jumps for her; but she could turn in almost any position, so you can see many off-balance turns for her in ballets he made for her. He really made ballets *for* all of his dancers, true, but it was clear Suzanne was special and inspired him the most in those years.

It was while he was creating *Jewels* that Mr. B. started using me to demonstrate for the boys. I was only in the corps, but he was starting to be aware of what a quick study I was during his classes. I have poor eyesight and was always pushing my way to the front to watch his combinations. Balanchine's classes were always interesting and were never the same twice. As a musician, he was also training us to have a musician's ear. He would sometimes give steps that were three counts against music written in four, or he would use a four-four measure and then give a combination to be counted in five or six. Consequently, we really had to concentrate. This was not the kind of class to see how high we could jump or how many pirouettes we could do. In fact, as already noted, he would never let the men do more than two pirouettes in class. Any more than two was just a trick, he'd say, and he'd often say that seals could do much better tricks anyway, like balancing beach balls on their noses. Instead, he concentrated on cleaning up our techniques by emphasizing *glissade*s and *pas de bourrée*s—"just like brushing your teeth," he'd say. He would also stretch our memories by giving us combinations that took as much mental power as muscle power. This facet of his training seemed to be the most difficult for European-trained dancers, except for Violette Verdy and, years later, Ib Andersen. Both understood Mr. B. right off and clearly loved taking his classes.

In my first years with the company Jacques was the absolute master of the men at picking up Mr. B.'s challenging class combinations. He and I would often get into playful arguments when Balanchine showed us brain teasers. I would think the combination was one way and Jacques would insist it was another. Balanchine seemed to be amused watching me, the new boy, disagreeing with Jacques, his senior star. He would sometimes have us both demonstrate some combination he had just given and then would say, "No, Jacques, he's right," or "No, Cleeeford, Jacques is right." Suzanne never participated in these classroom games. She always stayed aloof and waited until Mr. B. finished playing with us. I think he rather enjoyed playing King Solomon.

The spring of 1967 was simply perfect. Oh, I was well aware of the social upheavals churning all around me, hippies, drugs, "flower power," protests against the Vietnam War, and all that, but I was concentrating solely on my career, and a happy-go-lucky nineteen-year-old dancer in the NYCB was what you would see. All I wanted to do was *dance*. I took every daily company class, and some at the school, watched as many rehearsals as I could, and watched all eight shows a week, whether I was dancing or not. That was my whole life, and I loved it!

I was once again choreographing for SAB to some music I loved. It was the second movement of Tchaikovsky's Piano Concerto No. 1, and to this I was making an ultra-romantic *pas de deux* for Johnna Kirkland

and Michael Steele. This *pas* ended with Johnna bending forward in a deep arabesque *penchée, en pointe,* to kiss Michael on the lips as he was on his knee below her, holding her by the waist for support. Then, as their lips met, Michael let go, so that their only physical connection was their lips. It's an obvious gimmick, and I'm embarrassed by it now, but at that time I thought it very clever.

A weird thing about this, however, is that when Balanchine saw it he asked me where I had learned about this step. He said, "You know, dear, you *must* have heard about it somewhere. How did you find out?" He seemed a bit unnerved. I didn't know what he was talking about and told him so. Pat Neary was also watching that run-through and later asked me why I put that kiss pose in my *pas de deux*. She said that had shocked Mr. B. because it was virtually what he had done himself when he was a sixteen-year-old student in Russia. After that rehearsal, Balanchine told her that this actual pose, or something very similar, had been used over fifty years earlier by himself when he was in the Imperial School. Pat said Mr. B. thought I had heard about it before somewhere. But no, I told her I'd never heard about it. She said, "Well, I'll tell him. He's really freaked out." Some days later Balanchine came up to me and said, "It's very interesting because I did something like that once myself, but it's too obvious and too romantic. You don't need to be so literal." Twenty-five years later, in 1991, Tamara Geva, Balanchine's first wife and a member of his first performing group in St. Petersburg, described in an interview with Francis Mason a kiss pose in a ballet that Balanchine had choreographed for her in his teens. The way she described it sounded as if it looked remarkably like what I had done. Mason called me to tell me about what Geva had just told him because he already knew the story about this kiss pose from me. What with Mr. B. also wanting me to dance the Candy Cane lead in *The Nutcracker* and perform Katschei in *Firebird,* both of which had been his old parts, I got the feeling that he wanted me to follow in his footsteps, but this "kiss" pose was just too weird a coincidence.

Balanchine's support and encouragement were not without annoying side effects, though, which I had to ignore. Some of the bitchier male dancers felt that his interest in me was coming about as a result of my buttering up the "Boss." They pointed, for example, to my laughing at his jokes in class (which I genuinely thought were hysterical) or at this latest "evidence" that I was attempting to curry his favor by inserting into one of my ballets a pose that was apparently invented by him. They were understandably jealous. I wasn't disrespectful, just really independent. I didn't let them give me too much lip. I could hold my ground.

12

Balanchine's Last Seminar on Teaching

In June 1967 Balanchine taught his last full series of master classes, which he called "seminars." For some years, teachers from across America were invited to come to New York for a week each June to watch him teach his company class and explain his methodology. I believe the Ford Foundation paid for the teachers' flights and accommodations. These seminars occurred during our week-long layoff between the spring season at Lincoln Center and the four-week summer season in Saratoga Springs, New York. The seminars took place in the main rehearsal room of the State Theater (now known as the David H. Koch Theater). Chairs were set up for the approximately one hundred teachers in attendance, and Balanchine asked the dancers who were interested to come and take the classes so that he could use them to demonstrate. These classes were voluntary. Suzanne took them all, and, of course, so did I. Also present for every class were d'Amboise, Verdy, Mazzo, Morris, Leland, Estopinal, Mejia, Neary, von Aroldingen, Govrin, Schorer, Susan Hendl, Johnna Kirkland, Giselle Roberge, Delia Peters, Deni Lamont, Lynn Stetson, Lynn Bryson, Carol Sumner, Deborah Flomine, Robert Maiorano, and a few of the other dancers. I never understood why more dancers didn't take advantage of this great opportunity. These master classes would be illuminating because what Balanchine did not really explain in his company classes, he would go into in great detail during these seminars.

In his company class, Balanchine didn't often say why the steps had to be executed in a certain way. Every now and then he would go so far as to say, "Don't put your heels down, you should be like a cat." Then he told us that when he was a student in Russia the heels were never allowed to crash down. You did put them down, but you didn't bang them down. People so easily misunderstand this comment. If you accentuate "heel down," not only is it harmful, but you don't really get as big a jump, and you certainly cannot move, nor change direction as fast, as you can if you keep the weight on the ball of your foot. In Balanchine's works such as *Rubies, Tarantella,* and the scherzo from *A Midsummer Night's Dream,* there is no way to dance the choreography correctly with your heels planted down. You have to be like a boxer or a cat. That's one reason why Villella so pleased Balanchine. Eddie had been a trained boxer, and much of boxing is based on keeping your weight on the balls of your feet so that you can quickly change direction. A lot of Balanchine's ballets are built on speed, and all modern post-Balanchine choreographers, like William Forsythe, now take full advantage of this technique that Balanchine developed. Balanchine's training helped all dancers because this technique enabled dancers to move more quickly and cleanly.

Balanchine's first seminar class took two and a half hours, and we didn't get past *battement tendus* at the barre. He took apart the opening *pliés,* dissecting even the tempi necessary. He explained how to execute *demi-plié* to *grand plié* and why he wanted that done in one slow movement, not two. He clarified why he emphasized crossing our front and back *tendu* positions so that the leg and pointed foot were exactly to the front or the back of the center of the body. Everything he did, and I mean every little thing, had a sound and well thought-out reason.

In Suki Schorer's wonderful book about Balanchine's technique, *Suki Schorer on Balanchine Technique,* she very clearly and succinctly goes into great detail about Balanchine's training, so there's really no need for me to repeat that here.

I never found Balanchine's emphasis on being so precise to be a constricting influence. I found the discipline liberating. Some dancers were frustrated and said he wouldn't allow them to be "individuals." To my way of thinking, you're not supposed to be an "individual" while learning a technique. You can be an individual while you're performing and *applying* that technique. Balanchine was absolutely the most technically precise teacher I have ever known. Nothing could slide by. He saw everything. He was dismissive of dancers who substituted "emoting" for technique. For him, one can never be too neat or clean. There are many steps dancers slur over or take for granted. Balanchine could spend the entire class teaching just *glissades* or *port de bras.* Imagine a teacher doing that today. I had never heard him explain these things in such detail before these seminars. As it turned out, he never did again.

This does not mean that Balanchine only wanted brainless automatons, but his quest for technical perfection is the source of the myth about Balanchine being "mechanical."

The first day we made it through *tendu*. The second day we started again from the beginning, and it wasn't until the end of the week that we got to allegro work and big jumps. A few amusing things happened along the way. One was that Suzanne Farrell teased me for the first time.

As it happened, one day Suzanne and I ended up right next to each other at the barre. There was not a lot of space in the studio because of all the teachers' chairs taking up so much room. So there I was stretching my Bolshoi "attitude" (a very high back position of the leg) and really trying to get my line to look like Plisetskaya's, when Suzanne suddenly turned to me right before the adagio and said, "John, now don't get your leg up higher than mine." I thought she was kidding, of course, as I couldn't get my leg up nearly as high as hers, but she had a totally deadpan expression on her face. I said, "Don't worry, I won't." Then she gave me a Cheshire cat–like little smile and shrugged. I realized she was just making a joke. She has a very dry and witty sense of humor, but I hadn't yet seen that side of her. It was nice to see this from Balanchine's "Alabaster Princess" (his name for her).

Another incident at these seminars showed that many of the teachers came there just to be critical. Balanchine allowed questions to be asked at any time during the class, so one day, following *grand battement* at the barre, a teacher raised her hand and asked, "Mr. Balanchine, when your dancers are doing their *grand battement*, is it correct, when you're changing *battement* from front to side to back or wherever, to move the hand on the barre?" Balanchine asked, "What do you mean?" She continued, "Well, are you allowed to move the hand on the barre to adjust your change of weight?" Balanchine said, "No, no, it must remain absolutely at the same place on the barre." (Mr. B. was a disciplinarian, even as to how a dancer held on to the barre.)

The teacher then continued, "Oh, I'm so sorry, but I saw somebody move her hand and wanted to know if that was what you wanted." Balanchine said, "No, it's absolutely wrong. Never move your hand at the barre. Which dancer did that?" The teacher then smiled sweetly and said, "Oh, Miss Farrell did." It was such a petty and tacky remark to make. Suzanne blushed and looked embarrassed. Mr. B. glanced at her, smiled, and turned back to the teacher, and without missing a beat said, "Well, if Suzanne moves her hand, then it's all right!" Everyone laughed. No one could ever trip him up.

Mr. B. did become a tad annoyed one day, though, when all the teachers seemed to be picking on every little thing. He finally said, "You are invited here to watch the way I teach. I am like a chef. This is my kitchen. You come and you eat. If you like the food, you stay. If you don't like the food, you can go. I make the food I like to eat. This is how I teach. I teach the way I like to *see* dancing." He was very blunt about it. He was not trying to tell the teachers that they must teach his way. He was simply explaining how *he* taught ballet. Here was the man who was the direct link to the Imperial Russian classical ballet and to Marius Petipa. Here was the man who started to change the face of American ballet when he came to the United States in 1933, and here he was, offering his expertise to these teachers for free, and some of them had the nerve to criticize him. I thought they were very rude and disrespectful, to say the least.

When I came under Balanchine's influence, it didn't take me long to become his most ardent advocate. He had not tried to break my spirit, for instance, as Loring had. As mentioned, I had also been told Balanchine did not like individuality and personality, which I found ridiculously untrue. He encouraged it, but only if your technique could back it up. I had been told he disliked humor. Wrong again. He had a wicked sense of humor. Was he a perfect man? Of course not! Who is? But I found him to be a perfect teacher, at least for me.

The last day of the seminars was quite ironic. As I walked into the studio there was Eugene Loring, of all people, sitting in the front row! Knowing how he felt about Balanchine, I was surprised to see him there. I was also a little nervous because even though we had not gotten along that well when I was at his school, he had nonetheless been my teacher and I would now have to dance before him once again, this time representing the "enemy." I'm sure, however, that Mr. B. was amused to have Loring as a guest in his "kitchen."

That day proved rather humorous. Mr. B. had a very specific technique for teaching *grand jetés*. His was not the usual way, which was to kick your front leg, jump up to where it was, and then act as if you were going over a fence, rather like jumping over a high hurdle. Balanchine taught the step completely differently. In his training, dancers basically kept the legs in one position as they ascended. It wasn't so much the jump that was important to Mr. B. as it was the look in the air. He used to tell us how Pierre Vladimiroff would jump so high using this technique that he could look around while he was still in the air before deciding where to land. The audience should not see the jump but only the sustained position in the air.

Mr. B. surprisingly singled me out to demonstrate a *grand jeté* combination. I had not mastered any of his technique at this time so I was a bit nervous. I still couldn't do a *glissade* or a *pas de bourrée* anywhere near how he wanted it. Balanchine asked me to do a series of *grand jetés* across the room and he would then correct me. I think perhaps he picked me out for that very reason, because I wasn't doing it right—and perhaps to poke Loring. I did the combination as best I could, and all the teachers graciously applauded, except Loring. Loring used to smoke a cigarette in a long cigarette holder (smoking was still allowed in the studios in those days, before Balanchine banned it), and when Loring was nervous, he'd start crinkling his lips. It was almost a tic, and that tic was really going full blast that afternoon. Balanchine then proceeded to analyze my *grand jeté* and explain why he wanted certain things changed. He said that I was new in the company and had not been "taught correctly." Ouch. I couldn't even look at Loring after that. After Balanchine corrected me, he asked me to do the combination again. The teachers were to applaud if I had done the combination as instructed. I did it again, trying to apply Mr. B.'s corrections. The teachers were demonstrative in their applause for my second attempt, with the exception of Loring. I saw his face and he was furious. Following the class, I started toward him to say hello, but he left very quickly . . .

13

My First Principal Role, *Valse Fantaisie*

The SAB Workshop Goes Public

I was eager to get back to my Workshop ballets, but had lost interest in completing the ballet to the *L'Arlesienne* music, so Balanchine now gave me some new music to choreograph: Stanley Shapiro's *Partita in C for Piano*. After listening to it I thought it a terribly dry piece and told Balanchine I didn't think it was for me, but he said to do it anyway. I then asked Robert Irving, our eminent music director and lead conductor, why Mr. B. had given me this score. He said, "It's a test, Johnny." Ah ha! So Mr. B. wanted to see what I could do with music I didn't like. I did as he wished, and the ballet pleased him. I guess I passed the test. I also choreographed Maurice Ravel's *Pavane for a Dead Princess*, a *pas de deux* I made for two students, Linda Rosenthal—(not the Linda Rosenthal who later became Linda Merrill)—and James Bogan).

So much was coming my way. Looking back now, after all these years, I'm amazed at my luck. At the time, I scarcely took a moment even to think about it. I was having a ball, dancing the best choreography in the world, and choreographing under Balanchine's tutelage. It didn't hurt that I was in the company of those I considered the best dancers in America, in the most beautiful theater, and with the best orchestra. I was mostly just immensely grateful.

One day in Saratoga Springs, NYCB's summer home, Mr. B. stopped class and told us what had happened to him that morning at the Gideon Putnam Hotel, at that time a notoriously pretentious hotel on the grounds of the Saratoga Spa State Park. Its clientele was quite elderly, and many residents were there for the mineral hot springs. He said he had gone into the hotel's restaurant for breakfast with a couple of the dancers, and the maître d' asked them to keep their voices down.

Balanchine was a very quiet man to begin with, so to hear that he was being too loud seemed like a joke. Balanchine told us he had then looked around at the other diners and thought, "Why? I can't wake them, they're already dead." He told only us, his "family," this irreverent thought. Another incident of a similar sort occurred later that same season at a fancy restaurant where men were still asked to wear ties. Balanchine always wore a sports jacket with a western string tie. One afternoon he was there for lunch, and the manager told him he would have to leave because he was not wearing a regular tie. He never went to that restaurant again.

I'm offering these anecdotes because Balanchine always did his best to lighten up the atmosphere by telling jokes and funny stories during his class. I enjoyed going to his classes just for the jokes. For instance, if a dancer was tired, Balanchine would say, "Don't stop. You can rest in the grave," or "You should do the step full out now, because in ten minutes you might be hit by a bus crossing the street, then you'll never have done the step right, and you will never be able to do it again." Admittedly, his humor could be sarcastic and sometimes dark. (I just thought it was funny.)

He was making a joke, but subconsciously he may have been thinking about his then-wife, the ballerina Tanaquil Le Clercq, ("Tanny," as she was affectionately known). Tragically, this beautiful young ballerina had contracted polio in her prime and was now in a wheelchair. That alone would have made him cherish the gift of movement and stress the necessity of taking advantage of the time we had as dancers. Who knew when a tragedy could befall us, as had happened to his beloved wife? During my time in the company I saw her on only two occasions. Both were performances at the State Theater. Years later, when I was staging Balanchine's ballets for various companies, Tanny personally requested that I stage his ultra-dramatic ballet *La Valse,* which took me by surprise. It was one of her signature roles; Balanchine left her the rights to this ballet in his will. I had never really spoken to her other than being introduced once at an intermission. Perhaps Balanchine told her I'd be good at staging this highly theatrical story ballet because of my background in acting. Who knows?

The 1967 fall season was the breakthrough for my NYCB dancing career. Balanchine was preparing a new ballet called *Glinkiana,* which used four movements of music by Mikhail Glinka. It began with a "Polka," which was led by Violette Verdy and Paul Mejia. The second movement was a "Valse Fantaisie," led by Mimi Paul and John Prinz. This was a reworking of an earlier Balanchine version of the same Glinka music. The third movement was the "Jota Aragonesa," led by Melissa Hayden and a large corps de ballet, and the fourth movement was a bravura *pas de deux* to the "Divertimento Brillante," danced by Patricia McBride and Edward Villella.

By this time Prinz had already danced *Tarantella* and been one of the four demi-solo boys in the first movement of the *Brahms-Schoenberg Quartet*. Balanchine had also choreographed the "Pas de deux Mauresque" for him and Suki Schorer in his full-length *Don Quixote*.

Balanchine quite clearly meant to show him off in the bravura "Valse Fantaisie," but fate stepped in. During a rehearsal with Suzanne of the fourth movement of *Brahms-Schoenberg Quartet*, at a time when d'Amboise was injured and Prinz was filling in for him, John did a double character turn, landed wrongly, and broke his elbow. I was sitting just five feet away when this happened and heard the crack. It was an awful moment. At the time we wondered what would happen with "Valse Fantaisie," which was set to premiere the following week. As mentioned earlier, Balanchine rarely had understudies. Mimi came up to me later that day and said Balanchine had just told her I would be doing the part with her. I couldn't believe it. There were four good reasons why she had to be wrong:

1. I was still too new in the company. In those days you had to be in the corps de ballet for at least one solid year before you would be cast as a principal dancer in a world premiere. Now, of course, times have changed, but in those days everyone had to put in that first year, from Suzanne Farrell on down. So although I was shy of my year by just a month, it was enough for me to be certain this was a mistake. The only exception I heard of was when Gloria Govrin was cast in the lead of the fourth movement of *Western Symphony* after being in the company for only a month (but that wasn't a world premiere).

2. There were other male dancers in the company who were excellent, had seniority, and who I thought would have been placed before me.

3. Mimi Paul was too tall for me, although there is not a lot of partnering involved in this ballet. At five feet eight, I was a good two or three inches shorter than Mimi when she was *en pointe*.
4. I was a little nervous about the prospect of dancing "Valse Fantaisie" because I had twisted my ankle again a few weeks earlier and hadn't jumped full out since then. But if by chance I was wrong about the first three considerations, I wasn't about to let the last one stop me.

The next morning on the rehearsal schedule, my name and Kent Stowell's were written in to come to a rehearsal later that day. Kent was already a soloist, so I thought maybe Balanchine had changed his mind and Kent was going to dance it.

When Balanchine walked in to start the rehearsal, Mimi, Kent, Francia Russell (Kent's wife, as well as a company ballet mistress) and I were already in the room. Kent then immediately went over to Mimi and took her hand to begin, so I moved to the back of the room. Mr. B. began teaching but stopped when he saw Kent with Mimi's hand. He said, "Cleeeford, come here, you're dancing with Mimi. Why you stand back there?" Kent was miffed, to say the least, and Francia seemed embarrassed. I didn't know how to handle the situation. I didn't want to make an enemy of Francia, and I liked Kent very much. He was really a wonderful dancer, but Balanchine was the Boss, and he had asked me to start working with Mimi, so I was not about to say no. A not-very-pleased Kent and Francia slipped out soon after Mr. B. started working.

When Balanchine began teaching me the man's solo, it was as Prinz had been doing it, but after a few seconds he stopped and said, "No, maybe we do this way." He then proceeded to teach me a completely different variation from the one Prinz had been rehearsing. Everything except that man's variation stayed the same. Mimi and I went out for coffee after this rehearsal, and she said that the version Mr. B. had taught me was what he had originally started to make for Prinz but had changed it when John had trouble with it. The original solo had no turns but continual jumps and was very aerobic—nothing too tricky, just lots of repetitive (and exhausting) *grand jetés*. Evidently I must have mastered the *grand jeté* technique that Balanchine had had me demonstrate at the seminar, because he returned to that version of the

Above: Me in dress rehearsal of
Valse Fantaisie, 1967. Photo by
Martha Swope. Used with per-
mission of NYPL swope_779249.
Valse Fantaisie. Choreography
by George Balanchine © The
George Balanchine Trust.

Left: Me and Mimi Paul in
dress rehearsal of *Valse Fantaisie,*
1967. Photo by Martha Swope.
Used with permission of NYPL
swope_779249. *Valse Fantaisie.*
Choreography by George
Balanchine © The George Balanchine Trust.

solo. I don't know if he actually liked the *grand jetés* better than what
he had given Prinz or if the earlier version was just better suited to me.
Balanchine was always trying to make the individual dancer in front
of him look good. If a certain step wasn't working out, he used to say,
"Steps can be changed." However, he never allowed anyone else, ballet
master or dancer, to alter his choreography. That was his right alone.

On the opening night of *Glinkiana* I felt as if all my dreams had
come true. The "Valse Fantaisie" section went off without a hitch. Remember, the audience didn't have a clue who I was. At the end of

my solo, on my exit, when I instinctively improvised a *tour jeté* into a backward split, the whole audience gasped, and then I heard quite an ovation as I was panting in the wings. Hector Zaraspe, the popular teacher from the Joffrey Ballet, who was now becoming very well known because he was the teacher of choice for Fonteyn and Nureyev, was at the theater that night. He came up to me after the performance and said it looked as if I had "owned the stage." Quite honestly that was how it felt. From then on, whenever I performed, and whatever I danced, I tried to feel as if indeed I "owned the stage."

14

More Solos and Peter Martins's Début

That fall season of 1967 was tremendously exciting for me. There was my principal-lead début in "Valse Fantaisie" of *Glinkiana,* dancing with Mimi, one of the most respected ballerinas in the company. This ballet was the only one Balanchine kept after the first season of *Glinkiana.* He dropped the other three sections. I later danced this ballet with Allegra Kent, Gelsey Kirkland, Kay Mazzo, Sara Leland, Suki Schorer, and almost all the up-and-coming young ballerinas. That ballet became one of my signature roles.

John Prinz did dance it a couple of times when his elbow healed, and with Suzanne Farrell (Balanchine cast Suzanne in everything at least once), but other than those few performances, that part was only danced by yours truly until I left the company. I also performed the "In the Inn" section of *Ivesiana* with Sara Leland, which was very difficult musically but very easy technically. In an emergency, Balanchine changed the *pas de quatre* in *La Sonnambula* to a *pas de trois,* and I was the boy chosen. Delia Peters, one of the wittiest girls in the company, quipped, "What is this, the John Clifford season?" When I was given all those parts and the attention from Balanchine, I quite honestly felt I was working hard for it, and that these were my rewards. In those years I wanted nothing more than to dance for and to please Mr. B. His opinion was all that mattered to me.

After Balanchine's company class, I would go to SAB and take the men's class, and if I didn't have rehearsal, I would also take the *pas de deux* classes, often with Melissa Hayden as my partner, and sometimes even the evening "late-C" class. I would also perform practically every night. I was definitely a workaholic. If I were not dancing in a performance, I would go to the theater and watch, as I would continue to do until the day I left the company. Being in NYCB was my entire life, and I never felt a lack by missing other events occurring in New York. That city had everything: theater, musicals, dance, and opera, yet I was basically spending all my waking time at the company or at the school. Crazy? Maybe. Obsessed?

Certainly. But also very, very, happy.

The teachers at the school were now giving me even more attention. Muriel Stuart, Tumkovsky, Madame Danilova, Eglevsky, Williams—all of them really started pushing me. They knew Mr. B. had singled me out, and they all wanted to do the best that they could with me. I accepted any and all suggestions at that time, a veritable sponge. I needed to keep my guard up, though, with some of the older male corps dancers. They played a lot of pranks on me due to my great love for Plisetskaya. When I first joined the company, I had a large picture of her split *grand jeté* in *Don Quixote* taped to my make-up mirror. After the premiere of *Glinkiana* (with "Valse Fantaisie" still in it), this photo was ripped up and left at my place. There were a few who went out of their way to make life difficult, but I took that as part and parcel of the territory. One does not enter a major institution like NYCB and receive the attention I was getting without there being a downside. Luckily, my friendships with Renee, Ricky, Johnna, and Giselle continued, and now that gorgeous soloist Marnee Morris became a close friend. I don't know how I would have survived without them that first year.

That December I finally got to perform *The Nutcracker*'s Candy Cane lead, which Balanchine had wanted me to do the previous year.

Life was good. Not only was I assigned Candy Cane and Toy Soldier; I was given the Tea (Chinese) solo as well. Whenever I was not dancing the Candy Cane lead, I would be doing Tea, even if I were also dancing the Toy Soldier in Act I. Actually, I preferred Tea because there was more real dancing in it, and I didn't have to be so concerned about jumping through that damned hoop. Mr. B. put a lot of pressure on me to do Candy Cane exactly as he had, since it had been one of his prized parts when he was young. He coached me for my first performance and would always say, "I did it this way, dear." He also said it was played much faster in his day! There is a section near the end of the dance when the boy has to jump through the hoop twelve times while simultaneously traveling forward and turning. What I gathered from the senior ballet mistress, Una Kai, was that most dancers didn't

Me in a Martha Swope studio photo of the lead Candy Cane. *George Balanchine's The Nutcracker®*. Choreography by George Balanchine © The George Balanchine Trust.

make it in their very first performance without at least one stumble. Luckily, I made it through fine in my début. I must have done it well because Balanchine kept me in it for as long as I was in the company. This meant that even during my later years, when I was the Cavalier and dancing the *grand pas de deux* with the Sugar Plum Fairy, I was still dancing Candy Cane lead in other performances.

The most fun came on New Year's Eve. It was a company tradition that in that performance the dancers could pull some pranks, and the stagehands could have some fun too, such as dumping all the snow at one time on the heads of the dancers during the snow scene. Even our distinguished music director, Robert Irving, would sometimes indulge, coming out to conduct the second act wearing a mouse's head. One year Farrell blacked out her front teeth when she greeted all the dancers as the Sugar Plum Fairy. This was totally out of character for her and took the whole company by surprise. We couldn't stop laughing. Suzanne had her back to the audience so only we could see it, but the audience knew something crazy was going on.

What they had no idea of was that Balanchine himself would sometimes give the dancers suggestions as to what jokes to do. Once he told Christine Redpath, a particular favorite of his, to make mistakes purposely during "The Waltz of the Flowers," as in Jerome Robbins's

"Mistake Waltz" from his comedy ballet *The Concert*. We all thought Chrissie had gone way too far, but Balanchine loved every moment of her seeming "mistakes."

On my first New Year's Eve performance of the Candy Cane lead (and without Balanchine's permission), I decided to challenge myself. I followed the twelve turning jumps through the hoop going forward with six more going backward, just to see if I could do it. I did it, but I never risked that again. I was terrified through the whole dance that I would really make a fool of myself. Afterward Mr. B. said, "You know, dear, I never tried that, but it was still faster when I danced it."

That Christmas was also the first time that the whole company saw Peter Martins dance. Jacques d'Amboise was injured, so Peter, who had just danced *Apollo* (staged by John Taras) with his home company, the Royal Danish Ballet, and on a concert in Edinburgh, Scotland, with Farrell and other NYCB dancers, was the last-minute replacement. On Taras's recommendation Balanchine invited Martins to New York to dance with Suzanne for some *Nutcracker* performances. Jacques was aging, and it seemed Balanchine was looking around for someone to be her new permanent partner.

Peter Martins was extremely different from any of our other male dancers at that time. He was very tall, blond, handsome, technically flawless, and cold as an iceberg, but that was perfect for Farrell. Jacques could sometimes overpower her with his flamboyance, but that obviously wouldn't happen with Martins. No way could he upstage Suzanne. His first performance of the Cavalier was very impressive and left us all with our mouths hanging open. The Cavalier in Balanchine's version has no actual variation. The only real dancing he does is in the coda, which consists of basically three combinations. One is a jumped traveling step, usually *assemblés*, and then a *grand à-la-seconde* pirouette section, and then a series of *brisé volés*. In his début performance Peter did something that I'd never seen before and have never seen since. In the grand pirouette turns, and after building up tremendous velocity, he did one single *relevé*, then four consecutive turns with his leg in "*seconde*," and then he pulled his leg into a *passé* position and did ten more pirouettes—all without a second *relevé*. That was a total of fourteen consecutive turns from a single preparation! Ricky Weiss, who was standing next to me in the wings, practically started crying, not out of jealousy but out of wonder. Ricky was a big turner too, but nobody could do what Martins did that day. He never repeated that, but it didn't matter because we all saw it.

Martins seemed understandably reticent and shy around the company. Although he was a principal dancer in Denmark, to be invited as a guest by Balanchine must have seemed an incredible responsibility to the twenty-one-year-old. Peter must have guessed that Mr. B. was testing him as the new partner for Suzanne and wanted to have him as a full-time company member. However, unlike all the other principal men, Peter didn't have much individuality as a dancer in those early years, and it wasn't until the Stravinsky Festival in 1972 that he really emerged as a performer. If that sounds a little harsh, it's because Balanchine always wanted us to be "entertainers" (his word) as well as technicians. "Entertain!" he always told us in class. No matter, Peter was a wonderful match for Farrell, so he was needed and fully appreciated by Balanchine. Unfortunately, the appreciation didn't appear mutual when he came back a few months later as a regular company member. Right from the start, there was a lot of friction between him and Balanchine. Peter just never liked Balanchine's classes, at least not while I was in the company. (I heard later that in the last few years of Balanchine's life, Peter did take Mr. B's class more regularly.)

By late 1967 Mr. B. and I were beginning to spend more private time together away from the theater. He would often take me to dinner after the performances (Suzanne did not do late night dinners) and talk to me about many subjects other than ballet. He was quite open regarding how he felt about the other dancers in the company. For instance, he thought Peter had a great future but was irritated at Peter's not taking his class or even trying to learn his style. Balanchine put up with this because he was extremely patient and he really needed Peter for Suzanne. Mr. B. was always very practical.

Martins, in his memoir *Far from Denmark*, wrote that he did not understand what Balanchine wanted with his style of classical technique. Mr. B.'s classes were markedly different from what Peter was used to, and he was trying to hold on to his Danish (Bournonville) schooling. As Peter himself once told me, the speed of the classes made him feel as if he were out of touch with his training, and he felt "foolish" and "awkward" in Balanchine's class, and the brief-to-practically-nonexistent rehearsal times really annoyed him. In European companies plenty of time was given to rehearsals because these were government-supported companies with far fewer performances. In America money is always tight; therefore time is at a premium.

Peter and I were quite friendly during his first few years. We were not buddies, but we talked about ballet and Balanchine a lot. He saw that Balanchine and I were close, and he was curious as to why I was so loyal to him. By this time I was a total Balanchine convert and couldn't understand Peter's lack of enthusiasm for Mr. B. We could get into endless disagreements about this, although not actual arguments. Peter kept saying that if he followed Balanchine's wishes and tried to move as fast as Balanchine wanted, or did not put his heels down the way Balanchine taught—(that old misunderstanding, because one does put the heel down, just gently)—he would somehow lose his more "classical" technique. I pointed out that if he were going to lose it that easily, it wasn't all that secure in the first place. I tried to convince him that he could keep his earlier Bournonville training, absorb Balanchine's technique, and therefore have more range as a dancer. He didn't agree with me at all then, and as he was absolutely adored by the press, I could understand why I didn't get through to him. If he didn't want to learn from Balanchine, what could I possibly do?

Peter told me that Lucia Chase, the founder and director of American Ballet Theatre, was desperate to have him for her tall leading ballerina, Cynthia Gregory. He told me around 1970 that he was continually pressured by her, and others, to leave Balanchine. They wanted him to dance in the classical repertory, such as *Swan Lake* and *Giselle*. Luckily, Peter had the good sense not to make a move at that time. I also know that Lincoln was most influential in keeping him in our company. He advised Peter that if one had the chance to work with a genius like Balanchine it made sense to take advantage of that opportunity.

Plus, once Jerome Robbins returned to the company, he used Peter in nearly every one of his new ballets. Two choreographers of genius making ballets for you at the same time? Who in his right mind would leave that? Even though Peter stayed, things remained quite difficult between him and Balanchine for almost six years. It was a shame he passed up so many crucial years of absorbing Balanchine's aesthetic and taking full advantage of Balanchine's classes when Mr. B. was still relatively young and vital. By the time Peter came to understand and appreciate Balanchine's genius, Mr. B's health was already failing.

Here, I'd like to interrupt my story to speak about Mr. B. in relation to his male dancers. So much has been made of his obvious and well-documented attraction to young ballerinas that the myth of Balanchine being interested only in his female dancers and choreographing for them has been perpetuated beyond all reason. Because of Balanchine's several wives and his statement that "Ballet is Woman," many people believe he wasn't interested in choreographing for men. Not true. He has not been given enough credit for the advancements he made for men's technique and repertory.

Take it from me, Balanchine also respected and worked excellently with the men in his company. To realize how much Balanchine valued male dancers, all you have to do is look at *Apollo, Prodigal Son, Tarantella, Rubies,* Oberon and Puck in *A Midsummer Night's Dream, Who Cares?, Orpheus, The Four Temperaments, Harlequinade, Stravinsky Violin Concerto, Duo Concertant, Divertimento from "Le Baiser de la Fée,"* and *Valse Fantaisie.*

I think much of what Balanchine found interesting about choreographing for men, especially the tall d'Amboise and Martins, was that they could be an idealized version of himself. Balanchine felt inadequate about his height and facial features, but he could become the romantic hero by choreographing powerful parts for these men. According to Danilova, Mr. B. was an exceptionally good dancer in the school before his career-ending knee injury. He loved demonstrating during rehearsals, and, when he taught, he always partnered the girls himself. In short, he was a somewhat frustrated dancer. Indeed, he always referred to himself as a dancer.

15

Jacques d'Amboise and Edward Villella

Technique *and* Personality

When I joined the company the two reigning male superstars were unquestionably d'Amboise and Villella. They were extremely different in temperament, technique, and physique, and each was a huge audience favorite. They would get applause the minute they set one foot on the stage.

Jacques was tall and classically handsome, with heroic proportions (a well-muscled torso), an infectious generosity of movement and spirit, and a smile that could light up Times Square. When Jacques bowed he would throw open his arms as if to embrace the entire audience, and he did! What a joyful presence he always brought to the theater.

Eddie, on the other hand, was compact, dark, with a violent recklessness about him and an almost super-human energy level. Villella was the wild card, the pistol ready to go off. His speed and ability to change direction like lightning were unrivaled. Once I saw this ability, I knew it was something I just had to acquire.

Both had tremendous elevation, and for Jacques this was most unusual. Tall men do not normally have that much *ballon*. Jacques was greatly influenced by André Eglevsky and shared many traits with him, such as the ability to freeze in the air in jumps and do multiple pirouettes, albeit with a very low *passé* and half-toe position. The differences between Jacques and Eddie in terms of men's techniques would be hard to assess by today's standards. All of the routine classical ballet vocabulary was easy for them, but the look of the male dancer has now changed so much.

Certain technical things have also improved remarkably for men—most notably pirouette positions (the very high *passé* and high half–toe, for example) and much higher leg extensions, big arabesques, and the more exaggerated arched feet, common to all men today. Neither Eddie nor Jacques had great feet, although Villella's moved so fast that you could hardly tell, and neither had much extension. A below-the-hip leg was the norm in arabesque or in à la seconde for the men of that day.

Balanchine's favorite Apollo in my day was Jacques d'Amboise. Mr. B. tried for years to help Peter Martins understand that Apollo was really a demi-character role and not a *danseur noble* part. The original Apollo, Serge Lifar, was not by any stretch of the imagination a classical dancer. When Balanchine cut the two opening scenes of *Apollo* for Baryshnikov (when Baryshnikov was briefly a member of the company), he did away with most of the pantomime and strongest acting moments of the ballet. These were the sections where Jacques excelled. Villella and other shorter men have danced this role successfully, but it does have more impact when danced by someone tall with longer limbs and who actually looks like a god.

It took me some time to see the sense in this cut, choreographically speaking, and now I think that Mr. B. did the right thing, because now *Apollo* truly seems timeless. I do believe the ballet starts off much more strongly as a result of his eliminating the 1950s-era stairs and darkly lit opening pantomime; starting the ballet with the stronger "Apollo" theme by cutting Stravinsky's opening music; and opening the work in blindingly bright lights. Balanchine told me that since Apollo was the god of light and was represented by the sun, the audience should be almost blinded when they first see him.

Even though Jacques and Eddie shared many roles—such as Balanchine's one-act *Swan Lake, Tchaikovsky Pas de Deux,* and the *Nutcracker Grand Pas de Deux*—Mr. B. was a master at exploiting the differences between the two dancers. Jacques was more the romantic Cavalier and Eddie the Firecracker.

Balanchine made many great roles that made full use of Villella's speed and rebel persona: *Rubies, Tarantella,* Oberon in *A Midsummer Night's Dream, Harlequinade,* the third movement of the *Brahms-Schoenberg Quartet,* and *Bugaku* (in which he was uniquely intense as a Samurai). These roles were the most difficult I have ever danced, and it took me some time to develop my own way with them.

Eddie was a tough act to follow; impossible, really. Since I was closer to Eddie than to Jacques in height, I did not dance too many of the "Cavalier" roles. *The Nutcracker Grand Pas de Deux,* the third movement of *Brahms-Schoenberg Quartet, La Source,* and the classical *Grand Pas de Deux* in *Cortège Hongrois* were the only "Danseur Noble" roles in my repertoire. *Harlequinade* is really a demi-character role, as are Oberon and Puck in *A Midsummer Night's Dream, Rubies, Tarantella, Agon, The Four Temperaments,* and others. I suppose *Valse Fantaisie* is a classical role, but all of Balanchine's ballets were just about dancing for me, and I never really analyzed which parts were "classical" or "demi-character" when I was on that stage.

Jacques undoubtedly was my inspiration for the *Stars and Stripes Pas de Deux* of Liberty Bell and El Capitan. No one could equal his over-the-top comic energy in this ballet. Actually, I was often considered a "mini" Jacques. This flattered me, and when anyone thought I had gone too far in the area of "selling it," all I had to do was point to him.

By choreographing the third movement of *Brahms-Schoenberg Quartet* for Villella, and the fourth for d'Amboise, Balanchine pulled off a veritable tour de force. Who said Mr. B. neglected his male dancers?

Today most male dancers do cross training (as do women) and Pilates or Gyrotonics. In my day this wasn't even heard of, and we had to fend for ourselves to stay in shape between seasons. We also didn't have a physical therapist on staff, nor a jacuzzi on site, and we had to pay for our own massages. Since we performed at least 250 shows a year, we were all in pretty good shape, and serious injuries were relatively rare. I chalk this up to the more demanding classes taught by Balanchine and some of the teachers at SAB.

16

Slaughter on Tenth Avenue and That "Greek" Ballet

Slaughter on Tenth Avenue was set to premiere for the New York City Ballet's spring gala, April 30, 1968, starring Suzanne and Arthur Mitchell. Every year for the gala Mr. B. would premiere at least one new ballet, and we all looked forward to it. I was thrilled to be cast in the corps of *Slaughter* and was given a bit part as the first boy who gets "bumped off" at the beginning of the ballet. When Balanchine was making *Slaughter,* he noticed that I could do the jazz steps better than the other classically trained dancers. I must tell you that Mr. B.'s "jazz" steps were very amusing because they were basically a variation on the classical *balancé.* I was doing them in a slightly more authentic jazz manner, and he liked that.

Balanchine had not choreographed anything for the company lately like this Broadway-style ballet, and since my early training was in jazz, I was curious to see how Mr. B. would approach it. I knew he had done Broadway shows before, and I was aware that *Slaughter* was from the Broadway musical *On Your Toes,* which had set a high standard for Broadway dance numbers.

As Balanchine worked on the boy's tap solo, he kept saying, "Bolger did this," or "Bolger did that." The original dancer was Ray Bolger, and Balanchine's first wife, Tamara Geva, played the Stripper. After Balanchine had more or less set the ballet, he invited Bolger to come in and brush up some of the parts that he had forgotten. If Bolger remembered a step that was preferable to what Balanchine had set, Mr. B. changed his own step, a collaboration between Mr. B. and Mr. B. It was great fun to have this movie and stage icon (Ray Bolger was the Scarecrow in *The Wizard of Oz* film starring Judy Garland) in the studio for those three days. He seemed delighted to be there, and the rapport and mutual respect between him and Balanchine were very evident. He also showed Mitchell not so much how to tap (Arthur was already a good tapper) but the style that was necessary to bring that 1930s-era character to life.

Suzanne's role was as a stripper with high heels and fishnet stockings, exactly like the *Earl Carroll Vanities* show girls of my childhood, and she was great. She was showing a great amount of freedom and daring and taking even more risks than she usually did. As a matter of fact, she got so carried away in one rehearsal that, while doing an attitude *penchée*, she kicked Arthur in the eye with the spiked heel of her shoe. It was a complete accident, of course, but still scary to see. Arthur himself had been dancing wildly and was lucky to end up with only a black eye. When she kicked him, he first shrieked and bolted from the room. Balanchine immediately chased after him, but a few minutes later they came back with Arthur holding an ice pack over his eye. It was a close call, for sure. Dancing in high heels could be pretty dangerous at times—for the man.

The premiere of *Slaughter* was of course a great big hit. On that first night there was a man in the front row, obviously drunk, and when Suzanne started doing the bumps and grinds during the second *pas de deux,* he started whistling and yelling, "Go, go, baby! *Yeah!* Go, *baby, GO!*" What a riot.

Four months before *Slaughter* premiered at the end of April, in January Mr. B. had premiered his extremely modern ballet *Metastaseis and Pithoprakta,* to music by the Greek composer Iannis Xenakis. It seemed that after Balanchine went through a classical period, he would choreograph something in the more modern vernacular. For instance, in 1967 he had premiered *Jewels, Trois Valses Romantiques,* and *Glinkiana,* all more-or-less traditional classical ballets. Then in 1968, he revived *Slaughter on Tenth Avenue* by Richard Rodgers, just four months after premiering the Xenakis ballet. This kept his company and audiences always wondering what he'd come up with next. One could never really anticipate or predict his next moves for our repertoire.

The first part of what we called the "Greek" ballet, *Metastaseis,* was for practically the entire corps de ballet dressed in white unisex leotards. There was no soloist in this first section. The second section, *Pithoprakta,* featured Farrell and Arthur Mitchell and a smaller corps de ballet dressed all in black, and it was *very* sexy. Balanchine seemed to favor little fringed skirts on Suzanne at this time. In *Slaughter*, her costumes, both her pink and her black ones, consisted of very short-fringed skirts, and in *Pithoprakta* her tiny fringed skirt was a pale lavender. She also wore an abbreviated bra and very sheer tights that went from her bust to her feet, and her hair was worn loose. Arthur, in the original version, wore only gold bikini briefs, with everything else bare. With his muscular torso, it was a very hot *pas de deux* indeed. The corps de ballet had little to do but frame the principal dancers. I never saw the ballet from the front since I was always in it, but I am sorry it has not been revived by NYCB. It was really interesting and maybe ahead of its time: not unusual for Balanchine, I soon learned.

Balanchine loved the excitement of live performances even more than I did. He abhorred anything boring. In class he would always remind us that audiences pay for what they see. After a combination he would sometimes say, "Do you think people want to pay $7.95 for that? You have to show them something!" (In those days, the top price for performances of the New York City Ballet was $7.95.) A continual emphasis was put on exaggerating the movements so that the audience would be able to see it.

"Show, show, show!" he continually stressed.

For such a big stage, Balanchine emphasized the necessity for clarity even more. For instance, when one did a *port de bras* with the palm up, it was to give something to the audience. It wasn't just some movement with one's hands and arms; it had to *mean* something. When we did a *port de corps* (carrying of the body), it was not just to stretch or to make a line; it had to have a *reason*. Balanchine would always say, "Look down at the ground first, see something nice, reach over, pick it up, bring it up and look at it, bring it over your heads and throw it backwards when you lean back." Usually, he would say it was a flower, or our paycheck, or diamonds, or money! He felt that if we equated it with money, we would go after it with more vigor. When doing an arabesque, we had to put our hand straight in front of our nose and reach. Balanchine said, "Don't just stand there with hand like dead fish! Reach for it like you're reaching for a Cadillac!"

When we had to point our feet, he would say, "Press like you're pressing on the accelerator of an MG!" He was continually stressing and pushing for "more." Once you had accomplished one set, or a

Balanchine teaching, mid-1950s. Photographer unknown. BALANCHINE is a Trademark of The George Balanchine Trust.

series of exercises, he would double it, slow it down, or make it faster—usually faster. There was never a letdown in the striving for perfection. Whenever you thought you had reached your limit, he would show you something else that was needed. There was actually no such thing as perfection in a Balanchine class. I will never forget his voice trying to encourage us onward. "Faster! Slower! Show! Energy! Neater! More! More! More!!" Does this sound like drudgery? To me it was sheer heaven.

17

Age 20

My First Ballet for New York City Ballet

In January 1967 Balanchine asked me if I would like to choreograph to some of Igor Stravinsky's music. I said, "Of course, he's my all-time favorite composer."

The first composer I ever really felt passionate about was Stravinsky. At the age of fifteen I became enamored of his *The Rite of Spring*. I drove my mother half crazy playing the music over and over. As a matter of fact, when I was sixteen years old and choreographing *West Side Story*, I would listen to this during rehearsal breaks and play it at parties with all the lights off just to see the reactions of my young friends. (They usually freaked out at those eleven crashing chords in the second half, and I'd have to turn the lights back on.)

Balanchine first asked me if I would like to choreograph *Jeu de Cartes* ("Card Game") or Stravinsky's *Symphony in C.* The music for *Jeu de Cartes* I found very exciting, very danceable, but I didn't know how to play poker, and I also knew that Balanchine had already made a ballet to this music successfully in the 1930s. I thought I had better not try to choreograph a score with which Balanchine had had such success, so I went with the *Symphony in C.*

I choreographed the first movement for the SAB students, although the lead dancers, Patricia Neary, Diane Bradshaw, and Frank Ohman, were from the company. Diane was a young beauty from California, with a most infectious smile. Balanchine liked her very, very much. She had a solid technique and exceptionally slim and beautiful legs, and was another dancer who had been trained by Kosmovska, but I think it was that smile and sun-kissed California freshness that got him. She was a real Christie Brinkley look-alike.

I began the ballet with Pat Neary in the center and two lines of dancers making an inverted "V" as the opening formation. Coincidentally, a half-circle-opening formation with the solo girl in the center occurs at the opening of *Rubies,* which Balanchine was about to begin choreographing, also with Pat as his center girl. When she saw the way Mr. B. was beginning his ballet, which was very similar to what I had just choreographed for her and which Balanchine had just seen in my rehearsal, she thought it was one hell of a coincidence. I immediately changed the opening of my ballet. Nobody would believe it was only a freakish similarity, and once again people might think I was copying the Boss. If Mr. B. subconsciously happened to lift my opening pose for Pat and the corps for *Rubies,* then I was just flattered.

A week later Balanchine came to watch the completed first movement of my ballet, with Lincoln and Suzanne (as always) in tow. He said, "Not bad," but he added that I had missed the basic point of the music and that I was following the melody too literally. He told me I should focus more on the rhythm. He said the interesting thing that Stravinsky had done with this first movement was not to change the rhythm once during the entire nine-and-a-half minutes, and he wanted me to think about that and re-choreograph it. I had never been asked to re-choreograph anything and I was devastated. I thought Balanchine must have hated my work. I asked Lincoln about it, and he said, "No, George likes it, but why don't you just take in everything he has to say and then go ahead and do what you want."

I considered it my job to learn from and to try and please Balanchine, so I completely re-choreographed the first movement, this time with the emphasis firmly on the rhythm. I also eliminated Pat's solo role. I didn't want anyone to think I had copied his idea of a tall center girl soloist. Balanchine then came to see the new version a few weeks later, and he was extremely pleased. He told me, "You know, dear, I couldn't have done better myself." Wow! That floored me! Now I couldn't wait to do the rest of the ballet. He said, "By all means, keep going." So, of course, I continued working on this ballet off and on through the winter of 1968.

It was in the spring season of 1968 that Villella's new ballet to the *Prokofiev Violin Concerto* was to make its premiere. It was to be Eddie's second ballet for the company. His first, *Narkissos,* was not a success, but Mr. B. wanted to give him another chance. One day during a rehearsal of the Xenakis ballet, Balanchine called me out of the room into the hallway. He told me that Eddie would not have his ballet ready in time and asked if I could finish my Stravinsky so that it could be performed during the spring season. I couldn't believe it! At twenty years old I was going to have a ballet of mine performed by the New York City Ballet. I wasn't exactly nervous, and it never occurred to me to be anxious or insecure. I was just so excited that I couldn't wait to get started. When we went back into the room to continue the rehearsal, Balanchine then choreographed a special little solo part for me, its highlight a supported arabesque *penchée.* In those years I had a perfect split *penchée* and I guess he wanted to show that off. A boy doing a split *développé* was quite unusual in those years. Of course, I was on cloud nine.

I immediately started choreographing my new Stravinsky ballet directly on the company dancers. I set the first movement with Marnee Morris (replacing Diane) and Anthony Blum (replacing Frank), exactly as I had staged it at SAB in the revised version. Both Marnee and Tony were stronger dancers, so I wanted them to start the ballet with a bang. The second movement was an adagio for Kay Mazzo and eight boys using Balinese-styled *ports de bras* and silhouetted lighting effects. The third movement consisted of three *pas de deux* couples and a solo role for John Prinz. The fourth movement featured Renee Estopinal and the entire cast of twenty-six dancers. Costumes were dug up from the storerooms from an earlier version of *Concerto Barocco.* These were black leotards with fishnet tops and black short practice skirts, but stylishly designed, and they looked very Art Deco.

Balanchine gave me an enormous amount of freedom with the rehearsal time, and Robert Irving was incredibly helpful with the score. I had a small tape recorder and a small conductor's score that I carried with me everywhere. I would make notes in the score and work with the tape when I was not working with the dancers. Balanchine occasionally came into rehearsals to watch, but he never made suggestions. He would simply be encouraging. His favorite phrase was "Not bad, dear. Continue."

We would often work until 10:30 at night. After about three weeks I completely lost my voice, which I think was a relief to the majority of the dancers. As I look back on this time, I'm sure I was a royal pain in the ass. I was obsessed with the Stravinsky music. I was trying to show Balanchine, the dancers, and the world at large, that I was ready for this challenge. I think I was very much like that brash young choreographer in the film *The Turning Point,* played by Danny Levans.

John Braden, a costume and lighting designer brought in by Lincoln, did the lighting, which was very involved and ended up looking very psychedelic. He used red and green lighting explosions on the cyclorama, gobos, and everything else he and I could think of. This was the late Sixties, and I'm sure we were influenced by the acid rock phase in music at that time. I was never heavily into that kind of music and I never went to rock concerts, but when I began lighting the ballet with Braden, I did try to make it look "contemporary." Considering the lighting plot from today's perspective, I'm sure it would look very dated.

Based on the audience's reaction, the opening night was a big success. There were at least seven front-of-curtain calls in addition to the normal two or three full-stage bows. With the audience liking the ballet so much, I thought all was well with the world. I was only sorry

Anthony Blum and Marnee Morris in my *Strawinsky Symphony in C.* Photo by Martha Swope. Used with permission of NYPL swope_779456.

Left top: Corps de ballet (with Merrill Ashley) of my first ballet for NYCB at age twenty-one, *Strawinsky Symphony in C*, after the name was changed to *Stravinsky Symphony* and the costumes were simplified. Photo by Martha Swope. Used with permission of NYPL swope_779793.

Left bottom: Kay Mazzo and men in *Strawinsky Symphony in C*. Photo by Martha Swope. Used with permission of NYPL swope_779455.

that Balanchine was out of town for the premiere and didn't see that wonderful reception.

The very next day, from that wonderful high, came the worst possible low. The *New York Times* editor who headlined the Clive Barnes review "W Is for Weak" was mocking the printed program, which spelled Stravinsky with a "w": Strawinsky. Although all the principal dancers received very good notices, Barnes's review proceeded to demolish my ballet, which completely devastated me. I was totally unprepared for his disastrous critique of my first company work. I read his review in the morning, walked into Betty Cage's office, and asked if this meant I'd be fired. She laughed and said no, and said I should go and read some of Balanchine's early reviews. To my relief, I learned that it was Balanchine's policy not to take the critics too seriously; in fact, not even to bother reading them. I was from Hollywood and accustomed to the importance of film critics. Nevertheless, I took her advice and went to the Library for the Performing Arts at Lincoln Center and pulled out reviews of Balanchine's early premieres. I was amazed to find that many of his first ballets in America, and even in Europe, had received less-than-flattering opening-night critiques. John Martin's reviews in the *New York Times* were especially hard to read. Even so, those were about Balanchine, and I still felt like a complete failure.

To my relief, and quite surprisingly, literally all the other reviews of my ballet were very positive.

It turned out that many of the critics disapproved of the way Barnes had taken a twenty-year-old choreographer to task so severely. Some of these comments about his not looking realistically at my first ballet caused him to come back and re-review the ballet two nights later. He then did a very generous thing. The *Times* printed his new review, wherein he wrote that although he didn't "like" my ballet any better the second time, he saw that in criticizing me so harshly, he was inadvertently making a comparison between Balanchine and me. His argument was that if my ballets were going to be performed in the same theater and by the same company as Balanchine's, I should be judged on the same level. He mentioned the John Martin less-than-glowing review of Balanchine's *Symphony in C* and reminded readers that twenty years later, Martin had to go back and reevaluate his position. Therefore, even though Barnes was not apologizing for his earlier review, he obviously did not want to seem incapable of recognizing talent or, worse, to discourage a young choreographer. Barnes said that obviously he was criticizing only that one ballet. Fair enough. He more than made up for it later with his review of my second ballet, *Fantasies.*

Balanchine came back to town a week after this brouhaha, saw a performance of my *Strawinsky: Symphony in C,* and said he didn't like the costumes and that the lighting was too busy. He was right, as always, but then he asked why I had changed the choreography of the first movement. That really threw me. I told him I hadn't changed one step of the first movement because, "You said you liked it the way it was," I told him. He said it didn't "look" the same. He said maybe it was because the lead girl now wasn't Diane Bradshaw but Marnee Morris. Marnee at that time had the strongest technique of all the girls in the company, whereas Diane didn't, and I thought a stronger technician would be better. He said it was much more "interesting" when Diane danced the part because it looked like a struggle, and the audience would be with her, hoping she'd get through it. Marnee, he said, made it look way too easy. He also said it was too rhythmical! He suggested I change it again.

I said, "Mr. B., you said you wanted the rhythm emphasized. I can't just keep changing the ballet." He then looked at me rather sternly and said, "Why shouldn't you? I've been changing *Serenade* for over thirty years." He told me a few stories about the order changes in *Serenade*'s movements and about changing some of the choreography and costumes, and later adding repeats. He told me a very wise thing: "A choreographer must not be in love with his own work. It's a *craft.*" He told me there's an old Russian saying about "sucking your thumb until it bleeds." As a purely technical exercise, he wanted me to go back and re-choreograph the whole ballet again. What an eye-opener! Though he had said he liked the ballet in all the rehearsals, he wanted me to do it over again as an exercise. I thought it was a very expensive exercise, and it would be hard on the dancers to relearn it. Wouldn't he rather just cut it from the repertoire? He said, "Absolutely not." He thought I might start by changing Kay's adagio and making it a regular *pas de deux,* that I should change other sections as well, and that I should keep "working" on it.

That ballet became a nightmare for me (and I'm sure for the dancers) for the next year and a half. Yet every single revision of *Stravinsky Symphony* (he did let me change the name to *Stravinsky Symphony*) met with better reviews, not only from Clive Barnes but from all the other critics as well. We went through at least four different versions, including the lighting and costumes. I eventually became so confused as to what the ballet was supposed to look like that by the end, I couldn't even stand to see it or hear that music again. I asked for it to be dropped from the repertoire in 1970. I guess it evolved into a decent-enough ballet, but it was a very difficult, though useful, learning experience. I can see now that Mr. B. was wise to put me through that, but at the time it was torture.

During those early years I had a tendency so typical of youth: I took everything Balanchine said very literally. For instance, when he had advised me to redo the first movement in its SAB version, he suggested I concentrate more on the rhythm. Then, when he saw it after the premiere, he asked why I kept everything in the first movement so squarely on the rhythm! It seemed a complete contradiction. But

I found out, as I worked more and more with him, that he did not always say what he meant, or mean what he said.

Betty Cage told me a very funny story about the set design for *Glinkiana*. Balanchine had told the designer Esteban Francés that the "Jota Aragonesa" scenery should be in different shades of red. Señor Francés complied, and when he showed Balanchine the design, Balanchine asked, "What is all this red?" Francés said, "You said you wanted different shades of red." Balanchine retorted, "I may have *said* red, but I didn't *mean* red." The poor man was totally lost, but he did redesign the set.

When Betty told me this story, I said, "What am I supposed to do? He says one thing but means another? What does Mr. B. really want?" It took me a while to understand that in the case of Balanchine, or perhaps anybody of his genius, one shouldn't expect too literal a communication. Mr. B. could be blunt and to the point when necessary, especially in class, but I think when it came to his feelings about music or choreography, which he admitted could change over the years, his words were not capable of conveying his thoughts accurately. Balanchine would use varying means to accomplish a desired result. At that time I was young, and I so worshipped the man that I was confused as to how to please him. I think it was clear to everybody who knew me then that my devotion to Balanchine was beginning to transcend a mere pupil-master relationship. I didn't realize at the time that Mr. B. was becoming a father figure to me. I was not yet spending as much time with him as I would be in the next few years, but we were together in some private social situations. Mostly he took me to dinners at his favorite restaurants, the Russian Tea Room, Monk's Inn, and The Ginger Man (the latter two were both on West 64th Street, a block from the theater). He also took me to small dinner parties at Leslie Copeland's apartment.

Mr. Copeland, who was English and was affectionately known as "Ducky," was the wardrobe master for the men and a personal friend of Balanchine's. He was openly gay and flaunted it in a very Quentin Crisp kind of way. This was before it was more socially acceptable, and one could still be arrested just for being at a gay bar. (Once on tour, when our company was staying at a Holiday Inn outside Akron, Ohio, Ducky met us in full drag and make-up as we were getting off the company bus after a show and he invited Balanchine to have a drink with him at the hotel bar—Balanchine did.) Very often, normally on a Monday night, our day off, Ducky would cook dinner and Balanchine would invite a few select dancers. I was fortunately always on the guest list. These dinners saw Mr. B. at his most relaxed. Besides myself, regulars included Kay Mazzo, Suzy Hendl, Renee Estopinal, the striking redhead Linda Merrill who had just joined the company, and, as usual, Mr. B.'s right-hand man and the company manager, Edward Bigelow. Thinking back now, it occurs to me that Bigelow and I were the only men, aside from Ducky and Mr. B.

Mr. B. often added some dishes of his own, but it was just as common for him to take over completely and prepare the entire meal himself. Fine wine, delicious food, and lively conversations: these were Balanchine's domain, and all of us cherished these gatherings. What did we talk about? Would you believe quantum mechanics? Mr. B. was very well read and seemed to know about everything. No topic was off limits. After Suzanne married, and Mr. B. was at his lowest, these dinners at Ducky's became even more frequent, and they helped lighten Balanchine's spirits a lot. God bless you, Ducky!

18

Teaching at SAB

Gelsey Kirkland as Student—The Bolshoi Ballet in NYC

Just before I started choreographing for the company, Balanchine asked me to teach some classes at SAB. I had been with the company a little over a year and I was hardly older than the students. Call it what you will—ambition, brashness—I was not shy about teaching students as well as any professionals who might drop in. I figured that if Mr. B. wanted me to teach, he must know what he was doing, and so I didn't worry too much about it. Mr. B. told me quite bluntly that he was training me to be a "ballet master" in the classic sense of the word: someone who taught the company classes and directed rehearsals. Balanchine himself said he was a "ballet master." The term "artistic director," he said, was an American affectation. He was systematically teaching me how to handle all the areas that a good ballet master should cover. About choreography itself, he often said it was as much a craft as an art and that during the Renaissance artists were always considered "craftsmen." I was also happily being used more and more as a dancer. Mr. B. used to say it was impossible to be a choreographer without being a dancer first. Now Balanchine was requesting that I start teaching at SAB, and soon after that he had me teaching the company itself.

The first classes I taught for the school were the intermediate men's classes and one of the C-level mixed advanced classes in the evening. Many times dancers from the company, such as Allegra Kent, Violette Verdy, Melissa Hayden, or Jacques d'Amboise would come and take my class. I thought it odd at first that dancers of this stature would come and study with me, but I think what they liked was that even though I was preaching the Balanchine gospel, as it were, I did tone it down a bit. Because I was teaching young students, who were not dancing eight performances a week and therefore could not concentrate on just *glissades* for the entire class, I tried to teach a well-rounded and "dancey" class. There are class combinations similar to a musician's scales, in which a student practices or repeats an exercise in order to perfect it. Then there are certain other combinations that train a dancer to know how to string steps together, as in a variation for the stage.

I was floored one day when Allegra and Jacques came together to take one of my first evening C classes. Teaching students was one thing, but having these two legends in my class was quite another. I was nervous as hell. However, both seemed to like it, behaved very professionally, and came to more of my classes. Eventually many more company members would drop by, and this is probably why Balanchine started having me teach the company class when he was unavailable.

Many future company members were in my classes at SAB when they were young teenagers, and I was only a few years older than they were. Some of the youngest students went on to great careers—Gelsey Kirkland, Jean-Pierre Frohlich, Victor Castelli, Elise and Laura Flagg, Peter Naumann, Victor Barbee, even Fernando Bujones.

On top of everything else I was continuing to make more ballets for the school. For the 1968 spring Workshops performances I choreographed a ballet to a short piece called *Orzonyi Chastushki* by Maya Plisetskaya's composer-husband Rodion Shchedrin. The leads in this ballet were Elise Flagg, Kathleen Haigney, and the fifteen-year-old Gelsey Kirkland.

Gelsey was a phenomenon even then. Certainly when I first knew her, starting when she was just fourteen, it was clear that here was a girl who would become one of America's greatest ballerinas. She was abundantly talented and used her older sister, Johnna, as her role model. Johnna had been a promising dancer at the school, and was already in the company, and therefore Gelsey had to match if not surpass her. Her sibling rivalry was obvious to all and she was so ambitious that she actually seemed a bit manic. I was once quoted in a dance publication about my thoughts on Gelsey soon after her début in Robbins's *The Cage* (his ballet about lethal female insects that kill the male after mating), and I said, "Gelsey? She was born to kill." I was referring to her role in that ballet, but I suppose unconsciously I was referring to her laser-like focus and ambition. Nothing would get in this girl's way. Unfortunately, her mania for perfection caused her problems later, as she recounts in her autobiography, *Dancing on My Grave,* which, sadly, is an apt title.

The reason I take it upon myself to speak about her is because I choreographed some of Gelsey's first solos at the school and her first leads with the company (before Balanchine used her in *Firebird,* in 1970), and I was one of her most frequent partners, so I was intimately involved with her early pre-American Ballet Theatre years. There is no question that she was a genius-level dancer, and, before her drug use ravaged her and shortened her career, she was undoubtedly in a class by herself. I absolutely adored her in the beginning—and so did Balanchine.

Usually, if Mr. B. had his eye on a certain young dancer he would suggest to whoever else was choreographing for the company at that time, whether it be John Taras, d'Amboise, or myself, that we should cast that dancer in one of our ballets. This was the case with Farrell, too. She danced her first leads in ballets by d'Amboise and Taras.

Gelsey danced the second lead in *Orzonyi Chastushki* and, as expected, was brilliant.

This was not a strictly classical ballet; it was more acrobatic and jazzy. Gelsey had a great time tossing off some very difficult things, such as a double pirouette, then, before coming down, extending her leg to the front, grabbing her ankle, and doing another turn. She never missed it. Everybody loved watching this technical wunderkind. She also danced a lead in Alexandra Danilova's staging for the Workshop of *Les Sylphides* (which *Danilova entitled* "Chopiniana"), with Robert Weiss and Elise Flagg. We knew it would not be long before Balanchine took her into the company, which he did soon after that performance, and as he had done with Renee Estopinal and Lynn Bryson a few years before.

I didn't know then how truly difficult her relationship with her sister Johnna was, or how stressful their home life was. I found this out much later. At that time, all I could really think of was the arrival of the Bolshoi Ballet, about to open across the Plaza at the Metropolitan Opera House.

The Bolshoi was scheduled to be there for six weeks and I was really looking forward to seeing them again. I was going to try to take their company class, and it was a pure coincidence that the ballet I was doing for the Workshop was to music by Plisetskaya's husband. I hadn't seen her for three years, but I still kept her picture in *Don Quixote* in my apartment. The one I had kept on my make-up mirror had been torn apart, as mentioned, so I never kept her photo at the theater after that. But I still tried to dance like a male version of her. I wanted to invite her to the performance but wasn't sure of the best way to approach her.

One day destiny stepped in. Sitting at O'Neal's restaurant with a few other Bolshoi dancers was Plisetskaya herself. I tried to catch her eye. At first she didn't seem to notice me, but then her eyes widened and she realized she knew me, though it looked as if she wasn't quite sure where we'd met. I went over to her table, introduced myself, and told her I was now in the New York City Ballet and that I had just choreographed a ballet to her husband's music. I then invited her to come to a performance. She said,

"Da. I come." I was understandably thrilled.

Everyone in the company knew of my crush on Plisetskaya. My mannerisms and exaggerated attitude position smacked of "Bolshoi-itis." It wasn't until she arrived at our theater that people really believed I knew her. She came to see a performance of *Prodigal Son* in which I danced one of the two Friends, and she came backstage afterward to give me corrections—right in front of Balanchine.

He greeted her warmly, but then she turned her back to him to correct me. Yikes. He just smiled like a cat that had caught a mouse and seemed very amused. He told me at dinner later that night that he admired her as a dancer but that she wasn't his "type." She was much too earthy and womanly to interest him. He was always drawn to the more angelic types. I don't think anyone would call Plisetskaya angelic.

Maya was able to pull some strings and I was once again allowed to take the Bolshoi's company classes. Every day I had class with the legendary Asaf Messerer in the morning at 10:00, at the Met, and then dashed across the Plaza to the State Theater just in time to take Balanchine's company class at 11:00. He was often late anyway, and he knew where I was, so if I came in five minutes late, he was fine with that. There were a lot of similarities between the two men's classes: both their barres were very short, fifteen or twenty minutes at the most. Messerer's class had more jumps in the center and was perhaps more well-rounded, but the girls were never *en pointe*. All Balanchine's girls took the entire class *en pointe* because Balanchine taught, in effect, a pointe class. Some of the women from our company, such as Melissa Hayden, Patricia Neary, and Marnee Morris, were allowed to take the Bolshoi's classes too. Jacques d'Amboise was the only other male from New York City Ballet. Marnee would be *en pointe* for the entire class, doing all the steps easily. Melissa and Pat wore soft shoes for the barre, but not Marnee.

The Russian dancers seemed amazed that steps that were difficult enough on demi-pointe were being done by Marnee easily on full pointe. A few of the dancers asked me if she had been trained at the Kirov. As we know, Balanchine's original training was with the Imperial Ballet of the Mariinsky Theater of St. Petersburg, which later became the Leningrad-Kirov Ballet. There are stylistic differences between the Kirov and the Bolshoi that date back to long before Balanchine was a student.

The Kirov was then considered more classical and technically pure than the Bolshoi. The NYCB in those years was also a tad more refined than the Bolshoi, due to the Mariinsky background that Balanchine brought to it. In March 2004, when I taught and staged Balanchine's ballets for both these companies, their stylistic differences were still evident.

I was always more "Bolshoi" because of my love of Plisetskaya, but Balanchine never seemed to mind that. He never wanted his company to be bland. Almost daily, that old cliché about Balanchine only liking cold dancers was proven false. Balanchine never in any way kept us from having distinct personalities. He always emphasized letting our individuality shine through. This is not to say he didn't enjoy making little cracks about the Bolshoi, or other companies, for that matter.

When a dancer came to his class and started doing an arabesque with a slightly bent knee, which, in the Bolshoi, is acceptable, Balanchine would say, "This is not the Bolshoi. We do arabesque with straight knee here." Or, if a dancer's movements were a little imprecise, he would go over and start speaking in Russian. Then he would say, "Oh, are you in my company? The way you were dancing, I thought you were from that other company over there," pointing in the direction of the Met. He passionately loved his Russian training, but he also saw its faults. And there was always a rivalry between the Bolshoi and his original St. Petersburg school. It was fun, though, to have some "competition" dancing at Lincoln Center. What a great time to be a dancer in New York City, where there were always enough audiences to go around.

This same season my old friend Anton Dolin was in the city, and he came backstage after a performance of *Prodigal Son,* when I was still dancing his original role as one of the two Friends. Mr. B. greeted him warmly, but when Dolin saw me he pulled me over to him and Balanchine. He told Mr. B. how "naughty" I had been not taking him up on his offer to study at the Royal Ballet school. Mr. B. just smiled. Dolin then invited me to go with him to visit Olga Spessivtseva, one of the most celebrated Russian ballerinas of the Anna Pavlova–Diaghilev Ballets Russes era, who was now living at the Tolstoy Foundation's retirement home in upstate New York.

She had suffered several nervous breakdowns and serious mental problems, which curtailed her otherwise fabled career. When I met her she was extremely shy and fragile, and she spoke mostly in French. In their youth Dolin had been her partner and, according to him, had been madly in love with her, and he did seem totally devoted to her. She lived in a sparsely furnished tiny single room that had only a bed, a tiny breakfast table, desk, bathroom, and a small television. She proudly showed me her handmade dolls of her roles, including as Giselle, the central role in *Les Sylphides,* and Aurora in Diaghilev's *The Sleeping Princess* (*The Sleeping Beauty*) and others. When I told Balanchine of my visit he said she was the greatest of Diaghilev's three most famous ballerinas, Tamara Karsavina and Anna Pavlova being the other two. He said, "Karsavina had the technique. Pavlova had the soul. And Spessivtseva had both."

19

Fantasies

Mr. B.'s Suit—More Classes—*In-A-Gadda-Da-Vida*

I was still concerned about the negative Barnes review of my first ballet, but I was buoyed up a little by the fact that Balanchine did not care about reviews one way or the other. I now wanted very much to choreograph a ballet to music that I would choose, and on a subject or idea that was mine alone. Luckily, Mr. B. asked me for another ballet, so I saw an opportunity.

After the Stravinsky ballet, Mr. B. wanted me to do a new ballet almost immediately, so I started thinking about music I had loved for a number of years, the ultra-romantic *Fantasia on a Theme by Thomas Tallis* by Ralph Vaughan Williams. It had always suggested to me some sort of Druid wedding, or perhaps something about ghosts. I knew it would be quite different for the company—a story ballet to romantic English music was not typical for NYCB then or now. I'm a very verbal person, and when I start thinking about choreographing something that has a story, I talk about it to my friends. The more I talk about what I'm going to do, the more it crystallizes in my mind, which I think comes from being an actor.

A young dancer in the company, Linda MacArthur, was another good buddy in those years, and I spent many happy hours at her apartment talking about the ballet that later became known as *Fantasies*. I decided that this was a piece that I really *had* to do for the company. I approached Mr. B. and asked him for permission to start rehearsals or at least to start experimenting with a few dancers. When I told him I wanted to use the Vaughan Williams *Fantasia*, he was uncharacteristically negative. He didn't like the music, he said, because it was too romantic and too "mooshy." When that didn't seem to deter me,

Balanchine finally said it was impossible for NYCB's orchestra to play because it took too many strings—too many violins, cellos, etc.

I don't know what got into me, but I went to Robert Irving (who was English) and asked if he was familiar with the piece and how many strings it actually needed. He said he knew the music quite well, as he had conducted it for the BBC during World War II, and he loved it, and that, as a matter of fact, it could be done with the number of strings currently in our orchestra. I told Robert my problem with Balanchine and that I felt very strongly about doing a ballet to music of my choosing. I had used Balanchine's choice of music for my first company ballet, and I thought it would be fair if I could now do something to music I really loved.

Robert smiled at my brashness and said he'd see what he could do. The next night during intermission, Robert started to play the *Fantasia* quite loudly on the piano that was always kept in the wings. Balanchine noticed the little mini performance and asked him what he was playing. Robert told him it was the Vaughan Williams *Fantasia*. Balanchine shot me a raised eyebrow look and took Robert into a corner. A few minutes later Robert came back to me and said, "Well, he said you might as well start working on it." Thank you, Robert.

I started work on *Fantasies* in Saratoga in July 1968 during our summer season. The original cast was Kay Mazzo (with Linda Merrill, the red-haired new girl Mr. B. quite liked, understudying Kay's part), Anthony Blum, Melissa Hayden, and Conrad Ludlow. Sara Leland was Melissa's understudy and Johnna was third cast for Kay's role.

Melissa really threw herself into her part. I had taken a big chance by asking her to be in this ballet, since I was still a very young choreographer while she was the senior ballerina of the company and could be quite the "diva." This was similar to what happened in the film *The Turning Point*, where the young choreographer asks the star ballerina (Anne Bancroft) to dance in his new ballet. Luckily, Melissa didn't deliver the diva attitude Bancroft does in the film. Melissa wasn't being used too much at that time, and she realized that the story of *Fantasies* would work better with a mature ballerina in the part of the Green Girl.

This turned into an important education for me in star temperament. Melissa was never difficult; she simply expected to be treated in

Right: *Fantasies* with the original cast, Kay Mazzo, Sara Leland, Conrad Ludlow, and Anthony Blum. Photo by Martha Swope. Used with permission of NYPL swope_779640.

Below: *Fantasies* with the original cast, Kay Mazzo, Sara Leland, Conrad Ludlow, and Anthony Blum. Photo by Martha Swope. Used with permission of NYPL.

a certain way. I greatly admired her dancing and had enormous respect for her as a person, but it did take some adjustment to watch out for her feelings and ego. When dancers reach a certain age and are at the pinnacle of their craft, I think they sometimes become sensitive that they may not live up to others' (or their own) expectations. Consequently, when I gave Melissa a step she couldn't do right away, or felt uncomfortable doing, she became a wee bit tense, although she always worked her way through it. She was never uncooperative, but I learned quickly how to be tactful.

Years later Rudolph Nureyev asked me to give him some private classes when he was on tour with the Les Ballets de Monte Carlo. I spent a year with them in 1986 as a guest choreographer and teacher. He too was a consummate professional, and even though he had never had my class before and it probably was very different for him, he nonetheless behaved himself without one ounce of star ego. His only requests were to repeat some of my combinations. I'd heard that he could be quite a terror, but with me he was always a gentleman and he was still as big a flirt as he had been when we took Stanley Williams's classes together at SAB some twenty years earlier.

Now back to *Fantasies.*

Gordon Boelzner was my pianist for these rehearsals. When Balanchine was choreographing, he would continually confer with Gordon. Sometimes, when Balanchine was really on a roll and choreographing rapidly, he would get ahead of himself, and Gordon would have to slow him down. Balanchine never seemed to mind it when Gordon called him over to the piano to point out something that he might have missed. Once, when Mr. B. was choreographing *Rubies,* he miscounted a sequence, which was extremely rare. Gordon stopped playing and said casually, "Mr. B., that section changes to a six count and doesn't go back to a four count until the repeat." All Balanchine said was, "Thank you." He adjusted the counts and went on choreographing with no fuss or waste of time. This incident has always stuck with me as an example of how ego-less Balanchine was when it came to his choreography. Other choreographers would get embarrassed if they made a mistake and got called on it in front of their dancers. Not Balanchine. It was the work that was important; nothing else.

Gordon told me that Mr. B. always made his own piano reductions from the full score for all his ballets, and he also did this for some of the ballets choreographed by others. He did the transcriptions for all eight of my ballets too. For him, it was a relaxing hobby.

I finished choreographing the first section of *Fantasies* while the company was still in Saratoga and invited Mr. B. to watch a run-through.

He seemed pleased and said, "Go ahead, finish it," and I completed it when we were back in New York in the fall. When it was finished, I invited Mr. B. to look at it. I was a bit nervous since it was very different from anything I had done before or, for that matter, from anything currently in the company's repertory.

He watched the entire ballet at the next run-through without saying one word. Normally he would whisper something to me as a ballet was going along, but that day he was silent. Afterward he said he was surprised he liked it even though he still didn't care very much for the music—"too mushy" (or, as he pronounced it, "mooshy"). Then he told me it would be on that season!

His only criticism was that there was one lift in the first section with Kay and Conrad that he thought was a little bit "banal" (one of his favorite words). It was an overhead straight-arm press lift, which is commonly called a "bird," in which Kay lay flat out and was lifted up by her hips. It's the same climactic lift used in the film *Dirty Dancing*. This lift then went into a flip and down to a "fish dive." Balanchine thought this lift and flip was a bit of a cliché and too "Soviet" and wanted me to do something more unusual. Flips like that were common in Russian companies at that time, and Balanchine liked to put down the Russians by calling them "Soviet." He always made a distinction between the classical "Russian" ballet as he knew it and what he considered the bastardization of it after the Russian Revolution, when things became "Soviet." Anyway, that was how the "walkover" lift came in. Balanchine didn't suggest it; he just asked me to change that one place. To this day that "walkover" still gets a strong audience reaction. I am a bit concerned that it's too acrobatic, but that was what I came up with and it has stayed in ever since.

Another part of the choreography that gets a big reaction is the moment near the end when the girl in green goes sailing over the shoulder of the boy in blue, only to land in a sort of hug with the boy in green.

That is the dramatic climax of the music, and everything builds to that point. While I was choreographing it, I got to that part of the score and for the life of me couldn't think what to do. Whatever I choreographed would need to be dramatic enough to match the intensity and passion of that music. It would also have to be the climax of the ballet's story, which is the meeting of a man and woman, each of whom has a fantasy lover. I needed the fantasy figures to be as believable to the audience as they were to their human lovers. I also knew that by the end of the ballet I wanted not only the real figures to have gotten together but also that the fantasy figures should look as if they were going to be united. I wanted something incredible to happen at this place in the music, but I couldn't think what. I just wanted everybody to get together in the middle of the stage at this point and freeze into a tableau of some sort. I had to make this one statement of everybody being "together."

Sara Leland (whom everyone called Sally) was now dancing the Melissa Hayden part; Melissa unfortunately had to bow out because of a knee injury, which she received in another ballet, not mine, thank goodness. In this climactic moment, Sally had to run to Tony, the boy in blue. I needed Kay, who was dancing the girl in blue, to get out of the way, and I wanted Conrad, the man in green, to catch her, but I didn't know exactly how that was going to happen. I just told everybody to run at each other. What followed was hysterical.

Kay thought she would be trampled, so she kneeled and ducked. Sally tripped, and to catch her from falling, Tony picked her up, at which point I thought, *That's it!* I used what they had done naturally and built it into the tableau. That moment still elicits comments whenever *Fantasies* is performed because it is considered very slick, and it certainly is surprising. I should be honest, though. That moment comes from an accident and I just made it look as though it were deliberate. Other choreographers routinely let their dancers invent actual steps, but that is not my style, nor Balanchine's, nor Robbins's. However, we all allowed the spontaneity of rehearsals to come into play. Even Balanchine would sometimes utilize a dancer's mistake; not often, but it did happen from time to time. A prime example is in his *Serenade,* when a girl fell and he kept it in. It was magical how he could simultaneously know exactly which steps to use which to discard, and also to know how to let the dancers be themselves. Or maybe I should say it was alchemy.

The premiere of *Fantasies* was in January 1969, and it was totally nerve-racking, even though Balanchine had given my ballet his blessing. The music was English, and there was no other English composer represented in the company at that time. Frederick Ashton's *Illuminations* (to a score by Benjamin Britten of the same name) had been in the repertory earlier, but it was no longer being done. *Fantasies* had a small cast, only four dancers, and it was very different from my first ballet, the much larger Balanchine-influenced Stravinsky work.

The choreography of *Fantasies* is a bit like Antony Tudor's, in that it uses some natural gestures, but it also uses a much broader classical ballet technique. There are some big tricky lifts, which again were unlike the typical choreography for the company of that time—and it had a story! After the drubbing I had received from Clive Barnes for my first ballet, I was dreading his reception for my second.

The first showing took place at a dress rehearsal for the Friends of City Center, a support group for the City Center companies, including the New York City Opera and the New York City Ballet. They gave it a polite reception, but nothing great, which was not a reassuring sign. A week later, the night before the premiere, Balanchine invited me to a dinner party being given at the home of his good friend Lucia Davidova, whom I addressed as Madame, as I always addressed Madame Danilova and other European ladies of her generation. There are many photographs of Balanchine choreographing *Agon* in which you can see Mme. Davidova sitting with her back to the mirror. She was a most elegant, aristocratic lady, with jet-black hair, who looked as if she knew in technical terms exactly what the dancers were doing (and of course, and in fact, she did). Mme. Davidova turned out to be a very supportive friend of mine in my years with the company. At the dinner Balanchine seemed pleased about my upcoming premiere and specifically asked her to come. He said she should not miss this "important premiere." He also asked me what I would be wearing and told me there was going to be a big party afterward at Bert Martinson's apartment. Bert was a major supporter of the company and heir to the Martinson Coffee fortune.

Balanchine suggested that I wear something other than my usual tacky brown suit. After I told him that was my only one, Mr. B. took me over to his apartment the next day and gave me a suit of his. Amazingly, it fit almost perfectly. The jacket was a little too wide in the shoulders (Balanchine had broad shoulders) and the pants were a touch too big at the waist, but everything else was fine. He also gave me a pair of his shoes, which were a bit tight. I went quickly to a tailor and had the waist taken in and wore the suit and shoes to the premiere. I still have them.

At its premiere *Fantasies* received just three curtain calls, versus *Stravinsky Symphony*'s seven, and I thought it was a failure. Audience members weren't ecstatic, as they had been for my Stravinsky, but neither were they particularly cold. The company's dancers seemed to like the ballet quite a bit, but I didn't know what to make of the audience's tepid reaction.

After the premiere Balanchine took me to Martinson's penthouse, where a large party was already going on. Not only were New York City Ballet members there, but so were some dancers from other companies and a lot of Martinson's personal friends, and everyone congratulated me on my ballet. Around midnight the doorman called to say Clive Barnes was on his way up. Martinson came over to me and said, "Well, congratulations, you've got a good review." "What do you mean?" I asked. Bert said he had invited Barnes to the party, and the fact that he had shown up must mean exactly that. He said that Barnes wouldn't dare come if he were going to pan my ballet.

Balanchine then came over and said, "No matter what Barnes writes, even if it's very, very, good, don't thank him. We do *not* thank critics if they give us good review, nor do we say anything if they give us bad review. We ignore them." Just then Barnes came bustling into the party looking very happy. He immediately came over to me with a copy of the *New York Times* and thrust it into my hand. He said, "Well, my boy, it's a lovely ballet. Why don't you read this?" Hallelujah! It was as good a review as the one for my Stravinsky ballet was bad. Barnes declared that "of all the young choreographers surrounding George Balanchine, and their name is legion, John Clifford strikes me here and now as the boy most likely." Wow! What a relief. Since then, this ballet been performed by companies internationally, from Berlin to Buenos Aires, and from France to Italy . . . and it's always been a success.

The next day all the other papers and magazines echoed Barnes's rave. I went against Mr. B.'s advice, though, and thanked Barnes.

Balanchine normally stood in the wings for all the performances, but I noticed that for *Fantasies* he especially liked to check out how the new dancers were doing. A gratifying personal moment happened in the first season when I was able to cast Johnna as the Blue Girl for the last performance.

I'd always loved Johnna's beautiful legs, exceptional arabesque line, and soft phrasing, but also always hoped that she would come out of her shell a little more and be more confident and assertive. I admired her dancing, yet she was insecure about her own talent and compared herself to her much-more-ambitious younger sister Gelsey. She shouldn't have worried. Her back was already as flexible as Plisetskaya's, she had much better pirouettes and extensions than Gelsey, and at seventeen she was only at the beginning of her career. Her role in my ballet didn't need any great attack or big technique, so it worked with her shy personality. It relied almost solely on having beautiful quality and line, something that she and Kay Mazzo had in common.

It was a pity that her father, the playwright and author Jack Kirkland, had never approved of her dancing. He had wanted her to be an actress and hadn't come to many performances of the company. He made an exception, though, to see her début in this ballet, I think because it was her first leading role. When he died, the suit in which they buried him was the same one he wore to that show. Her mother found the ticket stubs from that performance in one of the pockets. Johnna was touched that her father finally saw her dance as a featured dancer and she really did have a brilliant performance that afternoon. There's a point near the end of this ballet where she had to do an extended backbend arabesque. Realizing Johnna's natural ability, I changed it a little to a more Bolshoi-style attitude position. Johnna knew this was her forte. When she got to that point she arched back and literally bent her body into the most beautiful line I have ever seen onstage. I was watching from the front that day and heard the entire audience gasp. It was that beautiful. It was a bit acrobatic, yes, but nonetheless gorgeous. I was so proud of her that day.

Balanchine then started to show more interest in her and wanted to see if he could develop her further, but she had a catastrophe of sorts waiting for her in the wings. Gelsey, who was two years younger, had just joined the company. It was bad enough when she was still at SAB, but now she would be dancing right next to her big sister in Balanchine's class and onstage too.

Returning to Mr. B.'s classes and the SAB workshop, Balanchine's classes continued to be heaven to me. Of the men, it used to be Jacques who got most of the attention figuring out Mr. B's brain-teaser combinations, but now that task was starting to veer a little toward me. I loved the challenge, and of course it didn't hurt my ego that I was now included on an equal footing with d'Amboise.

Balanchine continued to invent combinations in class to test who could pick them up the fastest. Jacques had always been the champ at this game, but now I was a serious contender. It was always a good-natured challenge, never an attempt to humiliate us or to break our spirit. It was just such an adventure to go to class. If anybody ever had the nerve to criticize Mr. B.'s classes or his choreography, I became furious. I became the worst New York City Ballet snob of them all. I firmly believed everything I was being taught, and I still do to this day.

This isn't to say I didn't appreciate and acknowledge other styles of ballet or other companies, and exceptionally great non-Balanchine dancers, such as Nureyev, Vasiliev, and Plisetskaya, or Cynthia Gregory at American Ballet Theatre. Still, for me, nothing could surpass the Balanchine aesthetic. I did not forget nor ignore my early training with Loring and Dolin, and those great Bolshoi company classes with Messerer and Plisetskaya, but now I was studying with the true master. Mr. B.'s ballet classes, for me, have never been equaled. Also, I've said I always found Balanchine very amusing. His little stories totally cracked me up. If you wanted to do something else, I thought, or were thinking about your laundry, or a lover—well, then, go across the street for a cup of coffee, or go to O'Neal's for a drink (a "Hooker," a whisky shot with a small beer as a chaser, was one of Mr. B.'s favorites), but please don't waste his time or yours in his class. We were there to *work*. And so was he.

His company classes were only one hour long, between 11:00 and 12:00, Tuesday through Sunday. Balanchine would usually walk into class five or ten minutes late, hoping that that dancers would have gone through all the basic exercises at the barre on their own. He didn't really care to give the first *pliés, tendus,* and *dégagés,* which are just basic exercises that professional dancers should be able do on their own. But if Balanchine happened to be on time, then he would really teach them, not just give them.

We were never allowed to blur the steps or the positions. If one couldn't articulate the subtle differences between steps, positions, or tempi, then a dancer, any dancer, would inevitably reduce everything to the lowest common denominator. Balanchine hated sloppiness.

*Battement tendu*s, for instance, couldn't be done too cleanly (or too quickly) for him. Pirouettes had to be done from a very deep lunge with a straight back leg, not from a nondescript *demi-plié* fourth position but from an actual huge lunge. Arabesques had to have perfect right angles, as in the back's relationship to the leg. If you wanted a higher arabesque leg, fine, but you couldn't lean forward to accomplish a higher back leg; not in his class, anyway. (Only Farrell seemed to be allowed to break a couple of these rules for arabesques, not the rest of us.) Balanchine was very big on precise degrees. He would say, "Lift your leg to a ninety-degree angle," or to a forty-five degree angle. He never said just to *développé*, or *fondu*, to some vague height. When he gave extensions in the adagio section of class, he sometimes allowed dancers to develop these as high as each individual dancer could manage, but the dancer would have to know precisely where the leg was going, if you understand what I mean. He would joke and say, of an arabesque *penchée*, "Go to 360 degrees," the joke being the image of the working leg spinning in a complete circle like the hand of a clock.

His teasing of some of the youngest dancers was also typical of his sense of humor. When young dancers joined the company fresh out of the school, they would come into class feeling that they had more or less graduated. They were, by and large, terrified of Balanchine, but they were also relatively cocky. Mr. B., of course, handpicked all the dancers, but he would sometimes pretend not to know who they were. He would go up to some fifteen- or sixteen-year-old girl and ask her where she had studied. She inevitably would reply, "At the school, Mr. Balanchine." And he'd say, "Oh, really? Which school?" She would look up at him and say, "Why, your school, the School of American Ballet." And he'd say, "Oh, really? They don't know anything over there. But now, now, *I* will teach you how to dance!" It was a good way of getting dancers to realize that they were starting absolutely from scratch. It could be intimidating standing right next to Violette Verdy, Melissa Hayden, Suzanne Farrell, or Jacques d'Amboise at the barre, and it could really shake someone up, but everyone seemed to survive just fine.

Those last years of the Sixties and the early Seventies were in some ways the last golden period of the company. There was only one authority figure: George Balanchine. Everyone, from top management down to the least important corps de ballet member, had a sense of purpose and knew exactly what he or she was doing and why they were there. Even the stagehands adored him, and he knew all their names and personal histories. I can't stress enough the importance of the loyalty there was to Mr. B. There never was a sense of unfocused energy. For some dancers, I know that this was a problem if Balanchine didn't seem to like you or wasn't giving you enough attention: it was as if the whole world had come to an end. I was one of the lucky ones, and in those years, I never seemed to be out of his good graces. I wasn't the only one, of course, but there did seem to be only perhaps twelve of us he seemed to gravitate toward, and aside from Jacques and Eddie Bigelow, the company manager, I seemed to be the only male with whom Mr. B. was actually relaxed. I never saw him socialize one on one, or in a confiding way, with Villella, Martins, or any other male dancers. Even Lincoln Kirstein and he didn't seem to have a personal relationship. I knew they both greatly respected each other, but I never saw them have dinner or even coffee together. He did like and have drinks with Ronnie Bates, who had married Diana Adams when Balanchine was in love with her for a time, so obviously it wasn't that he felt threatened by any heterosexual male competition.

I was now choreographing nonstop for the Workshop. For the spring of 1969 I choreographed two new ballets. One was to the fourth and fifth movements of the massive *Bartók Concerto for Orchestra,* and I cast Ron Neumann, Elise Flagg, and Gloryann Hicks (a powerhouse new corps dancer) as the leads. The other ballet was *In-A-Gadda-Da-Vida,* to the rock song of that name by Iron Butterfly. Balanchine was intrigued I had chosen rock music that was inspired by the music of India and that the title referred to the Garden of Eden. With this wild music I therefore used a lot of Indian-style dance movement, and it had a slight reference to the biblical story of Adam and Eve. Balanchine even helped me with the lighting rehearsals and took a great interest in the female lead, a gorgeous blonde from the South, Anne Field, as Eve. The male lead, Steven Caras, as Adam, was seventeen years old, black-haired, and handsome beyond belief, and later had a long and happy career in the company. He is now one of the top ballet photographers in the world.

The spring of 1969 also marked the début of a major new Jerome Robbins work for the New York City Ballet and a complete change in the environment of the company.

20

Dances at a Gathering

The Return of Jerome Robbins

When Jerome Robbins returned to the company, his first idea was to mount one of his already successful ballets. I know this because Balanchine told me he was the one who suggested to Robbins that he do something new. This was so typical of Mr. B., who always wanted new ballets rather than revivals. Taking his advice, Robbins decided to use several Chopin piano pieces for his new work. He had started an earlier version of this at Harkness House, the home of Rebecca Harkness's ballet company, using several students from her school. He then fleshed it out into a *pas de deux* for McBride and Villella. Balanchine saw this and said, "Do more!" and so he did, an hour's worth more.

To begin, Jerry chose twelve dancers for his first rehearsals, which were to be held during the company's normal winter vacation. Usually the company had a six-week layoff period between its winter and spring seasons. Jerry requested that a few of us (and I was ecstatic to be chosen) stay and work those weeks on his new Chopin ballet, which was still untitled at that point. In addition to myself, the dancers were Sara Leland, Kay Mazzo, Robert Maiorano, Anthony Blum, Patricia McBride, Melissa Hayden, Allegra Kent, Violette Verdy, Jacques d'Amboise, John Prinz, and Edward Villella. Eddie was not there for many of those rehearsals as he was doing a lot of concerts and wasn't available. Later on Jerry brought in some understudies, like Carol Sumner, but from the beginning it was just the twelve of us and our great pianist, Gordon Boelzner. For five hours a day we were all Jerry's. We'd start in the morning, work for three hours, have a lunch break, work for another two, and then collapse.

My awe of Robbins increased when I started working with him, at least in the beginning. For whatever reason, whether it was my obvious hero worship or just that I had a lot of energy, Jerry decided to choreograph many of the male parts on me, especially Eddie's demanding leading role. I was the most like him physically and I certainly had the speed.

Robbins started rehearsals choreographing the "Wind Waltz," teaching four couples the same steps simultaneously. Kay, Sally, Allegra, and Melissa were learning the woman's part, and Blum, Prinz, d'Amboise, and I were learning the man's. If one of the dancers could do one of the steps a bit better than the others, then Jerry would try to get the other dancers to look exactly the same as the one who did the step best. For instance, Melissa had a larger ribcage than Kay, and one step that is partnered by the ribs worked very well with Melissa, whereas with Kay it just looked awkward, but Jerry kept insisting that Kay make it look exactly as it did on Melissa. Of course, dancers should try to do any step as well as they can, but at the same time, if something is based on a physical structure, as in this case, it's a little unfair not to change the step to accommodate the dancer who's actually going to dance the part. But no one knew who would be dancing which roles because Robbins kept changing his mind. One dance I did not see him choreograph was the wonderful solo for Violette Verdy. That solo was so right for her, in mannerisms and the style, that no other dancer I've seen has ever looked as "right" in it as Violette. This seemed to be an exception to the way Jerry usually worked, because he obviously choreographed that specifically for this unique dancer.

I soon saw that Jerry's method of working was very different from Balanchine's. When Balanchine first started to choreograph, he knew which dancers he was going to use in which parts, and he used each dancer's abilities almost as if he were that dancer himself. Mr. B. always worked with each dancer individually. Jerry, on the other hand, would choreograph the same steps on a number of dancers and then later decide who would do the role. This dehumanized the process as we felt we had nothing at all to do with his inspiration. We were all interchangeable parts.

Luckily, Jerry seemed to like me, and I was pleased he was choreographing Villella's dances on me, even though I knew I was not going to be dancing that role. Villella was a major principal dancer and I was still only in the corps, but I loved being able to work on his role because it was quite a challenge.

After about two weeks we began to feel a lot of tension in the room. Robbins being the perfectionist that he was, and given that he didn't make the dancers feel special to the ballet, the normal fatigue after hours and hours of rehearsal got to be unbearable. There was no release, and no humor, as there was in Balanchine's rehearsals. There was no escape from Robbins's manic intensity. Balanchine would tell his little stories and jokes and always keep the mood in the room very light. Also, Balanchine didn't usually use all the time allotted. Sometimes he would be late, or he would see that everybody was tired and would finish hours early. There was never any feeling of failure in his rehearsals. With Jerry, every minute that was scheduled was used, and he never seemed to be pleased with what we were doing. We all thought it was our fault and that we weren't living up to his expectations. He seemed to take everything so personally, and if any of us made a mistake he'd snap at us and acted as if we had done it on purpose.

I took this very hard because I wanted so much to please him. There were plenty of tantrums starting with the dancers, too. John Prinz had quite a temper; at one point Jerry kicked him out but a week later changed his mind and brought him back. Hayden and d'Amboise bowed out of the ballet only a few days after rehearsals started, and Allegra also walked. She told me she sent him a telegram saying, "Dear Jerry: Goodbye." Jerry later talked her back into it, which was great for me because she was my partner in what became known as the "Giggle Dance," and I really loved dancing with her.

He was less caustic with Villella, McBride, Mazzo, and Leland, who later became his ballet mistress and staged his ballets for other companies for several years. He was smart enough to know he really needed those dancers if his ballet was going to be a success. For my part, I just got very depressed. One day at O'Neal's Baloon (purposely misspelled because a "Saloon" wasn't allowed in New York City then), a popular restaurant across the street from the stage door, Balanchine sat down next to me at the bar, and he noticed how down I was. He pressed for what was bothering me. I didn't want to say anything and sound like a complainer, something Balanchine detested. Finally, he said, "Dear,

Allegra Kent and me in rehearsal of *Dances at a Gathering* (with Jerome Robbins looking on), circa 1969. Photo by Martha Swope. Used with permission of NYPL swope_1211296.

you better tell me what's wrong, because if you're unhappy we're *all* in trouble." He said this because I was usually so upbeat. I finally told him I was exhausted from working with Jerry. He then told me that no matter how difficult things were, it was good for me to work with him. I said I knew he was a great choreographer and I was lucky to be in his ballet, etc., but he interrupted me and said, "No, dear, not that. He will teach you how *not* to treat people." It was a great line and one I remember to this day. He went on to say that someday I would have my own company, and then he said, "I'm teaching you how to be a real ballet master. Someday that will be yours," he said, pointing at the State Theater. "So, is good for you to know what *not* to do!" Whenever I'm choreographing a ballet and find I'm getting tired and short-tempered with the dancers, I remember Balanchine's sage advice. I don't ever want to treat people the way Robbins did.

I want to be very clear here. When Balanchine pointed to the theater and said, "Someday that will be yours," I did not take him literally. I knew there were others before me, like d'Amboise, Taras, Moncion, and even Robbins, who he hoped would one day be true ballet masters and run companies of their own. When he said this to me, he was only sixty-five years old and in relatively good health. There was no way either of us thought he'd be going anywhere. Did he expect that I would one day actually be his successor? Who knows? He really never thought that much about the future because he knew full well how things could change in a heartbeat. I do know, however that he was teaching me to be a ballet master following in his footsteps, no matter where that might be.

21

The 1969 Spring Gala Preview

Dances at a Gathering and *Prelude, Fugue, and Riffs—*
Suzanne Farrell Resigns!

That spring of 1969 turned out to be quite an eventful time. The SAB Workshop had premiered my *Bartók Concerto* and my Iron Butterfly rock ballet *In-A-Gadda-Da-Vida,* and the premiere of *Dances at a Gathering* was right around the corner. By this time I was dancing many solo and principal roles in the company. Even before *Dances,* I was starting to understudy a lot of Villella's roles. I was also learning the *pas de deux* in *Stars and Stripes,* which surprised me because I'd expected to learn the solo boy in the third regiment before I'd be taught the leading male role, one that was only danced by d'Amboise, Ludlow, or Villella. I was also dancing Eddie's role of Oberon in *A Midsummer Night's Dream,* rather than Puck, which I thought was right up my alley. I eventually danced both these roles, alternating between the two for all the performances of *Dream.* I was the first man ever to dance both these roles.

As if all this were not enough, I had started to choreograph my third ballet for the company, to Leonard Bernstein's *Prelude, Fugue, and Riffs,* one of his wittiest little gems, originally written for Woody Herman and his jazz band. My lead ballerina was Allegra, and I was using much of her playful personality and vibrant quirky style. Allegra hadn't danced anything like it in the company for quite a while, and she had a zany sense of humor that I wanted to show off to the public. I had seen her dance in a jazz style on numerous television shows (she used to appear often on *The Bell Telephone Hour*), and she and I were by now close friends.

Both my Bernstein ballet and *Dances* were scheduled to premiere on that same gala program, and Jerry insisted that she could only appear in

Above: World premiere of *Dances at a Gathering* right before curtain falls, full cast. Couples from left to right are Violette Verdy and me, Kay Mazzo and Anthony Blum, John Prinz and Sara Leland (*backs to camera*), Robert Maiorano and Patricia McBride (*backs to camera*), and Allegra Kent and Edward Villella. Photographer unknown.

Middle right: Me as Oberon and Jean-Pierre Frohlich as Puck in Balanchine's *A Midsummer Night's Dream*. Photo by Martha Swope. Used with permission of NYPL swope_789351. Choreography by George Balanchine © The George Balanchine Trust.

Bottom right: Me as Oberon and Kay Mazzo as Titania in a performance of Balanchine's *A Midsummer Night's Dream* (approximately 1972). Photographer unknown. Choreography by George Balanchine © The George Balanchine Trust.

Above: Me as Puck in Balanchine's *A Midsummer Night's Dream* with Robert Maiorano. Photo by Martha Swope. Used with permission of NYPL swope_789309. Choreography by George Balanchine © The George Balanchine Trust.

Left: Me as Puck in Balanchine's *A Midsummer Night's Dream*. Photo by Martha Swope. Used with permission of NYPL swope_789307. Choreography by George Balanchine © The George Balanchine Trust.

his ballet that night. He didn't want her to appear in anything else, especially dancing with the same partner, me. Balanchine then suggested I use Linda Merrill, the gorgeous redhead whom he was starting to groom as a soloist and who had been Kay's understudy in my *Fantasies*. I was lucky enough to be choreographing at all in such heady company, so of course I agreed. But I had other problems.

Lincoln had chosen a new young costume designer for my ballet, but sadly, the costumes he came up with were not what I had in mind, and they were wildly different from what we had discussed. They had to be scrapped; as a result, by the time we got to the dress rehearsal there were no costumes for my ballet. Balanchine was lighting that rehearsal, as was his custom with all my ballets. Despite what the program reads in that era, he always lit his own ballets and was involved in one way or another with everyone else's, except those by Jerry, who brought in a "name" lighting designer, such as Jennifer Tipton or Tom Skelton. Mr. B. asked me what I wanted the dancers to wear, and I said, "I'd like the girls in bright-colored bell bottoms and the boys in pants and T-shirts." Balanchine then went up onstage, took some money out of his pocket, and gave it to the dancers. He told them to go and buy their own clothes after the rehearsal based on the colors I wanted. How generous of him to save the day.

What nobody knew was that a bomb was about to go off because of the love affair between Paul Mejia and Suzanne Farrell. They had fallen in love the year before and were dating on the sly, which was obvious to everybody in the company, except Balanchine. We were all acutely aware of his obsession with her, and we all expected her to be the next Mrs. Balanchine. One of the most obvious statements of his love was the role he created for her in his full-length 1965 ballet *Don Quixote*. She was not only Dulcinea, the love object in this, but also the Virgin Mary, no less.

When Paul and Suzanne announced that they had married, Balanchine was devastated. He was visibly crushed by Suzanne's marrying a dancer, and one who was not only forty-four years younger than he was but also just as short. Balanchine was always sensitive about his height. He was only five foot, eight, and so was Paul.

After the marriage was made public, Balanchine disappeared for two weeks. None of us knew where he was. I later found out that he went to stay with Barbara Horgan's mother in Taos, New Mexico, a place as

Stage rehearsal of my
Leonard Bernstein ballet,
Prelude, Fugue, and Riffs,
with me and Allegra Kent.
Photos by Martha Swope.
Used with permission of
NYPL swope_779904,
swope_779907,
swope_779906.

far away from New York, and the press, as he could get. Everyone in the company felt Mr. B.'s pain, and it was as uncomfortable for us as I'm sure it was for both Suzanne and Paul.

Balanchine was as furious as he was hurt, but even so, he kept Paul in the company, although he did take him out of all his solo roles and didn't cast him in anything new for several months. That must have hurt Paul and infuriated Suzanne, but under the circumstances it could have been a lot worse.

It wasn't until the spring gala that Paul was cast again in one of his former solo roles, the third movement lead in *Symphony in C*. It seemed as if the storm had blown over and Mr. B. was finally accepting the marriage.

The original program order for this gala was *Symphony in C, Dances at a Gathering,* and *Prelude, Fugue, and Riffs*. At the last minute Jerry insisted that his ballet should close, which made perfect sense, since my little ballet was only seven minutes long, and a trifle, and *Dances* was a major, hour-long work, so the order of his ballet and mine were switched.

Linda Merrill was now in *Prelude, Fugue, and Riffs* instead of Allegra (because Robbins insisted Allegra not be seen in a ballet before his . . . and dancing with the same partner, me), but Linda was also in the corps of Mejia's movement of *Symphony in C*. This meant that there wasn't a break between *Symphony in C* and my ballet, as they were now back-to-back.

All this was happening on the very morning of the gala. Balanchine decided to cut the third movement of *Symphony in C* rather than throw another dancer into Linda's place. His thinking was that Linda wouldn't have time for a costume change and shouldn't be in a ballet right before mine without a rest. What this meant, though, was that Paul Mejia was now not dancing in the gala.

Suzanne hit the ceiling! She took it personally, feeling that Mr. B. was still holding a grudge against Paul. It did seem unfair, as there was no real reason to cut the whole movement instead of just replacing one corps girl. However, everything was happening so fast and at the last minute who knows if Mr. B. was even thinking of Paul at that point? It would seem very odd to have cast Paul, only to cut him out later.

Here is the sequence of events as I witnessed them, but of course I wasn't privy to what went on in other rooms.

The afternoon of the gala I was sitting in Betty Cage's office having tea with her (which I often did), when Suzanne burst in, crying and practically screaming (unheard of for her): "He can't do this to Paul and me. It's not fair! *I'm leaving! And Paul is coming with me! We quit!*" She then stormed out. She was upset because she'd just heard that Balanchine had cut the third movement, which was her husband's comeback in a principal role. Before Betty and I could say anything, Eddie Bigelow ran in and asked, "Has anyone seen George? Does he know? *Oh my God!*" And he dashed out. Next Robbins came in, looking as if he had seen a ghost. "Does George know? What are we going to do? My ballet premieres tonight! And now this?" And then he ran out.

Then Ronnie Bates came in and said, more calmly, "OK. Balanchine wants to replace *Symphony in C* with *La Sonnambula*" (*Symphony in C* featured Suzanne in the second movement; so when she left there was no one else prepared to dance it). Ronnie left, but seconds later Bigelow returned and said, "Well, *Sonnambula* is out because Jerry thinks the ending is too close to the end of his ballet, so now Mr. B. says *Stars and Stripes* with Milly and Jacques is in. We'll open with that, then Johnny's piece, and close with *Dances*." Finally, seeming as if he didn't have a care in the world, Balanchine casually strolled in and calmly said, "Cleeeford, shouldn't you be getting ready for tonight?" I said, "Oh, damn. I totally forgot. Bye." That whole scene was like a crazy Marx Brothers movie and I was glued to my seat.

The actual premiere of *Dances* was not scheduled until the following week, and therefore it wasn't reviewed, so Jerry didn't lose any of his precious opening night coverage, but Paul and Suzanne's resignation was met with a flurry of newspaper and magazine headlines the following day. All the reporters made the most of the scandal of Farrell resigning at the last minute, and most of the articles were at Balanchine's expense. Their age difference and his obvious obsession with her made him look like a petty, jealous old man. To this day people still think he fired her. He did not. Did he, in effect by canceling *Symphony in C*, cut her and her husband out of that performance? Yes, but he didn't actually fire anyone.

Things were already calming down until that fateful night. I believe that if Paul and Suzanne could have weathered the perceived insult, things would have normalized eventually. After all, there had been talented girls before her whom he had groomed and fallen in love with, and who had rebuffed his advances and married other men (Allegra and Diana Adams, for example), and he still kept them in the company, continued choreographing wonderful new ballets for them, and none lost their roles or standing. He had always licked his wounds and gotten over it. He always acted like a much younger man, and I don't believe he really saw his and Suzanne's age difference until that point. This time, though, his years had finally caught up with him. He was a fool for love if there ever was one.

I didn't know how his last wife Tanaquil Le Clercq felt about all this, as she was never around the theater much, but I imagined it must have been tough on her too. He had already moved out of their apartment before Suzanne's marriage.

In the following days Balanchine was calm, at least outwardly. He always said he didn't care about past or future, that all he was interested in was now. When Suzanne left the company, Balanchine lost his primary muse, and I don't believe he ever fell in love again.

However, since "now" was his primary concern, he immediately started to develop a new star, the incomparably delicate beauty Kay Mazzo.

Kay had been in the company since she was sixteen and had always been popular with both Balanchine and Robbins. She just needed the extra attention that was now heading her way to bring out the great dancer she eventually became. Besides Kay, other wonderful dancers were now getting more of Mr. B.'s attention, such as Sara Leland, Karin von Aroldingen, and that teenage phenom Gelsey Kirkland, who was just about ready for her big break.

Even though Paul and Suzanne's resignation happened the same day as the preview of *Dances at a Gathering*, that ballet was still a major event for our company. It had the longest ovation I can remember, eleven or twelve front-of-curtain calls. Happily, I ended up dancing the Villella allegro solo for that gala preview even though Eddie danced the official premiere a week later. None of us were surprised by the ballet's reception, but at the same time, it didn't feel as if that great

Me at an after-party for the gala preview performance of *Dances at a Gathering*. Courtesy of the author.

reception was for us at all. That applause was totally for Robbins. Jerry should have been ecstatic at the response, but his only comment to the cast when he came backstage was to criticize the ribbons in Kay and Sally's hair, saying they were all wrong. I remember this distinctly because both girls were almost brought to tears by his callousness. We were all emotionally drained, and a kind word, or some show of his appreciation for our hard work, would have been nice. No one in the cast seemed happy that night, only relieved that at long last that this premiere was over.

To our relief the season continued as usual and things returned to normal after Farrell left and Robbins had his big comeback. More and more often, however, I would be at O'Neal's having a burger before the show, and at 6:00 p.m. there would be a call that I'd have to dance Eddie's part that night. It wasn't too pleasant for me to stand backstage before the curtain went up and hear the announcement, "For tonight's performance, John Clifford will be replacing Edward Villella." I could hear the whole audience moan.

Villella was a huge star at that time, and the audience felt cheated when he didn't dance. I then had to come out and start the understated first variation knowing the audience was disappointed that they weren't going to see the star. But, no matter, I loved dancing any role in those days. Being on that stage is all I wanted.

I must admit I learned many great things about stagecraft, pantomime, nuance, dramatically based choreography, and, dare I say it, subtlety, because of Jerry Robbins.

However, I was always Mr. B.'s boy and Jerry knew it.

11

Monte Carlo and *Rubies*

In late June, immediately after this eventful spring season, the company was invited by Princess Grace of Monaco to dance for a week-long homage to the Ballets Russes of Serge Diaghilev. That company had been based in Monaco, and it was where Balanchine had created his first major ballets. Since he had also been Diaghilev's last ballet master, it was an obvious choice for Mr. B.'s company to perform. We were scheduled to dance first for a week in the ornate six-hundred-seat Opera House and then for a gala on a specially constructed stage in the courtyard of the Grimaldi Palace, with Princess Grace, Prince Rainier, and other international celebrities in attendance.

Air France donated a private plane for our flight. Balanchine told me that a musician he knew, the married mistress of the president of Air France, arranged for this free flight. The champagne never stopped flowing. The entire company, plus our patron Bert Martinson, another patron Ruth Dubonnet, and a lot of other NYCB supporters flew with us. Everybody was in high spirits, and Balanchine was making much of Kay and Karin now that Suzanne was gone. He had already taught Kay Suzanne's part in *Diamonds* (although it first went to Allegra Kent), and he was sure to include Karin and Kay with him in any photographs. It was also clear that he was not romantically interested in either. He treated Kay more like a daughter, and Karin more like a friend, and after what he had just gone through with Farrell, it appeared he didn't want any more romantic entanglements.

My dancing duties in Monte Carlo were originally not to have been too heavy. I was dancing, as usual, the third movement lead in Jacques d'Amboise's *Tchaikovsky Suite No. 2*, as well as the second *pas de trois* in *Agon*, and one of the two friends in *Prodigal Son*. On the day of the last show, the gala, I was sitting at the Café de Paris across the street

Me and Linda Merrill in the finale of Jacques d'Amboise's *Tchaikovsky Suite No. 2*. Photographer unknown.

from the opera house, having a cappuccino and strawberries after the morning class. Suddenly Eddie Bigelow rushed over, all out of breath, and said he had been looking everywhere for me (this was before cell phones) because Balanchine wanted to see me immediately. He told me that Villella was injured and couldn't dance *Rubies* that night. He said Balanchine wanted to see if I could learn it, and he wanted to start teaching it to me right away. By this time everyone knew I was a quick study, but this was ridiculous! *Rubies* is one of the most demanding male roles in the entire repertoire, and I'd never even understudied it. Mejia had danced it once or twice before he left, but no one else had. The ballet involves a long opening movement, a very tricky *pas de deux,* and an exhausting third movement. Not only did I not know whether I could learn it in one afternoon—I wasn't sure I had the stamina or technique even to make it through. Of course, I said I'd do it. I never said no to Balanchine.

I ran to the rehearsal room and there found Villella, who was limping terribly (I never found out how he hurt himself); McBride, with whom I had danced only in *Dances* when I replaced Villella; and our pianist Gordon and Balanchine. Originally the thought was that Eddie could dance the *pas de deux* and I would just dance the first and third movements. But Eddie could barely walk; it was clear that there was no way he'd be able to dance at all. On the spot Mr. B. decided to teach me the whole ballet straight from the beginning. We only had two hours for this rehearsal, so I thought I'd use a trick I learned when I was an actor memorizing lines in a hurry. I blocked out absolutely everything except Balanchine's voice. I just tried to absorb what he said and the choreography, like a sponge. I put myself in a kind of Zen state. The rehearsal lasted exactly two hours and somehow, I learned the whole ballet.

We got together once more at 6:00 p.m. and had a run-through onstage with the full cast, but Villella didn't show up to that rehearsal. I could have used his help, but he seemed in great pain and was probably at the hotel with his foot in a bucket of ice. For that performance, the closing night gala at the palace (no pressure), my adrenaline was running higher than ever. I was determined not to let Mr. B. down. After all, he was risking a lot by taking a chance that I would deliver a performance worthy of the occasion and wouldn't screw up the choreography. Princess Grace, Prince Rainier, and even the actor David Niven, not to mention all those company patrons who had accompanied us, would see me either blow it or succeed. However, all I really cared about was pleasing Balanchine.

What I was planning on doing was just to copy-cat Villella and be at the right place at the right time. Forget about selling it.

I was doing fine in the performance except for one entrance in the finale. At one point, from opposite sides of the stage, Patty and I had to make an entrance after five counts of eight, of which the first four counts were silent. That was pretty tricky. I was in the wings counting correctly, and knew when to come on, but I forgot what the hell the step was. I went totally blank. *Panic.* The stage was too big to run all the way around (behind the backdrop) and ask Patty what the step was, so I kept waving to her. She is somewhat nearsighted, and she thought I was signaling that I didn't know what the count was. I knew the damn counts but I just didn't know the damn steps! I ran out after the five eights not having a clue what I was going to do.

Luckily, by the time I got to my place I remembered the steps, and everything went fine. That really was way too close for comfort. I only made one mistake that night, when I kicked on the wrong side of Patty and she kicked my hand. After the bows, Balanchine came backstage

Me with Patricia McBride in *Rubies*. Photos by Martha Swope. Used with permission of NYPL swope_781683, swope_781684s. Choreography by George Balanchine © The George Balanchine Trust.

absolutely beaming. I had never seen him so happy over a dancer's performance. I'm sure he was that way with Suzanne, but I wasn't Suzanne! It was one of the greatest outpourings of warmth I'd ever seen from him, and his smile was huge. He honestly seemed shocked that I had done so well. His usual compliment was a dry, "Not bad, dear," but not so on this occasion. He kept saying, "Wonderful!" over and over. Eddie came backstage too, though his only comment was, "I can't believe you actually did that, Clifford." I decided it qualified as a compliment of sorts. I just was relieved to have made it through *Rubies* with honor, and by Balanchine's reaction I knew he was pleased and proud of my dancing. That was worth everything. Oh, and of course I sold it. You can take the boy out of Hollywood but you can't take Hollywood out of the boy!

13

Teaching at SAB

Gelsey Kirkland's Rise—*Reveries,* My Fourth Ballet for NYCB at 22

With only a week off in between, our annual four-week summer season at the Saratoga Performing Arts Center in upstate New York followed the high times in Monte Carlo. This five-thousand-seat amphitheater on the grounds of Saratoga State Park was always a joy to return to, and lots of performances came my way. To say I was busy would be an understatement. The conclusion of the Saratoga season normally marked the start of the summer layoff period, although for some summers we'd play a week each at other large outdoor venues, all normally five thousand seats or more, such as the Ravinia Festival outside Chicago, the Blossom Music Festival outside Cleveland, the Merriweather Post Pavilion near Baltimore, and the Wolf Trap Performing Arts Center near Washington, D.C. These performances were always great fun, even though in those years we didn't have our own portable sprung floor and those theaters had rock-hard stages. After those tours, we usually had the month of September off.

In 1969, however, Stanley Williams was going to return to Denmark for the month to teach at the Royal Danish Ballet, so Mr. B. requested that I take over all of Stanley's classes at the school while he was away. Even though I had taught sporadically at the school before, this was to be my first month of daily classes.

Mr. B. specifically asked me to teach the boys how to pirouette quickly (Stanley had them turning too slowly for Balanchine's taste), to waltz like a ballroom dancer, and most especially to move faster in general. The school had just relocated to the luxurious new Juilliard School, right next to Lincoln Center, and had much more room than at its old facility on Broadway and 82nd Street. I taught both *pas de deux* classes and two weekly advanced men's classes, and this time I taught a few jazz classes. As if that weren't enough, I was also preparing to choreograph another ballet for the company.

My fourth ballet, *Reveries,* premiered in December 1969. I had originally thought I'd call it *Homage à Petipa,* to honor the great nineteenth-century classical choreographer Marius Petipa. Balanchine had suggested I use the *Tchaikovsky Suite No. 1* for this ballet, and, as I learned with my Thomas Tallis ballet, it was very difficult in those days to use music for a new ballet if Balanchine didn't approve of it.

I was a "house" choreographer; that's what we were all called in the press. Before my time, John Taras, Frank Moncion, Todd Bolender, Jacques d'Amboise, and Ruthanna Boris all choreographed ballets for the company as "house" choreographers. Mr. B. said since we didn't sleep in the theater we really weren't "residents," so he never liked that title, "resident choreographer."

I ended up naming my new ballet *Reveries,* based on the first movement's overtly romantic opening. This was a very dreamlike interaction of one man (representing a choreographer) and twelve surrounding women, the corps de ballet, all moodily lit under a star-filled sky by Ronnie Bates. (Even though Ronnie was our lighting designer, he based all his plots loosely on the work of Jean Rosenthal, the company's original brilliant lighting designer.) The principal man in the first movement was Tony Blum, who was also in my first and second ballets for the company and who was my alternate for my third, *Prelude, Fugue, and Riffs.* The second movement was an adagio for Johnna and Conrad. It was her first real principal part, choreographed just for her. Conrad had also been in *Fantasies.* In those days Conrad was just about the strongest partner we had. He was paired with Farrell whenever any ballet had very difficult lifting duties, such as in *Don Quixote, A Midsummer Night's Dream,* or *Concerto Barocco.* The third movement was the *Marche Miniature* for the then-sixteen-year-old Gelsey Kirkland, with Susan Hendl, Susan Pilarre, Giselle Roberge, and Deborah Flomine. This was also Gelsey's first principal role with the company and the start of her legendary career.

Anyone watching Gelsey that first night knew that here was a major talent, a shooting star. Luckily for the state of their sibling rivalry, her sister Johnna had an equally big success.

The last movement brought everybody back together in a big, choreographically complicated finale that always brought down the house. This ballet was an unquestioned hit, and it further cemented my reputation as "Balanchine's Prize Prodigy, a choreographic wunderkind," as Walter Terry put it in the *Saturday Review*.

Although Balanchine had first suggested the Tchaikovsky music, he was not pleased by the first rehearsals of the opening movement. Of course, it was fine with him that I was using Johnna and Gelsey. He loved what to him was the gimmick of casting sisters, but he asked me why I had not choreographed the first movement using the "Russianness" of Tchaikovsky's score. He said the music represented the "vast steppes of central Russia." What? How would I possibly know that? Then it hit me. If Balanchine were going to suggest a piece of music, it clearly would be music he already knew well, as he'd made the piano reduction for rehearsals and probably had his own idea of what the ballet should look like.

He must have had very definite ideas in advance, especially about this particular Tchaikovsky music. At one rehearsal I got a bit annoyed and spoke up. After a run-through of the second movement adagio he said, "Show me something that's never been seen before. This is too banal." He was paraphrasing, of course, what Diaghilev used to say to him: "Étonne-moi!"—"Astonish me!" I said to him, "Mr. B. how can I show you something you've never seen? You've seen, and done, everything!" He said, "Well, there's one part I don't really like." I asked him to tell me specifically what was wrong with it. He said that the sequence repeated itself and what I had done, choreographically speaking, was to repeat too literally what had come before, and also that it was too "mooshy" (that word again). And on top of this he said my steps looked as if they could be done to any other piece of music.

Now that really did it. I couldn't leave that comment unanswered. I said, "Mr. B., when *you* are choreographing a ballet with classical steps, *you* sometimes repeat the same steps and sequences too." Oops. I might have gone too far. I stubbornly continued, "Some of your own classical choreography could easily work with another piece of music." He said, "No, that's not true. In my ballets, a step would *not* fit with different music." He was starting to get rather annoyed. Who could blame him? Of course, Mr. B. used *sauté,* step-*jeté,* or *piqué* arabesques in every classical ballet. I guess I was having a bad day, and in my frustration I decided to give him an example of what I was talking about.

I said, "In the middle of the second movement of 'Bizet' (*Symphony in C*), where you have the ballerina being lifted across the stage in those *grand jetés* and then she goes into the adagio section, that sequence would fit perfectly into this Tchaikovsky score." He said, "Nonsense, it would not fit." So, being as obstinate as I was, I put on the recording of the Tchaikovsky music and proceeded to dance the ballerina choreography of the second movement of Balanchine's *Symphony in C.* Now looking back, I was really being quite a brat. I'm sure a lot of people wondered why he put up with me. Anyway, I did most of the second movement and said, "There, you see? It fit." (Actually, it worked out perfectly.) The musical and dance phrases matched exactly and even better than I had thought. It wasn't genius, but I had proven my point.

What an idiot I was, trying to prove a point to Balanchine. I thought we were just having a friendly disagreement, but Mr. B. turned red and said, "No, you cannot do that! That's not fair!" I was laughing, but he was serious and then told me that the second movement of *Symphony in C* was supposed to be the "Dance of the Moon!" Now, that stopped me cold. Balanchine had always said his abstract ballets were just "dancing, no story." Now he was saying that the second movement of the Bizet was the "Dance of the Moon?" What? Balanchine had gone on record as saying that there were no hidden meanings in his ballets, but he never said that he himself didn't have a personal inspiration. Evidently the lifted *grand jetés* were meant to represent the moon's arc across the sky. After his comment, all I could say was, "Well, Mr. B., you really got me. I don't know what to say." I didn't think he'd be so touchy. What I didn't realize at the time was that he was being criticized daily in the press for not being as successful as Robbins with his latest ballets. My timing couldn't have been worse. Later I had Lincoln look at my ballet because I wanted a second opinion, and luckily, he loved it.

Many classical ballet choreographers, like Frederick Ashton, use the same standard classical vocabulary over and over. Balanchine, however, was able to take the most banal combinations of classical steps and put them together in surprisingly new ways, even though the steps them-selves were sometimes very ordinary. For example, we all used to laugh when Balanchine was choreographing and got stuck (which was rare) and would simply put in a *sauté,* step-*jeté.* And it's not that it's done just once; it is usually repeated in a fugue or a canon. It was funny when he said to me that his steps *literally* could not be done to different music. A classical step can always be re-used, but its position in a sequence and its relationship to the music are what make it unique.

I don't want to leave the impression that Balanchine and I didn't also have some contretemps over other ballets of mine. It was not always a honeymoon between us. One example was when I choreographed Stravinsky's *Symphony in Three Movements* for the school. This was a couple of years before Mr. B. created his masterpiece for the 1972 Stravinsky Festival. I loved this music and asked him if I could make a ballet to it for SAB. He said yes, so I choreographed the first move-ment and second movement adagio before I invited him in to watch. I had an Adam and Eve creation-of-the-world kind of theme, wherein the first movement was the creation and the adagio was for Adam and Eve. It wasn't literal, but it was in the subtext.

When he saw it he was not at all happy. Normally he'd be pretty encouraging, but for this, just as for the Tchaikovsky music of *Rever-ies,* he had a clear and explicit feeling of what the music represented. It was not abstract music to him by any means. The Tchaikovsky score represented rural Russia, and this Stravinsky score was "about World War II," he said. I was thoroughly dejected. I felt there was no way I could really know what he felt about a particular score unless he told me, which he never did until after the fact.

I decided I might as well just give up choreographing then and there. I so wanted to please him that if I couldn't, I just didn't want to try.

I was also rather angry, so I boycotted his morning classes. This was during a rehearsal period, and if I didn't have a rehearsal I also didn't hang around watching him work as I usually did. After a week Renee told me Mr. B. had asked her where I was, and why wasn't I coming to class. I guess I had made my point, and I didn't want to push it too far, so I planned to go back to his class the next day.

Later the same day, as I was having my tea break with Betty and told her I was going to get back to Balanchine's class, she said that would be a smart thing to do. Betty told me Mr. B. was upset with himself that he had upset me! Unbelievable. She went on to say he had told her what had transpired with the Stravinsky rehearsal and that maybe he had been wrong. She said he told her maybe he was being "old-fashioned" and possibly he was too close to the Stravinsky score and had been wrong in expecting me to hear in it what he heard. How amazing! So the next day I was in class on my best behavior and working my butt off.

He smiled when he saw me come in, but when he saw me working a bit maniacally, fiercely doing my *frappés* like a machine gun, and pulling up to look as tall as I could, he came over and said, "What are you doing, dear? You're going to kill yourself." I said, "Just trying to work harder, and look taller." He said, "Relax—all geniuses are short. Me [tapping his chest], Hugo Fiorato [our secondary conductor)], and Hitler!" When he said "Hitler" I doubled over laughing, and all the tension was gone. However, I stopped working on that score, and after seeing what he did with it for the Stravinsky Festival, I was so glad I did. No way could I have even touched the greatness he did.

Now back to *Reveries.* Later on, after he'd seen the ballet onstage, Balanchine seemed to like it quite a bit and kept it in the repertoire for years. (The name was later changed to *Tchaikovsky Suite No. 1*; more about why later.)

The reviews of *Reveries* were great, too. Clive Barnes wrote in the *New York Times:*

> What Mr. Clifford shares with Mr. Robbins is very clear indeed—both of them have accepted the choreography and genius of George Balanchine and made the necessary accommodations to live with it. Both have been influenced by Balanchine—the very much younger Clifford more perhaps, yet there again, not that much more, than Robbins, but both have absorbed the influence, digested it, and used it. For the very young Mr. Clifford this is a particular triumph.

One of the interesting things about casting Johnna and Gelsey in *Reveries,* now that I think about it, was that it resulted in both sisters making their débuts in the very same ballet as the creators of leading roles for New York City Ballet.

The Kirkland sisters, Conrad Ludlow, and Anthony Blum in *Reveries*. Photo by Martha Swope. Used with permission of NYPL swope_780165.

Johnna Kirkland and Conrad Ludlow in the second movement of *Reveries*. Photo by Martha Swope. Used with permission of NYPL swope_780152.

Gelsey Kirkland in the third movement of *Reveries*. Photo by Martha Swope. Used with permission of NYPL swope_780143.

Gelsey and Johnna had grown up in a very tumultuous household. They were the daughters of the playwright who adapted *Tobacco Road* for the stage, Jack Kirkland, and their mother had been an actress in this play. Evidently their father fell in love and married all the actresses who played the part of young the girl Pearl. How very Balanchine.

When I started choreographing *Reveries,* the process clearly intensified the existing rivalry between the sisters. Gelsey had strong jumps and turns, but she didn't have the high extensions she later developed, whereas Johnna had a much warmer quality, prettier legs and feet, and a perfectly proportioned arabesque line. Johnna was also more feminine than her younger sister. During performances Gelsey would stand in the wings for the adagio movement and watch Johnna and quite literally cry over her exquisite line and the way that she could move so seamlessly between positions, like liquid. I asked Gelsey why she was so upset because I couldn't believe she was that jealous. It was obvious that in Gelsey's future she was going to outshine Johnna, mainly because she was more ambitious. Gelsey said she'd do anything for Johnna's extensions and arabesque line. I told her, "Gelsey, Johnna would give anything for your jumps." Then it would be Johnna's turn to watch her sister from the wings. She would moan and say, "I'll never be that strong. I'll never be able to jump like that. Mr. B will never like me."

She was wrong. Balanchine kept casting Johnna, but the more Gelsey's star rose, the more insecure Johnna became. I think one of my strengths as a choreographer is that I'm able to bring out some of the better qualities in dancers. With Johnna I emphasized her line, the way she could work through her feet, and so forth. The fact that she was young and beautiful didn't hurt. When the costume designer Joe Eula came to watch an early rehearsal, he was smitten with her and said, "Where did she come from? She's gorgeous!" And in fact, she was. At first I thought this jealousy between the sisters was harmless, but then I realized it was getting out of hand. Both were wonderful dancers and each received her share of curtain calls and bravos. Actually, at one performance after the second movement of *Symphony in C,* which came right after a performance of *Reveries,* Johnna received two solo bows after her adagio, whereas the ballerina dancing the adagio in Symphony *in C* (I forget who) received only one after hers.

If only Johnna had had more confidence, who knows how far she could have gone in that company?

But Gelsey had that fire in her belly that made her unstoppable. Balanchine even re-choreographed his famous 1949 version of *Firebird* for her.

Though Gelsey was an unbelievable technician, she did not, as yet, have much stage presence. So, in this new *Firebird,* she was unfavorably compared in the press to Balanchine's original ballerina, the already extremely experienced Maria Tallchief. I thought this was most unfair. Tallchief was an adult, and had great personal magnetism, whereas Gelsey was just a teenager getting started. The reviews said she was technically proficient but a bit bland. What did the press know? I thought she was great. She soon started to feel the pressure of being Balanchine's latest "discovery," and the lackluster reviews didn't help. Gelsey and I were very close in those years, and she asked me to help her with *Firebird.* Since I had a reputation for being a ham yet was still seen as one of Mr. B.'s favorites, she thought I could help her get some fire into her *Firebird.* I was cautious about sticking my nose into Mr. B.'s ballets because he did not like anybody to influence his ballerinas: however, I did have a track record of successfully coaching some of the dancers.

For instance, during my first year in the company Balanchine didn't seem to be paying much attention to Marnee Morris. He saw that we were friends and that I had cast her in my first ballet, so he asked me to see what I could do to "light a fire" under her. Marnee was having a difficult time in her personal life (marriage problems) and it showed in her dancing, so I helped her just to be more "Marnee" and believe in herself. That's all it takes with so many dancers: to have someone there who really *believes* in them. Dancers have told me over the years that I'm very "supportive." When Mr. B. noticed that she was dancing with more authority and confidence, he asked her what had gotten into her. She told him I had been coaching her.

Later, after Farrell left, Sara Leland was cast in *La Valse,* and I also worked with her on that. Mr. B. asked her if someone had been coaching her and she said, "Johnny helped me with it." Balanchine said, "Very good, why don't you work with Cleeeford some more." She only needed more self-assurance; after all, Farrell was a tough act to follow. Normally Balanchine was very possessive of his dancers and didn't like it when they were "coached." But since it was obvious to everyone by then that I was his protégé, other dancers started asking me for help. Again, most of this was just about giving them confidence. I would never dare change a step. Why mess with perfection? Since he was having me teach more company classes, this coaching just seemed a natural progression, and he encouraged it.

Gelsey was then just coming into her prime. Though she was only seventeen, she was technically the strongest dancer in the company, and perhaps even in the world. Balanchine was in an expansive, creative mood, and he was absolutely delighted with her. He seemed to have mostly gotten over Farrell and was focusing more and more on his youngest ballerina. He revived the fiendishly difficult *Theme and Variations* for her, which was the last movement of his new *Tchaikovsky Suite No. 3*, and I was given a principal part in the third movement, the Scherzo, with Marnee as my partner and with a large corps of twenty-four girls.

This was a tour de force role for me as I was the only man. I asked him one day at O'Neal's if I was supposed to be something, and he said, "Dear, you're a 'French Tickler' for all those girls." I told you he had a really naughty sense of humor. He also told me to learn the lead in *Theme*, but he never wanted anyone else to do the Scherzo movement, so sadly, I never got to dance that wonderful role. I'm thankful I've gotten to stage it for some of the world's major companies.

In just one season Balanchine cast Gelsey in the second movement in *Symphony in C*, the female lead in *Harlequinade*, and the adagio lead in *Concerto Barocco* (with Johnna dancing the soloist role), and she continued dancing in every performance of *Theme and Variations* and *Firebird*. She handled all these demanding ballets terrifically well. In *Theme*, which is already quite difficult as it is, he started adding different challenges, which was totally against his regular philosophy. He added triple turns instead of doubles and bravura *gargouillades*, instead of the normal *pas de chats* for her in the solos. She was so spontaneous about everything that he was having a great time testing her to see how far she could go. He did much the same thing with Merrill Ashley ten years later, and then again with Darci Kistler, whom I consider the last true Balanchine-trained ballerina. He really loved challenging his dancers, especially those who were young, talented, and could handle it.

Me and George Balanchine in rehearsal. Photo by Martha Swope. Used with permission of NYPL swope_1211737s. BALANCHINE is a Trademark of The George Balanchine Trust.

When Alicia Alonso was a guest with my Los Angeles Ballet in 1980, I asked her what Mr. B. was like to work with when he choreographed the original *Theme and Variations* for her in 1948. She said he always seemed to be "challenging me." If she could do one of his more difficult combinations easily the first time around, he would invariably change it and make it even harder, much the way he later worked with other great technicians, such as Gelsey and Merrill. He wasn't being sadistic: for him it was just playtime. He approached both teaching and choreographing as if he were playing a game with himself and the dancers. He'd bat the ball to us, and we'd hit it right back. It was fun.

24

Gelsey Kirkland and Maggie Black

After Suzanne left the company the classes became a bit more well-rounded, and when Gelsey entered the company Balanchine immediately started teaching class for her. When I say he taught class "for" her, I mean he molded the class around her and stretched her natural abilities, thereby gradually developing her inborn gifts. Gelsey was a great jumper, which Suzanne definitely was not, and consequently Balanchine started teaching class with many more allegro combinations and jumps.

Gelsey was concentrating solely on her technique in her early years, but she still seemed to be having the time of her life. And yet, she was so intensely driven she could be a bit off-putting. I had seen that syndrome once before at Loring's school, where one girl nearly had a nervous breakdown trying to be too "perfect." If one looked very closely, one might have seen the early signs of the manic perfectionism that later led to Gelsey's drug use and eventual tragic downfall. None of us knew of her demons then. All we saw was an incredible talent on the verge of greatness. At fifteen through seventeen she was lock, stock, and barrel, a "Balanchine" dancer. In those days she was not at all pretentious, and the temperament she later exhibited was nowhere to be seen. She was a total delight.

I blame the bad advice and the drugs she received once she entered American Ballet Theatre for her eventual downfall. The atmosphere there was rampant with drug use in the early 1970s, when she joined them. Balanchine kept a tight lid on drugs in his company, but ABT's management appeared more lax about (or perhaps unaware of) the drugs used by their dancers, and even some of their senior staff. I believe the non-dancing sycophants and fans who always seemed to be surrounding her were also part of the problem. To make matters worse

Gelsey's alcoholic father had a violent temper, which I witnessed during one family dinner I attended. I am positive that this also added to her problems. Gelsey joined NYCB in 1968, when she was only fifteen years old. Other dancers had joined at that young age before, but none had her set of problems.

Around this time a new teacher appeared in the city, Maggie Black. She seemed to come out of nowhere (she had not been a known ballerina with any major company), but she soon developed quite a following. Violette Verdy, Johnna Kirkland, Michael Steele, and Melissa Hayden were some of the first New York City Ballet dancers who took her classes. Natalia Makarova, then in her prime, was another of Maggie's early regular students.

Maggie taught at a small studio directly across the street from Lincoln Center, and, curious, one day I went over and took her class. She was definitely not a Balanchine-trained nor even a Russian-styled teacher, but her class was very thorough and she seemed enthusiastic about the dancers, which is always a plus. Her classes were two hours long, and whereas Mr. B.'s sometimes seemed rushed, Maggie's were slower-paced, and therefore there was more time to go over the combinations and really "work" them. She repeated every exercise at the barre twice, both right and left, which was quite unusual. I thought her class was quite good for me to take once a week on our day off.

At first, she didn't try to change my "sculptural Balanchine" hands, which other companies' dancers considered a bit flowery. She didn't try to change the deep-lunge, straight-back-leg position for pirouettes, which Balanchine preferred: for the first month or so, I really thought Maggie was a good find. However, I made one of the biggest mistakes of my life when I took Gelsey over to take her class.

From the first class Maggie focused all her attention on Gelsey and made her a sort of protégée. Gelsey returned the compliment by making Maggie her sole mentor. It was a ballet version of Svengali and Trilby. There are certain teachers whose livelihoods and reputations are based on famous dancers taking their classes. In New York City it's a big business. There are many amateur dancers who will never be in a professional company but feel they are part of the action because they can take a daily class with some of the stars of the ballet world, and I find nothing inherently wrong with that. Also, many professional Broadway dancers like a daily ballet class, which was true of the TV dancers of my youth. Unfortunately, I've seen some rather mediocre teachers stroke a star's ego just to keep them coming back. At first, Verdy, Makarova, and Hayden were Maggie's regulars, but they soon dropped away; and when Gelsey became her student on a daily basis, all of a sudden many more non-professionals started showing up. Because of Gelsey, Maggie's classes became *the* place to study in New York City.

Although Gelsey continued taking some classes at SAB, mostly with Stanley Williams, she took less and less of Balanchine's. She needed and wanted a teacher or coach totally dedicated to her, one who would give her undivided attention. She soon seemed almost addicted to Maggie's classes and coaching. It got to the point where Gelsey wore her hair in the same style and actually dyed it to match Maggie's dark brown color. She also began dressing in the same peasant-style blouses and long skirts as Maggie wore. It was as if Gelsey were gradually becoming her clone.

Maggie did not initially try to change my style, but she did try later, which was why I stopped taking her class, and she was certainly doing so with the much younger and more malleable Gelsey. It started to worry me after a while, because Gelsey was completely changing her whole "look." This was obvious to everyone, especially Balanchine. She no longer danced like a New York City Ballet dancer, and she started to get oddly bitter when talking about Balanchine. He had never been anything but kind and supportive, but she started speaking about him as if he were some kind of enemy. Things came to a head when Gelsey started inviting Maggie to watch private stage rehearsals at the theater. This was definitely not done in Balanchine's "house." No outside people were ever allowed in unless he invited them, or at least cleared them.

Early in the preparation of a ballet, dancers would rehearse in the rehearsal studios with Balanchine or the ballet mistress. Later a dancer could request a pianist and go over a role alone onstage or privately with a partner.

Maggie started showing up regularly at Gelsey's onstage "private" rehearsals. She would sit in the back of the theater, where she thought she couldn't be seen, and she would give Gelsey corrections afterward, or sometimes Gelsey would even run out front to confer with her during the rehearsal itself. Maggie actually coached her right under Mr.

B.'s very nose on several occasions. He would be onstage with Gelsey while Maggie was hiding in the back of the house. This became just too much.

When I saw this happening, I invited Gelsey over to my apartment to speak to her in private. I said, "Do you really think it's smart to have Maggie come over to the theater and coach you in Balanchine's ballets, and when he's standing right there? Maggie has never danced or even studied with Balanchine, and Mr. B. is your employer after all." Gelsey blew up at me and said, "You don't understand classical ballet and neither does Balanchine!"

"Neither does Balanchine?" This was worse than I thought. "Criticize me all you want," I said, "but saying 'Balanchine doesn't understand classical ballet' is way over the top." She then stormed off.

Balanchine immediately saw this change in her. In the rare classes she still took from him, she would stubbornly do his combinations in a more Maggie Black style, right in front of his face: two bent knees for pirouette preparations, instead of the straight back knee, and things like that. It was blatantly obvious that she was getting some other training. He eventually found out it was Maggie teaching her, though I'm not sure how. I certainly didn't tell him, as I was the one who took her to Maggie in the first place.

Because of Gelsey, some other younger dancers started going to Maggie's classes too, and Mr. B. was *not* happy about that. He started making sarcastic cracks in class. For instance, he would say to a dancer, "Oh, I see you've found black magic!" Despite his bantering tone, I knew that Balanchine was not only insulted but also hurt to his core that Gelsey, his pride and joy, had deserted him for this teacher with what can best be described as a checkered ballet background, and a nonentity compared to a Danilova or a Tumkovsky. Had she been someone of that stature he might not have minded one bit.

Down on Tenth Avenue not far from the theater was a late-night bar (almost a dive) where he and I would often go after performances. One night he brought up Gelsey's name and said, "Well, dear, *you* danced very well tonight." It was rare for Balanchine to give so direct a compliment, and he emphasized the "*you*." (I had danced the third movement of *Brahms-Schoenberg Quartet* that evening with Gelsey.) "But," he said, "You know you were dancing with a *zombie*." I said, "She'll get over it." Under Maggie's influence Gelsey was developing a rather stiff and old-fashioned stage manner. (She had even changed the way she wore her hair for performances from the high French twist, which most of the girls in the company used, to a 1950s-style low bun.)

Although we danced together a lot, Gelsey and I were not getting along at all. She was my most consistent partner in those years, but once she got under Maggie's spell, I found it impossible to continue. Balanchine asked, "Who is working with her?" He knew very well who (and I didn't want to be the one to drive in the final nail), so I said, "I'm sure she gets a lot of input from various people." I really didn't want to get in the middle of it, especially as I was still kicking myself for having introduced Gelsey to Maggie.

A couple of days later Gelsey came up to me, furious, and said she'd heard that I had told Balanchine she was being coached by Maggie. I said, "Gelsey, I didn't, but the whole company knows. You even look like her twin. Why do you think I would tell him since I'm the one who took you to Maggie in the first place!" We had another private onstage rehearsal that same day for Jacques' *Irish Fantasy*, and we could barely manage two steps without her running out to the back of the house to check with Maggie. One simply cannot rehearse that way. Truly, she could not get through one sequence without running out and asking Maggie's advice. The relationship was very reminiscent of the famous one between Marilyn Monroe and her acting coach Paula Strasberg.

Finally I'd had it and said angrily, "Are we going to get through this rehearsal or not? Would you *please* stop running out to check with Maggie?" Gelsey said, "She's not here." I said, "Oh, come on. I can even see her." "Well," she said, "I need her and you just don't understand." I then went over to the stage manager and had him bring down the asbestos (front) curtain so that we could rehearse once straight-through without stopping. Gelsey blew up when I did this and said she refused to dance with me, and she said again that her friends said I didn't know anything about classical ballet. I said, "That may be your friends' opinion, but we're cast to dance together, so let's try and get through this *please.*" She stormed offstage.

Gelsey at that time had a large clique forming around her who praised her every move. Some fans can be quite aggressive and feel they have a right to give their opinions on subjects about which they know nothing. Gelsey was still very young and insecure, and in need of confidence, so she was easy prey for these people. It was as if they were vampires feeding off her fame, and I was at a loss as to what to do about it.

That evening in the performance of Jacques' ballet she did some pretty outrageous things. There was a section where we needed to do a back-to-back little Irish jig step, but when we turned to face each other I saw that she had left her position and was pretending to hide behind some corps de ballet girls in the back. She was pantomiming to the audience that finger twirl by the side of the head saying "he's crazy." This made me look like an idiot, doing the step full out by myself. Obviously it was pretty unprofessional of her to do that during an actual performance, and lucky for her Mr. B didn't see that show.

Although we often still danced together, she refused to speak to me cordially until we were cast in the premieres of *The Steadfast Tin Soldier* and *Coppélia*. Then she seemed to relax a bit, but I now think it was because she had already made up her mind to leave the company to dance with Baryshnikov, who had recently defected from the USSR and joined American Ballet Theatre. What she says concerning Balanchine and SAB in her autobiography *Dancing on My Grave* is unfortunately full of inaccuracies (I'm assuming the book's title refers to her role as Giselle). Since I was a sober, non-drug-using eyewitness to most of her accounts, I saw things much differently.

When I left New York City Ballet in 1974, I had no idea that she would be leaving the company a month later. It was too bad; at one point, we were very close friends, and anyone who saw her dance in the late 1960s and early 1970s saw her at her peak. Of course, such classics as *Giselle* or *La Sylphide*, which Gelsey danced after she left NYCB, are performances that set a very high bar for her generation and generations of young ballerinas to come, but to see her dance for Balanchine while she was still in his company was to see her in her unaffected first flowering. Her artistry may have deepened during her ABT years, as normally happens when a dancer matures, but I think the same would have taken place if she had remained with Balanchine and avoided her drug period. Who knows what glorious new ballets he would have made for her? Such a pity.

Besides *Coppélia* (which he had originally planned for me and Gelsey), I do remember Balanchine was thinking of doing a new *Sleeping Beauty* for her around 1969, when she was sixteen. In the mid-sixties he told me he had thought about doing it for Farrell, and years later he told me he wanted to do it for Darci Kistler when she was sixteen. The reason he never did this ballet was because the State Theater stage didn't have the trapdoors and other stage equipment he remembered from the Mariinsky production in which he appeared as a child. If he couldn't do it "right," he didn't want to do it at all, he said.

When I founded my Los Angeles Ballet, I was very lucky to have Johnna Kirkland as my principal ballerina and partner. She brought a style and technique directly from the Balanchine tradition; and even though she never really went that far in New York City Ballet, rising only to soloist level, in Los Angeles she started to live up to the potential that Balanchine had seen in her.

The first time Balanchine saw Johnna dance with my company was in Avery Fisher Hall at a Promenades Concert with the New York Philharmonic. He was very pleased and said to her, "Why didn't you ever dance like that for me?" That was the greatest compliment that Mr. B. could have given her, or me.

Thinking about my long-time partnering of Gelsey and Johnna brings to mind some of the other great ballerinas I have had the privilege to partner. Mimi Paul was the first ballerina with whom Balanchine placed me, but that was in an emergency situation. Violette Verdy was the first ballerina with whom both Jacques and Balanchine paired me for several principal roles. I was not a very strong partner physically, but luckily Violette was a very gracious lady. She really helped me get through my first *Nutcracker*. She also seemed to enjoy working with someone with a sense of humor. Until the day she died Violette remained one of my closest friends, and she was always an inspiration as an artist.

After *Nutcracker*, Violette was my partner again for *Stars and Stripes*. It was unexpected that in *Stars* Balanchine cast me in the *pas de deux* instead of as the soloist in the third movement men's regiment. Usually, a dancer comes up through the ranks from corps de ballet to soloist, to principal dancer. But I didn't go through the soloist level, and this was a relief; the way casting was set up, the soloist level was almost a no-man's-land. Sometimes the soloists actually danced less than corps de ballet members, and one could also get stuck in that rank and not be promoted. Fortunately, although I was listed as a soloist for two years, I'd actually been dancing as a principal soon after joining the company.

By the time I got *Stars* I was a more seasoned dancer, but still there were many older and more established dancers in the company who didn't appreciate that I was allowed to dance major parts so soon. Once, when I was onstage dancing *Stars and Stripes* with Violette, an older principal man was standing in the wings talking to Balanchine. Gloria Govrin was near them and heard this exchange. As she told me later, the dancer said, "Mr. B., how can you let Johnny go out there and carry on so much? He's such a ham!" Balanchine said, "No, dear, he's just having fun." When Gloria told me this, I knew Mr. B. really "got" me.

25

Allegra Kent

What makes a performer a legend? Those who saw Laurette Taylor on Broadway in the 1940s, or heard Maria Callas sing in the 1950s, or heard Glenn Gould play Bach in the 1960s routinely use the adjective "legendary" when describing these artists.

For me only Maya Plisetskaya and Allegra Kent really rise to that level. The irony is that Kent and Plisetskaya were polar opposites as performers. I've already written at length about Plisetskaya; here I focus on Allegra and what made her so special.

Most great dancers "dance out" to the public. By this I mean that their personality reaches out over the footlights and they bring themselves to the audience. Such was the case with d'Amboise, Nureyev, Villella, Hayden, Verdy, obviously Plisetskaya, and other wonderful dancers.

Then there are the rare few who seem to draw the audience in to them. It's as if the dancer is able to make the audience zoom in, as in a film close-up. Allegra Kent was the master of this magic. Galina Ulanova and Margot Fonteyn also had this ability, but Allegra certainly used it to maximum effect. On television in her youth, she did dance out, but when I was twenty and first watching her from the audience's perspective—she had returned after her third child was born—she developed this drawing-in ability and took it further than anyone I've ever seen.

In Jacques d'Amboise's autobiography *I Was A Dancer*, he relates a story that Balanchine, late in his life, once told him about Allegra. Jacques asked Balanchine who was the most talented and most unusual ballerina he'd ever worked with. Without hesitating, Balanchine said, "Allegra. She is the most gifted—but something stops her from being consistent." Sadly, this was all too true, but when she did dance, she was unforgettable. And she's almost impossible to define.

Plisetskaya had tangible attributes that are easier to nail down: her big jump, pliable back, amazingly liquid *port de bras,* unstoppable energy, and dramatic acting that burst over the footlights. This was not Allegra Kent. Her gifts were much more subtle.

So what then made Allegra Kent so special?

Let's start with her physical appearance. She is quite petite, only five feet three. She does not have the especially long or thin legs that are so in vogue today, but she has exceptionally delicate hands and feet. Her thighs are well rounded, similar to Alicia Alonso's, and her neck is not particularly long. She has a small head and an exceptionally beautiful face.

In her youth Allegra had a big jump (in her autobiography, *Once a Dancer,* she writes that jumping was her favorite thing) and brilliant *batterie* (*entrechat sixes* were no problem for her, and Balanchine put eight consecutive ones just for her in the third movement of his *Western Symphony*). She was not a powerhouse turner like Maria Tallchief, but her perfectly split arabesque *penchées* and her extreme flexibility were unique to her for that time. Balanchine took full advantage of this ability in his choreography for her in *Ivesiana* ("The Unanswered Question") and *The Seven Deadly Sins* (with Lotte Lenya playing her alter ego) and when he made her the virginal Japanese bride on her wedding night in *Bugaku.*

Her physical delicacy and uncanny ability to look as if she was not quite real or "there" (she always looked transparent, as if one could see right through her) made her Sleepwalker role in *La Sonnambula* and her doomed heroine in *La Valse* stand out from all other interpreters. Farrell, Mazzo, McBride, Paul, and others were also excellent and gave lovely performances in these same ballets, but to my eyes they all still looked human, whereas Allegra didn't.

Even in roles created for others, such as the *pas de deux* in *Agon,* second movement of *Symphony in C,* and *Swan Lake,* she brought a certain mystery that seemed to elude all the other NYCB ballerinas at that time. Also, when she was *en pointe* it looked as if there was a thin layer of air under her toes. In *Scotch Symphony,* where her role is that of a Sylph (fairy), this ability to float-in-air looked especially magical. The only dancers I saw who came close to this same ability were Irina Kolpakova, Evelyn Hart (the great Canadian ballerina), and Gelsey Kirkland in her prime.

I first came under Allegra's spell when I was eleven and performing the Nutcracker-Prince to her Sugar Plum Fairy in Balanchine's *Nutcracker*. At that time it was her physical and facial beauty that got me. It wasn't until I was in the company and watching her from the front that I began to understand why she was so revered in the company and beyond. True, I had seen her dance on television quite often on *The Bell Telephone Hour* and other variety-styled programs, but they never did her justice.

When she returned from her third pregnancy, in 1968, Balanchine cast her to dance with me in *Valse Fantaisie*. I thought it almost cruel of Mr. B. to put her into this very taxing jumping role after she had just come back from giving birth, but, as she told me, "He just wanted to throw me into the deep end." Actually, in her first performance, she fell flat on her stomach as she performed the circle of *grand jetés* near the end of the woman's solo. Instead of being upset, she just laughed and laughed all the way through the rest of the ballet. We soon became fast friends, partners, and she has remained my life-long muse.

During these years, as she relates in her memoir, she was also going through a messy divorce from her husband, the celebrity fashion photographer Bert Stern (his photos of Marilyn Monroe are iconic). Her personal problems were the major reason she canceled performances so often and got the reputation of being unreliable. Even so, Balanchine was always ready to put her back onstage when she was able. He seemed almost grateful whenever she could bring herself to perform, which happened less and less in her mid-thirties, right when many ballerinas are reaching their prime. The audiences loudly applauded her every appearance, and Robbins and d'Amboise created new works for her, as did I, but we were never sure when she'd be able to dance a full season.

Balanchine wanted her to be in *Who Cares?* when he was first thinking about doing this ballet. I know because when he was planning this work he had her name written on a paper bag he placed on the piano before class one day. I asked the pianist what this was, and he said, "Mr. B.'s new ballet to Gershwin." Allegra's name was written next to "The Man I Love" and "Fascinating Rhythm." In her book Allegra says she needed cosmetic surgery because of the revealing costume in *Bugaku* and didn't feel she could take on the *Who Cares?* role. Patricia McBride ended up replacing her (I don't believe she even knew Balanchine was first thinking of casting Allegra), and Patty was truly magnificent in it, but I can clearly see an apparition of what Balanchine might have made for Allegra.

The amazing thing was that even though she began to jump less, and to eliminate her more physically taxing roles, her technique remained rock solid. She was always very appreciative of her early training in Los Angeles with Carmelita Maracci, so we shared that in common. I soon realized in partnering her in several ballets that I barely needed to touch her: her core strength was so solid that she seemed always to be on balance, and this was something that Carmelita excelled in doing as a dancer and emphasized as a teacher.

I remember watching Allegra do an almost slow-motion triple pirouette *en pointe* in *Bugaku,* which stopped dead and on full toe. Instead of coming down, she stayed securely on balance that seemed to last forever, raised her *passé* knee up (as if to prove a point), and then slowly came down.

In the 1973 Berlin filming of the second movement of *Symphony in C* (a role she hadn't danced in years), Allegra pulled off five unsupported pirouettes in the finale! The thirty-six dancers surrounding her broke character and cracked up because at the end of the turns she did a quick *sous-sus* and raised her hands in triumph, like an Olympic gymnast after executing a perfect vault. We then heard Balanchine's voice over a loudspeaker saying, "Let's do this again, please," and it sounded as if he too was laughing.

Even years later, when she was fifty-one and I had brought her out of retirement to dance with my chamber touring company, Ballet of Los Angeles, in a rehearsal of *Apollo* (she danced her last Terpsichore with us), she did a huge perfect *entrechat six.* When all the dancers gasped and then applauded, she quipped, "I only do one a year." I told her, "Save it for the show."

Watching her coach young dancers when I've taken her with me for my staging of *Bugaku* (the Royal Ballet), *La Sonnambula* (Sacramento Ballet), and *Apollo* (my Ballet of Los Angeles), or having her personally teach me how she danced *Agon, Concerto Barocco,* or *La Valse* (when I've staged these for other companies), has shown me how all of her dramatic effects were calculated, not truly spontaneous. This rather surprised me. She looked as if she was improvising onstage in her performances, but working with her as a coach made it clear that she had really thought out all her roles. She once told Darci Kistler to "throw your eyes out of focus" when dancing the Sleepwalker in *La Sonnambula*. She used the word "echolocation" for describing how the Sleepwalker could "see" her way. Brilliant!

What she also brought to all her roles, and to her coaching of young dancers, can only be described as good taste combined with a heightened theatricality. She innately understood that in some of the more sensual roles that Balanchine created for her—such as *Bugaku* and *The Seven Deadly Sins* (both ballets had revealing costumes and strong sexual imagery and undertones)—her performance would be more powerful if she played down the erotic elements. She knew the value of "less is more." This actually elevated the drama in these ballets past any tawdry elements. In Balanchine's truly bizarre ballet to Charles Ives's music *Ivesiana*, in "The Unanswered Question" section, she was dressed only in a white leotard with hair loose and bare legs and feet; held aloft by four men and never touching the ground, she was clearly the myth of the unattainable female. A shirtless man contorted himself and writhed at her feet, hoping to gain her attention—but she never acknowledged him. She stayed aloof and implacable. That Allegra could inspire Balanchine to create such a role speaks volumes about her power as an artist.

In the macabre and dramatic *La Valse* (originally created for Tanaquil Le Clercq), where the heroine is seduced by Death himself and succumbs to her own vanity, Allegra brought to the beginning part an innocence and vulnerability that turned horrific in the second section when she gave in to the weaknesses we all have (such as greed, and vanity) as the character of Death enticed her. When she plunged her arm into the long black glove that the death figure offered her, at the climactic surge in the Ravel score, Allegra made it into a metaphor. Here is where all others who have danced this portray how the once-innocent girl fully gives in to the figure of death, but Allegra alone made this movement almost sexual, which no other ballerinas I've seen interpreted quite this way. The innocent girl becomes a wanton woman with that one gesture. The way she did this, by throwing her arm behind her as if it had a life of its own, while continuing to stare intently at the black glove, and then by slightly turning her head back (almost as in ecstasy) as her hand slid sensually into the glove like a snake into its lair . . . well!

As a choreographer I studied all her performances closely because the power of interpretation when danced by an artist of her caliber was an education in itself. Mr. B. always said it wasn't just all about the steps. She was the living example. She didn't just dance these ballets—she lived them.

Allegra is highly intelligent (she has authored many essays and several books), and possibly because of her intellect she does not suffer fools easily. She was usually quite nervous before she performed, but I saw that her habit of dealing with this was to act out. This usually meant non-ballerina-like behavior, such as stretching in outlandish positions, acting hyper, or withdrawing completely into herself and ignoring everyone around her.

More proof that she was unique was that after Farrell resigned, Balanchine cast Allegra first in Farrell's iconic role in *Diamonds,* causing much unhappiness for Violette Verdy and Melissa Hayden. On the very same day I found Violette at the school and Melissa at the fountain at Lincoln Center, each of them in tears. When I asked what was wrong, each said she thought it was so callous and downright disrespectful of Balanchine to give this plum role to Allegra, who at this point was notorious for being unreliable and for canceling performances at the last minute. Both these senior ballerinas had asked Balanchine for this part after Suzanne's departure, but he gave it to Allegra, even though she had been dancing less and less on a regular basis. The common thinking at the time was: will she or won't she appear? What could I say? Clearly he thought that highly of her. Needless to say she was magnificent in it. She didn't have Farrell's long legs, but her innate magic and unique delicacy made up for that easily.

Ten years later, right before Balanchine's triple bypass surgery, when he was already quite fragile, I happened to be standing next to him in his favorite spot during performances, the downstage right wing. This was at the Kennedy Center Opera House during the matinee of Baryshnikov's last performance with the company. The ballet he was dancing was *La Sonnambula,* and his partner was an especially nervous

Bugaku, with Allegra Kent. Courtesy of the author.
Choreography by George Balanchine © The George
Balanchine Trust.

Allegra Kent. She was shaking quite a bit on the supported promenades
and I think she was aware of what a big deal it was to be Mischa's last
NYCB partner.

Suddenly Balanchine grabbed my arm and asked me to go with him
out front. He needed my physical support because there were a lot of
staircases to maneuver and he was unsteady on his feet. We needed to
stop occasionally for him to catch his breath, but I couldn't understand
why he needed to rush out to the front of the house. Once we got there
he watched for a few minutes, and then said he wanted to go backstage.
On the way I asked him why he needed to see the ballet from the front.
He said he needed to check on the lights for Allegra. When I asked
why, he said simply, "Because she is very special."

26

"Coach" Balanchine

Mr. B. understood all of us, sometimes more than we did ourselves. For example, during one very cold Saratoga season, Balanchine bought horse blankets (Saratoga is the home of a famous racetrack) for all the dancers to keep warm in the wings. He then gave all the dancers horses' names, which were also stitched onto the blankets and based loosely on their real names. Some weren't too kind, so I'll leave those out. Luckily, mine was "Cliff-Formidable Pinto." I asked why "Pinto" and he said it was a small horse that was very, very fast! That was fine by me and I loved the "Formidable" part.

There was one rule, simple but powerful. The only thing a "Balanchine dancer" had to do was to work hard and listen to Balanchine. If a dancer was a little bit more exuberant, on one hand, or reserved, on the other, that was not necessarily a bad thing. It meant that there was more diversity in the company. That's what made the New York City Ballet so great.

However, music always came first, and God help anyone who changed Balanchine's choreography without his permission!

Mr. B. was as noted for what he didn't say as for what he did say. Often, he would take rehearsals and never say a thing to the principal dancers. He'd spend the precious time on the corps de ballet, doing away entirely with rehearsals for the principals, expecting those dancers to fend for themselves. He confused many young dancers by saying, "Just do the steps," and "Don't think!" What he meant was don't *analyze*, and above all, don't *calculate*. He was speaking here only of how one should approach the steps but not how one dances a dramatic or character role. For those parts he liked the dancers to dig deep into any dramatic elements. For instance, when Mr. B. cast me as Puck I wanted to approach it very differently from the approach of the dancer for whom he created the role, Arthur Mitchell. Arthur danced it rather regally; which suited his personality to a T. I asked Balanchine if I could do it more like Mickey Rooney in the 1935 Max Reinhardt film. Mr. B. was quite shocked that I knew this old film. I reminded him I was from Hollywood and had once been an actor. I told him I loved Rooney's almost manic, totally boyish approach, and that I had once played Puck in the Benjamin Britten opera (a spoken-danced role), when I was sixteen. He said absolutely to do it like Rooney if that's what I thought would be best for me. Years later, after Balanchine's death, and after I had been gone from the company for years, I was amused to see a NYCB telecast where the man doing Puck used practically all of my shtick. I'm sure he wasn't aware where it originated.

Balanchine's classical ballets—*Raymonda Variations* or *La Source*—do not need any interpretation from the performers. If a dancer with a strong personality, say Melissa Hayden or Violette Verdy, seemed to "interpret" a Balanchine ballet, Mr. B. would sometimes feign annoyance, but he really wasn't upset, or he wouldn't have kept casting them in those roles.

One evening I was standing with him in his usual place in the downstage right wing during a spectacular performance by Violette in *Tchaikovsky Pas de Deux*. During her solo Mr. B. turned to me with a twinkle in his eye and said, "Well, she does tell a story." Does this mean that he was displeased with her? I don't think so, since he was smiling and his eyes were laughing. He knew his dancers inside and out, and Violette's habit of playing with the music obviously pleased him. Why else would he continually cast her in this and other abstract ballets, such as *Episodes* and *La Source,* which he had also choreographed for her? He knew what she would do beforehand and did not feel any coaching was necessary. His more serious modern works were another story. Mr. B. usually spent a great deal of time rehearsing the corps in *The Four Temperaments* and *Agon,* and when there was a new cast in *Apollo,* he would sometimes spend time on each variation.

Let me give you a few of my coaching experiences with Balanchine.

As already noted, I first danced *Valse Fantaisie* as an emergency replacement for John Prinz. For my first performance I was concerned with just doing the steps correctly. During rehearsals Mr. B. taught me the basic choreography, but nothing more. During the first performance

I did add one inflection of my own, totally spontaneously. On the exit after the male variation, I did a *tour-jeté* split into a backbend before I exited into the wings. The *tour jeté* was choreographed, but opening my legs to a split in the air before I landed, and the backbend as I turned on the exit, were my idea. It was not planned. It just happened. After this first performance I went to Balanchine and apologized for my tacky addition. I felt embarrassed for letting myself get carried away like that. Amazingly, he said it was fine and to leave it in. Gradually I added more beats and a greater sense of rubato, using Violette as my example. Each time, I asked Balanchine what he thought, and each time he said the changes—which were not actually changes, but more like embellishments—were fine. Since he kept me in this ballet for my entire career with the company, I guess he liked me in it. On other occasions, for other ballets, when I inadvertently added something he didn't approve of, he would say that was "buttering the bacon." I got the hint. However, I never made any additions to the modern works: *Agon, The Four Temperaments, Symphony in Three Movements.* I considered these works sacrosanct. I still do. To me, making any changes would be akin to brightening up the background on da Vinci's *Mona Lisa.*

In 1968 there came a turning point for my dancing career with the company. I had been mesmerized by the "Melancholic" variation in *The Four Temperaments* from the first time I saw Richard Rapp dance it. I had never wanted to dance anything so badly in my entire life, even though I thought I was totally wrong for the part (too young and basically an allegro dancer). At that point I had already danced *Valse Fantaisie,* "In the Inn" from *Ivesiana,* and the leads in Candy Cane and Tea, as well as the Toy Soldier in *The Nutcracker,* all upbeat allegro solos and very different from the angular, somber "Melancholic." One day I gathered up my nerve and asked Mr. B. if I could possibly understudy it. To my surprise he said yes, but I never thought I'd actually get to perform it. I only wanted to feel those steps in my body and dance to that beautiful Hindemith music.

A week later there was a rehearsal and I followed Richard like a shadow in the back of the room. I noticed Mr. B. was watching me. A few days later, right before the ballet was set to go, Richard hurt himself, and I was on! I did the stage rehearsal the day of the show, but I was very tentative because I still wasn't completely sure of the steps, let alone of any "interpretation." After that rehearsal, Mr. B. said he wanted to see me in the small rehearsal room at six that evening. Was he actually going to coach me? I had never seen him coach anybody at that point. When he asked to see me privately, I thought maybe I had been awful and he wasn't pleased. At six he walked in, rolled up his sleeves (a personal habit of his) and said, "Let's begin."

"Melancholic" starts with the man doing a *grand jeté* onstage from the wings. He then *relevés* up to an arabesque immediately on the same leg he's just landed on. In the rehearsal I purposely did not jump too high. I had two reasons: one, the variation was called "Melancholic," and I thought a big *grand jeté* would be inappropriate; two, it's damned hard to *relevé* on the same leg after landing from a big *jeté*. Mr. B. stopped the pianist after this first jump and said, "No, dear. It must be a big jump. Enormous! Then *relevé* into a big arabesque, and with *energy!*"

I asked him if I should be melancholic at all in this solo. He said, "Absolutely not! The dancer is not melancholic." Mr. B. proceeded to lead me step by step, and note by note, through that entire solo, and it was quite different in style and energy from what Richard had been doing.

Everything had to be done with maximum force and energy. Mr. B. also said he wanted "contractions" in this dance, so I approached it in Martha Graham, modern-dance terms, using what I had learned in my Martha Graham technique classes at Loring's school. As Deborah Zall taught me, a Graham contraction can be explained like this. Imagine that you have a cord attached to the inside of your navel, which comes up through your throat, and out of your mouth. When someone pulls on this cord, then that is a contraction. It is not a downward, sinking, or collapsing movement. A Graham contraction goes *in* and *up*. When I showed this to Balanchine, in this rehearsal, he said, "That's exactly right."

When the performance came that night, I was immensely excited and very hyper. Mr. B. had told me exactly what to do. I was given the chance to dance against type, and I was not going to let him down. As I stood in the wings watching the first three *pas de deux* that begin this masterpiece, I actually started to shake, but not from fear. I was beginning to feel that Balanchine's ballets had a direct, almost supernatural, link to . . . well . . . the universe.

It's hard to explain. His combination of steps, added to the music, created something new, another kind of reality. I was going to be a participant in some sort of sacred ritual. This was more than mere dancing, more than just performing; this was something entirely new for me. I was going to be, in a few seconds' time, the vessel through which Balanchine would worship his God.

Imagine that you are staring straight into a cyclone. This storm is going to pick you up and carry you high above the earth, but after this wild ride you will land safely. Nothing to fear.

He often compared the theater to a church. When I leapt onto that stage, I was not going to be myself. I, me, the ego, would disappear. There would be no John Clifford. I was going to be quite literally Mr. B.'s steps and Hindemith's music.

The piano played the entrance notes, "ba-dum," and I was off. I don't really remember that first performance except that at the end, when I got up off my knees, my legs nearly gave out. I had never done that solo straight through, and now, using all that Balanchine had just shown me, I had no idea of how brutal that solo was on the legs. I had to push myself up from the floor with both hands, and the exit truly looked limp, exactly the way Balanchine wanted it. (It wasn't until the next day that my back felt as if it were broken!) After this first performance, Mr. B. took my hand as I cleared the wing in the deep backbend of the choreography, and he quite literally held me up. (He did this for all my subsequent performances.) There was a surprisingly long ovation from the audience. I asked him if I should bow, but he said no, so I just stood in the wings next to him and listened. It seemed to go on and on, and all he did was smile and nod his head.

Later that night Renee and I had a late dinner at Monk's Inn. We were the last diners, or so I thought. As I was paying the bill the waiter came over with a magnum of champagne and said, "This is from a fan." I looked around the restaurant but couldn't see any other people. I said, "No, seriously, who sent this?" He motioned over his shoulder to a small alcove in the back. I went to investigate, and there sat Balanchine, grinning like a Cheshire cat. He was with a beautiful blonde who was not a dancer. He introduced me and told her that tonight had been my début in "Melancholic." He then said, "And, it's never been danced better!" You can imagine my shock! I hadn't been in the

Studio portrait in a pose from "Melancholic" from *The Four Temperaments*. Photo by Martha Swope. Used with permission of NYPL. Choreography by George Balanchine © The George Balanchine Trust.

company that long, and this role was very different from anything I'd been given to dance before. He must have meant what he said, because that role remained mine alone until the day I left the company. Mr. B. even brought me back several times to dance it as a guest artist, and that ballet has always remained immensely important to me personally.

21

Balanchine's Tastes

Even though one of the key ways to understand Balanchine is to accept the fact that he was, in a way, unknowable (he used to quip, following the Russian poet Mayakovsky, that he was a "cloud in pants"), there were some clues to his character that I was lucky enough to pick up simply because I spent so much time alone with him. Many books and articles about him miss crucial points of his nature, plus misunderstand completely how he handled his dancers.

Balanchine often said he preferred to choreograph for dancers he'd like to "take out for coffee." What he meant was that he liked working with intelligent people with whom he could have a conversation and people whose personalities intrigued him. Whether or not they were great technicians was beside the point. He knew he could teach them to be that if they applied themselves.

It also became clear that he preferred grooming a dancer who had a natural (instinctive) movement quality rather than someone who had a perfect technique, and who was, as he would say, "boring." It seemed that nearly all his favorites were natural movers before they became good technicians. What Balanchine demanded most from any of his dancers was that they had the desire—the absolute passion—to dance, the discipline to work at it, and complete and utter loyalty to him. As he has often been quoted, "I don't want people who *want* to dance, I want people who *have* to dance."

It was an enormous disappointment for Balanchine when dancers who had been primarily trained at his school, and whom he had hand-picked for his company, decided that they did not want to "worship" at the same church. He took it very personally. For dancers who came to him from a European school or company he was more forgiving, as in the cases of Peter Martins, Jean-Pierre Bonnefoux, or Mikhail

Baryshnikov. He always had the most respect for dancers who came from the older ballet traditions. Still, when they came into *his* company, he expected them to adjust themselves to *his* world. I looked at this very pragmatically. He was our employer, after all.

The ideas of Balanchine only liking tall girls with long legs and small heads, or his not liking short boys or dancers with strong personalities, are myths, which he himself sometimes perpetuated because whomever he was interested in at the time became the "ideal." He had some preferences, as we all do, but what Mr. B. liked most—and I'm basing my opinion on a great deal of personal observation and many conversations with him—was the "selflessness" that was necessary to open oneself up to receiving his knowledge and the ability to translate what he was offering you into something individual.

He wasn't kidding when he said dance was a "vocation," much like being in a religious order. I'd see him over and over again working with a dancer who didn't have the perfect body or strong technique, simply because he found something unusual and interesting in them that he could develop. Karin von Aroldingen was a perfect example. This German born and trained dancer had been a gymnast as a child, and therefore had a very limber back, but was outwardly the very antithesis of a "Balanchine" dancer. Her body was very muscular for a woman, and her broad back, large feet, short legs, and slim, almost masculine hips, would seem to be everything Balanchine wouldn't like; however, she was the hardest worker I've ever seen, and she worshipped Balanchine. She did have a beautiful face and a big jump, so Mr. B. took her natural attributes and molded her into something quite exceptional. He took what would seem to be her flaws and made them into assets. He used her gymnastic abilities to maximum effect in the first *pas de deux* in *Stravinsky Violin Concerto* and in *Variations pour une Porte et un Soupir,* and her innate sweetness and beauty were showcased in his *Davidsbündlertänze,* the first movement of his *Tchaikovsky Suite No. 3,* and *Vienna Waltzes.* These five roles he made for her were *inspired* by her. I cannot think of another dancer anywhere who would have had the same effect on him resulting in his creating these masterpieces.

Balanchine often used the metaphor that ballerinas were flowers and the male dancers were gardeners. I think this was really Balanchine's own relationship with his ballerinas. A flower is beautiful because it exists. What a gardener does is nurture (water and feed) and protect the flower and arrange the shapes and formations of the garden in which the flower is displayed.

One morning I was having breakfast with Mr. B. in Evanston, Illinois, where the company was staying during its annual season at the Ravinia Festival. I had brought a newspaper to the table and was reading a review of *Serenade*, which the company had danced the night before. The critic remarked that the corps de ballet had not been in unison. I told Mr. B. I didn't understand this carping because I thought it had been a beautiful performance. "You know, dear," he replied, "I don't want them to be 'together.' I want them to be a field of different flowers, wild flowers, all moving in the wind at the same time."

I thought that was a particularly personal and beautiful glimpse into his tastes.

On another occasion in class, when Mr. B. was talking about how high to get the leg in a *développé*, he said he didn't care how high the legs could get. What he cared about was that the dancers' feet all hit the floor at the same time when they were dancing in unison. Their being together musically and rhythmically was more important to him than their being together visually. Balanchine was always more interested in the energy and sweep of movement rather than a series of static photos or an overly regimented corps de ballet.

28

Stars and Stripes . . . and "Panache!"

Back to the story: I was thrilled when Balanchine cast me with Violette for my début in *Stars and Stripes*. She'd been doing the *pas de deux* for years with several different partners, and had all her little mannerisms down pat, but I, on the other hand, could only offer my energy.

Our first performance was not smooth, but neither was our first performance of *Nutcracker*. In that, I had almost dropped Violette on the final "fish" dive, the last action in the *pas de deux*. We had never rehearsed in costume or onstage. I was wearing Villella's costume, which didn't really fit. Both her costume and mine were made out of satin, and since we had never rehearsed in these costumes, I didn't realize that satin on satin would be so slippery, but I found out. When we got to the fish dive, I was supposed to catch Violette by the waist by wrapping my arms around her. What happened instead was that she slipped right through my arms and only saved herself by slamming her hands on the floor and going into a step that looked as if it were straight out of Jerry Robbins's comedy ballet, *The Concert*.

Since there had also been no stage rehearsal time or costume run-through for the principals in the *Stars pas de deux*, I hadn't realized how exhausting it actually was. I probably should have been more aware of this at the time, but I was just having so much fun!

In that first performance of *Stars* everything was going terrifically well. All the partnering had been smooth, and there weren't too many lifts, so I didn't think I was overly tired, but in the end of the coda, there came a moment when I thought I was going to pass out.

Stars and Stripes was originally choreographed for the City Center stage, which is not as big as the State Theater's. I was never more aware of just how large that stage is than during the really huge, almost thrown, *grand-jeté* lift that ends this *pas*. When Violette and I took the mad rush to the wings that precedes this big lift, somehow I just couldn't keep up. I lifted Violette as best I could and held her up as long as I could, but we both fell hard on the exit. I just prayed we had cleared the stage. I worried that we were we still visible when we keeled over (rather than flew) into the wings. Instead of being upset, Violette just laughed and laughed and giggled all the way through the finale.

Clive Barnes reviewed the performance that night and unexpectedly gave our *Stars and Stripes* a rave. He said if the word panache had not already been invented, it would have had to be, after my performance.

The next night, as I was putting on my costume to dance *Stars* again, Balanchine asked if I had read the Barnes review. He said he was just reading a copy that Ducky had given him. "I saw your review, dear. 'Panache!' There would be none if it weren't for you?" He asked me if I knew what the word panache actually meant. I said, "Not really." "Don't get too excited," he said. "It's just a little feather. A feather that the French used to put in their hats. That was a panache. It's only a feather, dear." It was just like Balanchine to give me a little compliment and at the same time play it down.

By then it was a habit of ours to have dinner together after almost every show. His asking me out in front of the other dancers was sometimes embarrassing, like the time I was in the men's corps bathroom and Balanchine came in looking for me. He asked the other guys where I was and then actually came into the bathroom to tell me he'd be waiting for me downstairs. Of course, they all heard this. That sort of thing can totally alienate the company against one. Our friendship was really a double-edged sword, but at that time I didn't care what the other guys thought of me. There were so many good things coming my way that any bad things instantly vanished.

My fifth ballet for the company, which also premiered in 1969, was a minor work to two Debussy piano pieces as orchestrated by Maurice Ravel, *Sarabande and Danse*. It consisted of two contrasting *pas de deux*. The first was a very acrobatic but also romantic *pas de deux* for Johnna and Earle Sieveling, and the second was an upbeat dance for Violette and myself; it was full of bravura steps, tricky partnering, and big throws. Surprisingly, this little ballet received some of my best reviews. Frances Herridge, then the dance critic for the *New York Post*, said I was "a chip off the master's block," and Anna Kisselgoff said in the *New York Times*, "Clifford's new ballet is so original it is truly

Johnna Kirkland and Earle Sieveling in the "Sarabande" from
my *Sarabande and Danse*. Photo by Martha Swope. Used with
permission of NYPL swope_780205.

startling." I thought that was a bit much for something so inconse-
quential as my two little *pas de deux,* but I was happy it was successful.
Both critics were especially taken with the Kirkland-Sieveling more
unusual opening *pas*; I think the success of this came from my early
acrobatic training with my father. I always had the uncanny ability to
retain almost anything I saw or was taught. This has certainly come in
handy when restaging Balanchine's ballets for the last fifty years.

29

The Goldberg Variations Rehearsals and *PAMTGG*

Unfortunately, the latter portion of the period 1969–1972 was not the best time for my boss. Jerry Robbins had followed up his 1969 mega-hit, *Dances at a Gathering*, with another successful ballet to Chopin's piano music, *In the Night*, which premiered in 1970. Then came his setting of Bach's *Goldberg Variations*. Not only was this a very long ballet time-wise (well over an hour straight through, and it felt as if Robbins used every repeat), but it also took him a long time to choreograph. Rehearsals began over a year prior to its premiere in late May of 1971.

As originally performed, Robbins's staging of *Goldberg Variations* started with a theatricalized "Minuet" by Renee Estopinal and Michael Steele, dressed in elaborate eighteenth-century-looking black-and-white costumes. After they finished, they left the stage in opposite directions, and in walked Sara Leland in a mint-green leotard and practice skirt. She proceeded to do the first of the variations. She was then joined by two men (Robert Maiorano and Bruce Wells) for a *pas de trois*. As they finished their dance, Gelsey Kirkland, Robert Weiss, and I came out to replace them and perform another *pas de trois*. The ballet built from there.

Robbins started choreographing this in the SAB studios in the Juilliard School building, and I was one of the first dancers called to the rehearsals. Even though Jerry knew I couldn't stand his rudeness, he nonetheless still cast me in his ballets. I was still feeling some animosity left over from his horrible methods of treating dancers in *Dances*, and I didn't think he liked me that much as a dancer anyway, so I was surprised, and frankly not that happy, when I got called for his new ballet. Spending hours in a studio with him again was not my idea of a good time. Mr. B. had definitely spoiled me.

Jerry's first rehearsals of his new work consisted of a lot of walking steps, and he called these versions A, B, and sometimes up to C and D. Mostly there were only miniscule differences between these versions. He would then say, "Do four bars of A then switch to B for two bars, then go back to A for three bars, then go to C to finish." It drove all of us nuts. Switching back and forth between extremely similar sections of choreography, using only our memory, was incredibly difficult. No one enjoyed these rehearsals since it was clear to all of us that Jerry couldn't make up his mind between the different versions and was spending hours of precious time trying to decide.

I tried to dance well, when there was any actual dancing, but none of us had the sense that we'd be kept all the way through to the premiere. This was especially hard for a company that had Balanchine as our leader, a man who never wasted a second and always showed his dancers the utmost respect. I'm sure some of the other dancers didn't feel this way, but I had put Robbins on such a high pedestal for so many years that I magnified any flaw in his character way out of proportion. I behaved pretty badly, and I'm ashamed of this now.

Balanchine had liked *Dances at a Gathering* tremendously but had fewer kind words for *Goldberg*. Referring to the length of the piece, he said, "It looks like Robbins is trying to build a monument to himself." He also said "*Dances* was like milk that turned to good yogurt. *Goldberg* was like milk that just turned sour." At those first rehearsals, I had no idea how long this ballet would be. The rehearsals seemed to drag on forever. Then an unfortunate thing happened to Jerry that gave us all a short rest.

One afternoon a few weeks into rehearsals, Gelsey, Ricky, and I were all working on an allegro section and Jerry was jumping around a lot. Suddenly we heard a loud *pop* and he doubled up and fell over, grabbing his ankle. It was quite a horrific thing to see. I ran to the desk and asked them to call an ambulance, as it was obvious he had torn his Achilles tendon. Kay and Sally arrived to start their rehearsals just as a nurse was bringing in a wheelchair. I can't remember which girl said, "Well . . . so he was finally struck down!" It sounds callous, but there you have it. Neither of these girls had a mean bone in her body, but Jerry certainly had that coming to him. Amazingly, after only one week

Above: *Goldberg Variations* leading jumps in front. Photo by Martha Swope. Used with permission of NYPL swope_780584.

Left: *Goldberg Variations* complete premiere cast (I'm on knee to Peter Martins's right). Photo by Martha Swope. Used with permission of NYPL swope_780562.

Jerry was back choreographing, but from a wheelchair. I had to admire him for that. He was so damned determined!

By 1971, dancers from the school had started moving into positions being vacated by older members of the company, which was now taking on a newer, sleeker look. When I joined in 1966, there were still a few dancers who had less-than-ideal bodies, and varying levels of technique, but now all that was changing. Every one of the new ladies in the corps de ballet was physically more appealing than the next, and the men were also getting much more refined.

In addition to these new dancers, Balanchine still had all his great principals, and Gelsey Kirkland was fast on the rise. Also, now dancing as a beautiful team were Kay Mazzo and Peter Martins. Helgi Tomasson had come on board, and Sara Leland and Karin von Aroldingen were coming into their own. As for me, I had no complaints. I was dancing more than ever and only principal roles.

Meanwhile, Mr. B. was going through a significant slump in his career. I don't know why, but there were a few miscalculated ballets on his part that did not go over well with the press or the public, while at the same time Jerry's were being praised to the heavens. Jerry had been a guest choreographer for *Dances at a Gathering*. As he continued to choreograph, he started to move into a more prominent part of the repertoire, and new Balanchine ballets weren't needed as much to fill out the schedule as they had once been.

Balanchine's biggest mistake of all was a ballet that will go down in infamy: *PAMTGG!*

One day Balanchine came into class whistling the tune "Pan Am Makes the Going Great," which was a popular advertising jingle for Pan American Airways.

I guess he thought it would be a fun little tune to choreograph, so he commissioned composer Roger Kellaway, the composer of the closing musical theme for TV's *All in the Family*, to write a three-movement ballet based on that Pan Am jingle.

A few days later I heard some pop-sounding music coming from inside a studio. Peeking in, I saw Balanchine listening to a piano recording. Speaking for myself, the music sounded really second-rate and not something that Balanchine would normally consider. Mr. B. didn't seem too thrilled, either. I asked him what it was, and he said, "New ballet. Let's wait for the orchestra."

Unfortunately, the first orchestra rehearsal was a mess. I was there because I was now the lead in the third movement of this new ballet and was curious to hear what the music sounded like with the full orchestra. I don't know what the actual problems were, but it sounded pretty bad, as if Kellaway had composed it for certain instruments—which would have been miked for TV—to carry the theme, but now they could not possibly be heard over the rest of the orchestra because we didn't use microphones with our live orchestra. Robert Irving, who was conducting, really had to keep forces in check in order not to drown out the solo melodic lines. Mr. B. was visibly irritated and almost angry. He even snapped at Robert. This was totally uncharacteristic and showed me he was under enormous stress.

Mr. B. had also commissioned Hollywood film costume designer Irene Sharaff to do the costumes and Broadway set designer Jo Mielziner to design the elaborate futuristic sets. It was a very expensive production, loosely set in an airport, with some dancers dressed as flight attendants and others as all types of travelers. The bottom line was that it didn't work, but Balanchine was stuck with it. It wasn't New York City Ballet's habit to cancel a new ballet's premiere, and the premiere was already announced, so there was nothing that could be done about it. Balanchine was starting to get really testy, which was not like him at all.

I think what was really making him unhappy was a combination of many things.

For one thing there was Jerry Robbins to contend with. His ballets were being lauded everywhere, and he could be emotionally draining even for Balanchine. Also, contemporaries and friends of Mr. B.'s were aging and dying (most notably Stravinsky), and he was not romantically interested in any of the girls. There was no new Suzanne Farrell, and for someone who needed a muse, this was especially hard. He was inspired to a degree by Gelsey, Kay, Karin, and the others, but none were his whole world the way Suzanne had been.

I guess he thought he'd have a nice upbeat and popular success with *PAMTGG*, along the lines of *Slaughter on Tenth Avenue*. The word was out, though, that despite an obscenely expensive production, this ballet was just no good. And to make matters worse, the opening night was

Me, Sara Leland, and group in *PAMTGG*. Photo by Martha Swope. Used with permission of NYPL swope_780540. Choreography by George Balanchine © The George Balanchine Trust.

picketed! A picket line at State Theater? Not your usual sight. I don't know the details, but it had something to do with being anti–Pan Am Airways.

The ballet's first movement principals were Kay Mazzo and Victor Castelli, a new and wildly talented eighteen-year-old fresh from the school. I had taught Victor in many classes there, and we had become close friends. He even called me "Mr. C." He and Kay were the Young Lovers. The second movement was danced by Karin von Aroldingen and Jean-Pierre Bonnefoux, as sort of New Age Hippies, and the third movement was led by Sara Leland and me as the upper-crust Jet-Setters.

As expected, it got totally panned by all the critics. Almost every newspaper and magazine critic, except *Newsweek*'s Hubert Saal (the only loyal one out there), asked some version of, "Why doesn't Balanchine just hang it up?" They all more than hinted that Robbins should take over the company because Balanchine was getting old and perhaps just couldn't cut it anymore. How could the press turn on him like that? I was disgusted and hated it.

One night shortly after *PAMTGG* premiered, I was dancing the third movement of *Brahms-Schoenberg Quartet* and had a sort of cathartic

Above: Me and Gelsey Kirkland in *Brahms-Schoenberg Quartet*. Photographer unknown. Choreography by George Balanchine © The George Balanchine Trust.

Left: Me and Gelsey Kirkland in *Brahms-Schoenberg Quartet*. Photo by Martha Swope. Used with permission of NYPL swope_780859. Choreography by George Balanchine © The George Balanchine Trust.

release. I grabbed Mr. B. after I got offstage, hugged him, and very emotionally told him that all of us dancers only wanted to dance for *him* and only in *his* ballets. The critics could just go to hell! This was Mr. B.'s company and no one else's and we were *his* dancers. I told him I would quit dancing rather than work for anyone else. I probably looked like an idiot, but I was so ecstatic to be able to dance this great Balanchine ballet again that it all just poured out. For once he didn't look embarrassed by my emotional outburst. He very quietly put his hand on my shoulder and said simply, "Thank you, dear."

To our relief, *PAMTGG* only lasted one season. Before the last performance Balanchine seemed to be in a better mood and said everyone in the ballet could just wear anything we wanted. He jettisoned the set and costumes, and we all wore our most outlandish outfits. Bonita Borne wore a white *Swan Lake* tutu. Bobby Maiorano dressed in a leather jacket motorcyclist ensemble straight out of a Marlon Brando movie. I wore blue star-studded bellbottom pants, a red-and-white-striped shirt tied at the waist, white socks, tennis shoes, and dark glasses. The audience did not know what to make of all this. There were thirty-six dancers on a bare stage, all in bizarre attire, ranging from regular dancewear to street clothes. When it was over, and there was quite a big ovation at the end, Mr. B. seemed quite pleased and was beaming as we filed past him in the wings after the bows. He knew how to take it on the chin and let it go.

Unfortunately though, Mr. B. still was not completely his old self. He spent a lot of time away from the company, in Geneva, Zurich, Hamburg, or Berlin, and I was feeling a little lost. It just wasn't the same without him standing in the wings and teaching his daily class. John Taras took over those and they were rather dull.

My *Fantasies* was a solid success; *Prelude, Fugue, and Riffs,* to that jazzy score by Leonard Bernstein, had served its original purpose as a light-hearted filler for the Spring Gala, and it was still being included in the repertoire. *Sarabande and Danse* and *Reveries* were also very successful, so I had nothing to complain about. I was still only twenty-three years old.

As fate would have it, *Reveries* was scheduled one night on the same program with Robbins's *In the Night.* Both used a very similar lighting plot, and even though my ballet was premiered before his, Ronnie

Elise Flagg and Conrad Ludlow in *Tchai-kovsky Suite No. 1* (formerly called *Reveries*) Photos by Martha Swope. Used with permission of NYPL swope_780947, swope_780949s.

Bates said we'd need to change the lighting for my ballet because it was too similar to Jerry's. "Wait a minute, I did my ballet first," I said, "Yes," he said, "but Jerry is insisting you change your lights."

Both ballets used tiny electric lights as stars on the backdrop.

Mr. B. was standing nearby so I said to him, "This isn't very fair, because my ballet really needs that lighting and after all, I did do mine first." "Well, dear," he said, "Don't worry, you're young and Jerry's just a guest. You're a ballet-master here." I was? Balanchine had never actually called me that before; he'd only said he was training me to be one, which was quite different.

Mr. B. told me that the stars should be on the stage, not on the backdrop, and that if my ballet wouldn't work with different lighting, well then, it wasn't very good to begin with. He told me about how many times he'd changed the costumes and lights for *Serenade*. "A good ballet should look good in practice clothes and work lights," he said. I didn't really have much choice, so I decided to change the lights to a simpler light blue, add two sections of the Tchaikovsky score as solos for Gloria Govrin that I had originally cut, change the costumes into a simple practice look (these were later recycled for Balanchine's revival of *Square Dance*), and even change the title, to *Tchaikovsky Suite No.*

1. That made Balanchine happy since he always preferred using the music's title anyway, and surprise, surprise, the ballet went over better than before. Balanchine was right once again, and I proved that my ballet was choreographically sound, without any superfluous elements. Even all the critics said it looked better.

I did begin to worry, though, that all my ballets were beginning to be (at least visually) too "Balanchine," because of not being allowed to dress and light them the way I wanted. I knew even then that there was only one Balanchine and that copying him was a dead end, creatively speaking. However, I was privileged to be in my position, so I was more than happy to continue learning all I could from him, and let my concerns about looking too "Balanchine" pass.

30

Choreographing Elsewhere
San Francisco and Royal Winnipeg Ballets

Up until 1970 I hadn't been commissioned to do any ballets for other companies except for one quick chamber piece I did for Marvin Gordon. He had a small group of dancers in New York City called Marvin Gordon Ballet Concepts. He asked me to do a piece in 1968. I used the *Havanaise* by Camille Saint-Saëns, a short number that served its purpose for his group and has long since been forgotten. I was now creating new works only for NYCB and SAB. I was also so busy carrying a full dance load that there just wasn't time for me to work elsewhere. Besides, I really wasn't interested in choreographing for other companies or building a reputation as a choreographer. I believed then that my whole life would be spent with Balanchine and his company.

The first commission I had from another major company was from the San Francisco Ballet. This West Coast ensemble had close ties with the New York City Ballet from its inception. Lew Christensen, its cofounder and director, was the first American *Apollo* and had been the principal man in many of Balanchine's American ballets in the 1930s. I don't know why this company commissioned a ballet from me, but my guess would be that Mr. B. or Lincoln had something to do with it. I had not yet seen the San Francisco Ballet at that point (it was then a medium-sized company with around forty-five dancers), but I thought it would be a good experience for me to work with a company other than NYCB.

The first thing I did was find the music, and after listening to various scores I settled on *One Night in the Tropics,* a large symphonic work by Louis Moreau Gottschalk. Balanchine had used his music for *Tarantella* (Gottschalk was America's most famous virtuoso pianist-composer of the 1860s). I thought this was very danceable music and would provide the basis for a classical display piece for a company, even one I had not yet seen. I had only two weeks out of my New York schedule to choreograph the ballet, so I knew I would have to work quickly.

After I arrived in San Francisco I first watched their class and was pleased to invite their senior ballerina, Jocelyn Vollmar, to be my lead ballerina. She had been in the New York City Ballet years before, and she still had that Balanchine look: sleek and long-legged. She was nearing the end of her career, but I didn't care about her age, which I guessed was somewhere in her mid-forties. (She was born in 1925.) She still had supreme elegance and beautifully high extensions.

I then cast Leo Ahonen, an exciting allegro dancer who had a quicksilver technique and an infectious stage manner, for the second movement, which had various fun Latin American rhythms, hence the title *One Night in the Tropics.*

The costumes were designed by Robert O'Hearn (who had previously designed the costumes for my *Fantasies*), and they were exceptionally beautiful. He later designed the sets and costumes for my Los Angeles Ballet's full-length *Nutcracker* production, which Clive Barnes called "one of the most lavish in the country."

Unfortunately, I never saw an actual performance because I barely had time to set it and get back to New York. The reviews were favorable, but the critics commented that this ballet would probably have looked better on the New York City Ballet. In those days, the local San Francisco critics were rather hard on that company, but I don't know why; they had some really good dancers.

The next ballet I did for a company other than NYCB was in 1971, for the Royal Winnipeg Ballet. For this Canadian troupe I choreographed the *Concert Fantasy* by Tchaikovsky. It's a relatively obscure piano concerto in two large movements, and I don't know why this beautiful music has been so overlooked. It's great for dancing.

Costumes and set designs were by Tom Pritchard, and lighting was by Gil Wechsler. At this time Gil was the lighting designer for the Harkness Ballet, and both Tom and Gil were my close non-dancer friends (along with Aidan Mooney, who was like my brother and later became a right-hand man for Jerome Robbins). It was actually I who brought Aidan backstage and into rehearsals to view my ballets. He

Colleen Neary in the first movement of my
Kodály Dances. Photo by Martha Swope. Used
with permission of NYPL swope_780356.

quickly became a fixture of the company. Gil later became the lighting designer for the Lyric Opera of Chicago and then for many years he was the resident lighting designer for the Metropolitan Opera.

This new ballet was a thoroughly classical, Petipa-styled display piece. Arnold Spohr was the Winnipeg ballet's artistic director, and he was very happy with the result. Once again, though, I never got to see this ballet in performance because of my duties in New York. The reviews were good, but again the critics said it looked like a NYCB ballet. I took that as a compliment, of sorts. Perhaps they were trying to tell me something, but I didn't realize it at the time.

Around this time I also made *Kodály Dances* for NYCB, which was a fun little Gypsy-influenced number. The original leads were Renee Estopinal for the first movement (Colleen Neary was the alternate) and Allegra Kent and Anthony Blum for the adagio and finale, but, alas, Allegra was injured at the last minute, so Johnna Kirkland did the premiere. Clive Barnes didn't especially care for it; actually, neither did I. Against my preference, Lincoln insisted on an elaborate set, and Balanchine wanted me to cut some of the score. Barnes admonished me for "not letting my hair down" (as a choreographer), but if he'd seen the original version, before Lincoln and Balanchine got their hands on it, and seen how great Allegra had been in it, his criticisms would have been answered. It wasn't a complete waste, though. The costumes were later recycled by Balanchine for his Ravel ballet *Tzigane*.

31

Berlin

Irina Kolpakova and Yuri Soloviev . . .
and Perhaps My Own Company!

In 1972 John Taras was the ballet master of the New York City Ballet, but he was also the artistic director of the Deutsche Oper Ballet in Berlin. Taras was a fine ballet master, a decent teacher and choreographer, but he never seemed very happy, or very satisfied, working under Balanchine. He could be quite sharp with the dancers when Mr. B. wasn't around; when he was, Taras just seemed to melt into the background. Working for a genius like Balanchine could take the wind out of one at times.

Much to my surprise, one day Taras asked if I'd like to do a new ballet for the Berlin company and to also stage my *Fantasies*. Of course, I agreed. I had never worked in Europe, and what an opportunity! This commission was possible only because it was scheduled during our annual winter layoff.

I flew to Berlin, and after watching and teaching the German company for a couple of classes, I decided to do a very American-style ballet to Gershwin's *Concerto in F.* At that time, half the company's dancers were Americans. This surprised me, but I've since discovered this was common for most German companies of that period.

There were approximately sixty-five dancers, and among them were a few personalities I really liked. One was the striking young ballerina Didi Carli, whom I cast in the second movement adagio with Klaus Beelitz. The dancer in that has a "Lady of the Night" persona, and the man is her "mark," and it was quite sexy-funny. There's no story or character, but the last few seconds of the *pas* make it pretty clear what their relationship is. It always earned an appreciative chuckle from the public when I recreated it for my Los Angeles Ballet six years later.

The first movement was led by Robert Blankshine, whom I knew when he was a principal dancer with the Joffrey Ballet in New York. He was now one of the Berlin company's principal men. The last movement was for a solo girl, a powerhouse named Heidrun Schwarz, who was joined by the entire cast. The ballet was a great hit in rehearsals. The dancers seemed to love it, and there were no artistic problems. "Artistic problems," I later learned, were the norm for that company, especially when guest choreographers were invited. The German and American dancers formed two very disparate groups, and they didn't ever seem to support a guest choreographer's work. The company atmosphere wasn't the happiest. I later learned why and unfortunately got caught up in all of that company's politics.

The company's teacher, however, was really brilliant, and I loved taking her class. She was always known by her last name, Shelisnova. I am ashamed to say I never learned her first name. Mme. Shelisnova was an East German dancer who had been trained at the Kirov. She was in her very early forties, or perhaps late thirties, and had been allowed to settle in West Berlin by marrying a musician in the orchestra.

Shelisnova's protégée was the future great ballerina Eva Evdokimova. At that time Eva was the darling of the German critics, so I felt I had made a smart decision by having her in my first European production of *Fantasies*. I had put her into the part of the Blue Girl, so Shelisnova came to all those rehearsals. Had she not approved, I'm sure Eva would have withdrawn from the ballet. *Gershwin Konzert* and *Fantasies* showed two sides of my work. One was dramatic and intimate and the other a big, jazzy, fun closer. What could go wrong? A lot, it turned out.

In those years in Germany the opera's ballet companies performed only one or two nights a week and only two full weeks of ballet performances a year. The rest of the time the theater was given over to the opera. For this *Balletabend* (Ballet Evening) the program was going to be my two ballets and a version of Béla Bartók's *The Miraculous Mandarin* by Ulf Gaad, a Swedish choreographer. Its plot loosely followed the original libretto, which was all about a Chinese Mandarin and a prostitute. In Gaad's version the Mandarin gets stripped completely naked by some robbers, then is strung up and dies at the end of a noose. The full-frontal nudity was pretty gratuitous, I thought. The dancers didn't care for it in rehearsals, and I didn't much like it either, even though I normally like Bartók's music. The dancers and administration at least liked *my* two ballets, Taras seemed pleased, and everybody was dancing well, so I expected clear sailing.

After about two weeks of rehearsals, Egon Seefehlner, the theater's general manager, asked me if I wanted to be the ballet's next director. Taras's contract was ending, and he was going back to New York City Ballet full time. Pat Neary expected to get the job, as I later learned, but was not in favor with the dancers or Seefehlner, so she was not even being considered, though I don't think she knew this at the time. She had left NYCB some years before and was now their ballet mistress. I told Herr Seefehlner that I was not going to make any decision without talking to Balanchine first. I was only twenty-five and, frankly, I felt one or two ballet nights a week and then one or two complete weeks of ballet per year were not enough to keep me satisfied. I was used to being in a company that had eight performances a week and close to 250 performances a year. Also, European audiences always demanded a certain quota of *Swan Lake, Giselle,* and *Sleeping Beauty,* not something I was interested in at that time.

Seefehlner told me there wouldn't be a problem about so few performances because there was another theater in Berlin currently being used for operetta; that was also coming under his management. He told me this theater was now going to be used exclusively for ballet performances, and I would be virtually in control because it would be the "ballet's house." Moreover, they had plans in the very near future to have the company tour more. I thought that was all very interesting and it would be a very different story if those things really happened. Seefehlner then added that I would probably be making a lot more money than I could possibly make in the United States. Fortunately (or unfortunately), money has never been all that important to me, and consequently I didn't think about that aspect of the proposal. What *did* attract me more than anything was the idea of being on my own. That may sound awfully cocky for someone aged twenty-five, and who had Balanchine's blessing and practically the free use of his theater and company. However, I was starting to feel that there was no way that I could be a true choreographer if I did not get out from under Balanchine's shadow. Perhaps those reviews from San Francisco and

Winnipeg saying my ballets looked very New York City Ballet (meaning Balanchine) had seeped into my subconscious.

Whether I made it or failed, the idea of going to a large, state-supported company, one that really wanted me, was certainly attractive. The very fact that I was so young meant it wouldn't be disastrous if it didn't go well. I also felt sure I could go back to Mr. B. if it didn't work out. I finished setting my two ballets several weeks before they were due to premiere, left Pat Neary in charge of rehearsals, and went back to New York to dance the performances for which I had been scheduled and to discuss the Berlin offer with Balanchine.

Well, Mr. B. thought it would be a big mistake if I went to Berlin. He told me the machinery of a German opera house would basically just "eat me up." He said that I would have no freedom to choreograph what I wanted, as I had with him (more or less), and that I undoubtedly would be very unhappy. He also didn't think that the offer of a second theater would happen, or that more performances and touring would actually come to pass. Since he obviously had more experience and knowledge than I had, I began to have serious second thoughts.

The opening night of my *Gershwin Konzert* and *Fantasies* in Berlin was fast approaching, and I wanted to go there to be with the dancers and give them some emotional support. When I asked Balanchine for permission to get out of my performances a few days early, we looked at the schedule and saw that there was a performance of *The Four Temperaments* the same night as the Berlin premiere, and for which I was cast, as usual, to dance "Melancholic." I said to Mr. B.: "I don't know what to do. Shouldn't I be in Berlin for my premieres?" "Well," he said, smiling slyly, "That's fine, dear, you just go to Berlin, and have a good time." "Do you want to get rid of me?" I asked half-jokingly. "No, but it's not that important for you to be here. Anybody can do your part," he said.

"Now, wait one minute. Anybody cannot do my part," I protested. "Oh yes, certainly *anybody* can do 'Melancholic.' You know we can have Deni Lamont do it, or we can have Helgi Tomasson do it," he said. "Oh no," I said. "If you really are going to put somebody else in my part, then I'll stay and skip the premiere." He just smiled that smile of his. Mr. B. could always get a dancer to do exactly what he wanted, often by saying the opposite. He was a master of reverse psychology. I stayed and danced "Melancholic," skipping my German premiere. It seems it was a good thing I did. I knew nothing about the storm clouds brewing there.

I had also been invited to dance in the upcoming Berlin ballet gala, which was to take place a week after the premiere of my ballets. This was going to be very exciting because Irina Kolpakova and Yuri Soloviev, the two top stars of the Kirov Ballet, would be performing. I had never seen them, but I knew that Soloviev had been Nureyev's rival when he was still dancing with the Kirov, and, when Nureyev defected, Soloviev became the company's supreme male classicist.

Besides Kolpakova and Soloviev, Bobby Blankshine would be dancing on the gala, as were Cyril Atanassoff (of Paris Opera Ballet), Maina Gielgud (of Bejart Ballet in Lausanne), Eva Evdokimova, and other European stars of that era. This would be my first time dancing with such a distinguished group of non-Balanchine dancers, and I wanted to see how I'd measure up.

The night of the Berlin gala was also in the middle of our season, but I had no ballets with NYCB that night, so there was no conflict. Besides, I was really looking forward to dancing in Berlin and on the same program as Kolpakova and Soloviev. Talk about chutzpah!

I decided instead of doing a Balanchine *pas de deux,* or something that had been seen, I would choreograph a new piece to dance with Heidrun, my third movement lead in *Gershwin Konzert.* She was a very strong allegro dancer, so I thought I'd make a cross between Balanchine's *Valse Fantaisie* and *Tarantella.* Both ballets were very "me." The music I chose was the *Ruslan and Ludmilla* overture by Mikhail Glinka.

Upon my return to Berlin, I intended to tell Herr Seefehlner that I could not accept the artistic directorship. As flattering as that offer was, I wasn't ready to leave Balanchine. As things turned out, I was sabotaged before I even got there.

Evidently, the week before the premiere of my ballets, someone leaked that I was going to be the next director, and the German press reacted very negatively. They felt strongly against having another American. They reasonably wanted a German director for their German company. Taras's directorship had not been successful and they did not want another NYCB—or "Balanchine-style"—director.

I had not agreed to be their director anyway, and the job offer was supposed to have been kept secret while I was making my decision.

Later I learned that Gert Reinholm, a German ex-dancer from the company and now in the administration of the ballet, had always wanted to be their next director and it seems he was angered that he had been passed over. He had been stirring up trouble behind the scenes and was probably the one who leaked my name to the press. I had all that going against me even before my ballets premiered, although I didn't know this until I showed up two days before the gala. When I arrived the whole place was in turmoil.

Bobby was in tears because evidently at the opening night of my ballets he had been booed (!) as was the whole *Gershwin Konzert*. *Fantasies* had not fared much better, except that the audience hadn't actually booed (probably because the public so loved Eva). The hit of the evening had been *The Miraculous Mandarin,* which took everyone by surprise.

The night I arrived, there was to be a performance of the now-controversial program. To say I dreaded going to the theater is an understatement. I was terrified.

Before the performance I saw that Bobby's costume, which was supposed to be a deep red, had turned out pink! A shocking pink unitard on the very slim Bobby Blankshine made him look like a plucked chicken. I went to the wardrobe mistress with him and asked if we could at least put him in something else—even just practice clothes. The answer was absolutely not, and that they could never change costumes after a premiere, which gave me my first taste of what Balanchine meant about a German opera house mentality. The New York City Ballet would change costumes five minutes before a performance if that was what the choreographer wanted.

In this company you had to go through lots of red tape, make written requests, and so forth. Sigh. As I've said, Bobby was so upset that he didn't even want to dance that night. He was now faking being sick (he was a very "sensitive" boy). I said, "To hell with all this BS! Give me the damn costume and I'll dance." When I said I was going on, Bobby pulled himself together and said, "No, John, if you go out there they're going to boo you. It's going to be a big disaster." "Oh, for God's sake," I said, "You can't be serious." But Pat Neary also told me it would probably be a very bad idea if I danced because my ballets were the "scandal" of the season, and I was now a "target."

I didn't know what I had gotten myself into. Bobby finally agreed to dance, and all I wanted to do was sit in the audience to get a real feeling of what the reaction actually was. Well, guess what? It was just fine. This was the third performance of this program, and the so-called scandal (if indeed there had ever been one in the first place) had disappeared. The first movement of the *Gershwin* went over quite well, except Bobby still looked ridiculous in the pink unitard. The second movement with Didi and Klaus was a big hit. She really pulled off the sexy Cyd Charisse style of my choreography (Charisse was my inspiration for several of my later ballets), and she received many bravos. The last movement with Heidrun was also a success. Where was all the brouhaha I had heard about?

Fantasies went over very well too. I couldn't quite understand why there was all this drama over the opening night. I didn't know at this point that it was all a set-up. Politics!

An American critic who had been at the theater on the opening night told me it was obvious that a claque had been brought in to boo the premiere of my ballets. He said there was a group of ballet fans who did not want another American director. Actually, he said, the ballets had gone over very well, and it was only a group of about fifteen people in one section of the theater who did the booing. No one else booed, just this group. He told me not to worry and that it was quite common in that theater for things like this to happen. I was curious as to who brought that claque. Some people thought it was Reinholm, who wanted the job himself. I never found out whether that was so; at that point I was just glad I didn't want the directorship.

I met with Seefehlner the following day and told him I could not possibly take him up on his offer. For his part, he said that since there had been such a negative reaction to the opening night of my ballets, it would probably be best if I did not take the job. The sabotage certainly worked.

To say I was not looking forward to dancing on the gala the next day after all this drama is an understatement. I wasn't even sure I wouldn't still get booed when I went onstage. No pressure! At any rate, to top things off, I had caught a terrible cold, and for some reason the jet lag had hit me hard. Probably I was just nervous about the whole situation. I did, though, go see *Giselle* being danced by Kolpakova and Soloviev that night and came away a complete Kolpakova fan.

Irina Kolpakova was just about the most exquisite non-Balanchine-trained dancer I'd ever seen. She didn't have great extensions, a big jump, or great turns, but everything about her went together so beautifully. She had a lovely quality that is hard to describe. She made the character of Giselle so real, yet she didn't look as if she was doing anything physically phenomenal.

Soloviev, on the other hand, just soared when he jumped. He really flew and had the greatest *ballon* I'd ever seen. I had never seen double *brisés* before his, either. Usually, a *brisé* is done with one beat and then you change your legs. In the second act of *Giselle,* Soloviev did a series of sixteen consecutive double *brisés*! (Two beats, instead of just one, before the landing.) Unfortunately, he couldn't act. He was as stiff as a board and looked utterly detached. He was just a dancing machine, whereas Kolpakova really was Giselle. I did a warm-up barre with him one day and noticed how sad he looked. He seemed truly miserable. He tragically died by suicide five years later. When I heard this, all I could think was how I knew something bad was in his future based on his deep melancholia in Berlin. So sad.

I had to dance on the same stage with these people in the gala the next night? *This is ridiculous,* I thought. Some people won't believe this, but I've never been that secure about my own dancing. I enjoyed myself, certainly, when onstage—too much, my critics say—but I've never ever been pleased, really pleased, with the way I've looked in any films or videos. I was so glad that I was in a company with two genius choreographers, Balanchine and Robbins, who both seemed to value what I had to offer.

The night of the dreaded gala finally came.

At the Deutsche Oper, one had to dance on a "floor cloth." A floor cloth is canvas that's stretched over the stage and painted (if it needs to be) for the scenic requirements of different ballets or operas, but I had never danced on one. In this case it was not nailed down tightly. It still had a little give in it. For the old-fashioned ballets, where there are not a lot of quick changes of direction and so forth, that's fine; but not for the *pas* that I had just choreographed the day before the performance.

It was all based on changes of direction (which were my forte), quick starts and stops and jumping without big preparation, and for these I needed the traction that a regular floor could give. Either wood or linoleum would have been fine, but a floor that would move, even an eighth of an inch, while I was getting ready to jump, was absolutely nerve-shattering. All the European dancers were used to it. I most definitely was not!

For the gala, Kolpakova and Soloviev danced the *pas de deux* from *Les Sylphides* and the complete third act of *The Sleeping Beauty.* Bobby and Monica Vadamm danced a sweet *pas de deux* that Taras had choreographed to Benjamin Britten's *Soirée* and *Matinée Musicales.*

Evdokimova and Attilio Labis danced the complete second act of *Giselle.* Maina Gielgud and Cyril Atanasoff danced the *Grand Pas Classique,* with music by Auber and choreography by Viktor Gsovsky. Didi Carli danced the *Black Swan Pas de Deux,* with Klaus Beelitz, and Heidrun and I were set to do my *Glinka Pas de Deux.* Our placement in the program was in the middle of the second section. The first section was *Giselle* Act II, in the middle section were all the *pas de deux,* and in the last section was *The Sleeping Beauty,* Act III. I felt totally outclassed, to say the least.

The company dancers warned me not to be upset if there were some boos when the curtain went up or if my new *pas de deux* did not go over well. The press had not yet announced who the next director was, so many people still thought I was in the running. Before our dance I really expected the worst. I watched from the wings while I was warming up and saw a beautiful performance of *Giselle* by Eva, and Soloviev and Kolpakova did a lovely *Les Sylphides.* Everybody was dancing wonderfully. I thought I was going to be a mess, so I made a little vow to myself as I was counting the minutes until this nightmare was over.

I thought: *I'm here representing Balanchine and the New York City Ballet, the greatest company on the planet. I've choreographed my piece in the Balanchine style, and I'm going to show these people what that's all about. I may not be as classical a dancer or as elegant as all these Europeans, but if I move fast enough, nobody is going to notice that, nobody is going to see that my feet aren't as good as Bobby's or my jump as high as Soloviev's.* I decided I would try to dance faster than I had ever danced before, and I prayed that the conductor, Ashley Lawrence, was going to keep up with me. I had never worked with him before, and every conductor is different, so it usually takes some time to build a rapport. I told him just to go as fast as he could.

The moment came, we took our places behind the curtain, and I was ready for the worst. The curtain went up, and there was . . . applause! I couldn't believe it.

The way my *pas de deux* started was with Heidrun and me both posed on center stage. (There was a little bit of the famous overture before the curtain actually went up.) We then broke apart from our pose and, as she exited, I ran upstage to begin my first solo. Then came a short section danced together, then again alternating solos, a short section together again, and then a wham-bam finale with her doing *fouettés* and me doing *coupé jetés* around her in a circle. We then finished suddenly back in our opening pose. My *Glinka Pas de Deux* went off without a hitch. After every solo we received applause, and at the end we had to take five curtain calls! Was I relieved? Better believe it.

After the performance Seefehlner came running up to me all smiles and asked if I could maybe change my mind about taking the directorship. Just based on my little *pas de deux,* that one success on that one night, he had decided that I *must* come to Berlin, that it would be the best thing for my career, and that I should think of how John Cranko had made his success with the Stuttgart Ballet. I could do the same thing in Berlin. *Thanks, but no thanks,* I thought. If they were going to blow hot and cold that quickly—one ballet doesn't go over and then the next one does—well, that was not for me. I hightailed it back to New York, very pleased to be back in Balanchine land. Soon after I got back from Berlin, the company first heard about the impending Stravinsky Festival.

32

The 1972 Stravinsky Festival

Balanchine Triumphant!

I was more than happy to get back to the sanity of Balanchine after the chaos of Berlin. Even though I had held my own among these impressive international stars, I was not in the least inclined to become one of them. I did have offers for more international appearances, but the thought of missing out on dancing any Balanchine ballet was out of the question. I made the right decision, for soon after my return, Mr. B. discussed with me his plans for the Stravinsky Festival and my unique participation in this historic event.

The 1972 New York City Ballet Stravinsky Festival was not only one of the milestones of the company but also one of the most important theatrical dance events of the twentieth century. If you think I'm exaggerating, you weren't there.

I'm sure everyone interested in dance is aware of the close working relationship between Balanchine and Igor Stravinsky. Tchaikovsky and Petipa worked together on *The Nutcracker* and *The Sleeping Beauty,* which were milestones in music and dance for the nineteenth century. (Petipa gave Tchaikovsky detailed notes.)

Their *Swan Lake,* the most performed of all the Tchaikovsky-Petipa ballets, however, was not a true collaboration. The original premiere in 1877, with choreography at the Bolshoi by Julius Reisinger, was not a success, but in 1895 the Petipa-Ivanov version premiered at the Mariinsky with Petipa's overall plan. Tchaikovsky had died two years before this revised version, but there is evidence that he met with Petipa and was going to work with him on this new *Swan Lake.*

In our time *Apollo, Agon, Orpheus, Stravinsky Violin Concerto, Rubies, Symphony in Three Movements, Duo Concertant,* and the list goes on, opened doors for what was still possible for the classical ballet. Without these Balanchine "neo-classical" works, William Forsythe, Mark Morris, Jiri Kylian, John Neumeier, Twyla Tharp, Alexei Ratmansky, Christopher Wheeldon, Justin Peck, and, even to some degree, Jerome Robbins, would not have been able to develop their art in the same way. When Mr. B. told me he planned a weeklong celebration commencing on Stravinsky's birthday, June 18, featuring all the current Stravinsky ballets in NYCB's repertory, plus a revival of *Orpheus,* and twenty-two (!) world premieres, I was understandably ecstatic. Stravinsky had passed away the previous year, which was one of the reasons Mr. B. had not been at his best. Obviously this tribute was of great personal importance to him.

When Mr. B. announced this homage to Stravinsky, the entire company realized its significance for him. We knew this was not going to be like anything the company had done before. We were not disappointed. This anticipated program seemed insanely ambitious. Balanchine would choreograph *Symphony in Three Movements, Violin Concerto, Danses Concertantes, Divertimento from "Baiser de la Fée," Duo Concertant, Scherzo à la Russe, Pulcinella* (with Jerome Robbins), and the *Chorale Variations on Bach's Von Himmel Hoch,* plus revive *Orpheus.* There would also be his *Agon, Apollo, Rubies,* and a revised version of his one-act *Firebird.* Other choreographers represented were Jerome Robbins (*Scherzo Fantastique, Circus Polka, The Cage, Dumbarton Oaks,* and *Requiem Canticles*), John Taras (*Song of the Nightingale, Scenes de Ballet, Concerto for Piano and Winds,* and *Ebony Concerto*), Todd Bolender (*Piano-Rag-Music* and *Serenade in A*), Lorca Massine (*Ode*), and Richard Tanner (*Concerto for Two Solo Pianos* and *Octet*). I'd be presenting my own choreography to Stravinsky's massive forty-five-minute first symphony, the *Symphony in E Flat.*

Luckily, I had been interested in this music for a long time; it wasn't new to me. When Mr. B. asked which Stravinsky score I would like to choreograph, I suggested this large work. He was very pleased. The music is early Stravinsky, ultra-romantic (my forte), and it sounded to me a lot like a cross between Tchaikovsky and Rimsky-Korsakov, Stravinsky's teacher.

I had already choreographed six ballets for the company by then, including the large-scale *Stravinsky Symphony in C* (twenty-six dancers) and *Tchaikovsky Suite No. 1* (twenty-five dancers), so the grandeur of this music didn't intimidate me. I had initially envisioned using different lead couples in each of the four movements, but when I discussed this with Mr. B. he suggested I just use Peter Martins and Gelsey Kirkland as the only principal dancers. He wasn't going to be using them that much (although he later changed his mind about Peter), and he didn't want to do any new ballets for Gelsey.

Gelsey was by now totally under the influence of Maggie Black, and she rarely attended any of Mr. B.'s classes. Peter was still hanging on by a thread, and the strain between him and Balanchine had nearly reached its breaking point. It was only during rehearsals for the *Stravinsky Violin Concerto* and *Duo Concertant* that Peter finally started working well with Balanchine. Gelsey, as it turned out, only danced Robbins's twelve-minute-long *Scherzo Fantastique* (originally I was to partner her), Taras's *Song of the Nightingale,* Tanner's *Concerto for Two Solo Pianos* (with yours truly), and my *Symphony in E Flat.* Except for my rather long work, her time onstage was quite limited in these other shorter ballets. This was such a missed opportunity for her, but she had made her bed.

To watch Balanchine choreograph at this time was mind-blowing. He was practically flying from rehearsal to rehearsal, and was choreographing five or six ballets simultaneously. It made his previous work on his three-act *Jewels* look like child's play. He would start on *Symphony in Three Movements* for two hours, race across the street to the school (where the company had co-opted extra rehearsal space), choreograph some of *Baiser de la Fée* or *Danses Concertantes,* then return to the theater and continue on *Duo Concertant* or another ballet. We other choreographers had only one or two ballets to work on. It was amazing how he could do all his ballets at the same time.

Even though I was also learning several new leading roles, I made time to watch Mr. B. work as often as I could. This was always revelatory, and an inspiration, even during the frenzy surrounding this festival. I also want to comment on the concentration and professionalism demonstrated by the entire company, and especially by the corps de ballet. Normally, in any given season, the dancers are in ballets they've already performed plus one or two new works. For this occasion they were asked to learn, rehearse, and perform up to ten new ballets! This is a staggering feat, and the company pulled it off in grand style. Mr. B. was our inspiration and Stravinsky was his. Stravinsky's music is not the easiest anyway, and simultaneously working with up to seven different choreographers could have been a nightmare for the corps.

Miraculously, no one complained or was injured. Mr. B. said Stravinsky was helping us. Who could deny it?

The financial burden on the company was also rather large. Because of all the new scores the orchestra had to learn, and the work needed on the stage, lighting, costumes, and rehearsals, the company suspended public performances for one week prior to the opening night. Each evening saw a complete orchestra and stage run-through of one of the programs. Seven different programs with complete changes of décor, costumes, and lighting were necessary. This was an all-out effort, Mr. B.'s "comeback," if you will, and it was more than worth it. (The 1982 Tschaikovsky Festival—the company was now adding that "s" to Tschaikovsky's name—was less complicated because a unit set was used for every program and fewer new ballets were scheduled.)

While I was very busy with my choreography of the *Symphony in E Flat,* that was not my major concern: dancing was. I was originally cast to dance Robbins's *Scherzo Fantastique* (or thought I was, because I did the majority of the rehearsals with Gelsey) on the opening program, but one day about two weeks before the premiere, Mr. B. asked Sara Leland and me to come to the small practice room because he wanted to do "a little something." He said he had come into possession of the scherzo movement of an early Stravinsky piano sonata and he wanted concert pianist Mme. Madeleine Malraux, his personal friend, to play this three-minute piece and for us to dance it. Mr. B. then choreographed this lovely non-bravura *pas de deux* at breakneck speed, barely stopping for a breath, and never letting us repeat a sequence to make sure we had it. He spent all of one hour and a half, seemed pleased, told us to go over it again with Mme. Malraux, said, "Bye, bye," and dashed off to another rehearsal.

When we began to rehearse this after Balanchine had raced away, we realized that Mme. Malraux had not been keeping up with him. What had happened was that she had repeated some sections of music because she thought he was re-doing certain sequences instead of just continuing. Consequently, certain sections didn't match what Mr. B.

had just choreographed. We basically had to accommodate these discrepancies, as we knew it would be impossible to catch Mr. B. on the fly, and this *pas* was so slight and unpretentious that we thought it was just a filler anyway.

We didn't even have any idea of where this piece was to go on the program because it hadn't been scheduled. The morning of the opening night, Mr. B. told Sally and me to meet him in the wardrobe room where he would pick out our costumes for "tonight." What? It seems that he wanted the first dance of the festival to be our little *pas de deux*! Talk about pressure! For Sally he chose a simple pearl grey costume that consisted of a plain bodice and a knee-length chiffon skirt, and small-heeled character shoes. I wore a white blouse, grey satin knickers, white tights under those, and white ballet shoes. I had quite a lot of *batterie* (small beats), so character shoes were not appropriate, even though this was definitely a demi-character dance.

June 18 arrived and the momentous premiere evening began with three orchestral works: *Fanfare for a New Theatre, Greeting Prelude* (Stravinsky's variation on "Happy Birthday"), and *Fireworks*. Mr. B. and Lincoln Kirstein then came out in front of the curtain, each carrying a shot glass filled with vodka. Mr. B. said it was a Russian tradition to "Toast to the health of the guy that died." While this was happening, a piano was rolled out behind the curtain and Mme. Malraux, Sally, and I took our places. Mr. B. and Lincoln thanked the audience for sharing this celebration of Stravinsky's music and left the stage. Mr. B. had one more thing to say. He immediately returned to the front of the curtain alone and told the audience he had a "leeetle surprise." He said he had found a Stravinsky piano sonata written before he was born, but he knew that Stravinsky had written it for him. He told the audience he had invited Madeleine Malraux to play it, and that it would be danced by "Sara Leland and Cleeeford." *Ha!* I thought. *I don't even get a full name.* But I loved the casualness of it all. Once again, Mr. B. was demonstrating how unique the relationship was between our company and our audience. Of course, he only needed to use my last name because the audience knew full well who I was—just as they knew all the other dancers. The audience was like our family. Mr. B. was the proud papa showing off his children. And how very like him to begin a potentially pretentious festival with this "leeetle something."

Mr. B. always compared himself to a chef; well, here, we were the hors d'oeuvres. The real meal was to come, and what a feast it was! Sally and I did our thing to warm applause, and so the Stravinsky Festival began.

After the sonata "surprise" came Robbins's *Scherzo Fantastique* led by Gelsey Kirkland, now with Bart Cook. I had done all the rehearsals; but when Mr. B. decided to use me in the sonata there was no time for a costume change, so Robbins put Bart into the part. The rest of the cast were Victor Castelli, Steven Caras, and Bryan Pitts. I didn't watch that ballet because I was changing so as to get out front for the premiere of *Symphony in Three Movements*. This was the one ballet about which I had been most apprehensive while watching in rehearsal. It is a huge work, with six principal dancers, who, for the premiere were Sara Leland and Eddie Villella (the *pas de deux*), Helgi Tomasson and Lynda Youth, and Marnee Morris and Ricky Weiss. In addition there were five solo couples, and sixteen corps de ballet girls. Musically it is one of Stravinsky's most rhythmically difficult works, and what Mr. B. had come up with choreographically made the complexity of *Agon* look simple. Fugues, canons, asymmetrical patterns, and the sheer output of energy place this ballet in a class of its own, which made it very difficult to rehearse.

During rehearsals it looked like a mess. I couldn't figure out what Mr. B. had in mind, but as usual he was calm and collected while working, and he was not fazed when rehearsal after rehearsal was ragged. Only at the very last onstage run-through did he bring it all together. It was truly magical. With the simplest of modifications, he straightened out all the tangles and confusion of the previous rehearsals. At one point, and while the whole cast was dancing full-out in the finale, he actually went up on the stage and walked around and in-between the moving dancers. I don't know how he avoided getting kicked. He would take one dancer by the hand and move that person over a few inches, or take a couple and move them slightly forward or back—seemingly simple things. I was watching from the front and these slight alterations brought the whole ballet into focus. It seemed as if he knew all along what to fix but hadn't had the time to do it until that last stage rehearsal. With these simple manipulations, all was made clear, logic made visible, genius on full display. Watching him do this simply took my breath away. I was sitting with Renee when this was happening and she turned to me and said, "He's not human!" I could only agree.

Above left: Me and Sara Leland in *Symphony in Three Movements*. Photo by Martha Swope. Used with permission of NYPL swope_781703. Choreography by George Balanchine © The George Balanchine Trust.

Above right: Me and Sara Leland in *Symphony in Three Movements*. Photo by Martha Swope. Used with permission of NYPL swope_781702. Choreography by George Balanchine © The George Balanchine Trust.

Leading the men in *Symphony in Three Movements* the year Balanchine added pants (he cut them the following season). Photo by Martha Swope. Used with permission of NYPL swope_781427. Choreography by George Balanchine © The George Balanchine Trust.

The premiere of *Symphony in Three Movements* was like an explosion. Lines were straight, energy was electric, and all the dancers danced better than I had ever seen them dance before. This was the first ballet of the festival featuring the corps de ballet and they were out for blood. Dynamite! As for the principals—perfection! The ovation after this ballet really sounded more like a football game cheer. And, joy of joys, after Villella's second performance, Balanchine cast me in his role, and only I danced it until I left the company.

In fact, Mr. B. brought me back many times as guest artist to dance this, one of my favorite ballets.

Balanchine then scored a theatrical coup by premiering the *Stravinsky Violin Concerto*, a more intimate, possibly more accessible work, right after the much bigger *Symphony in Three Movements*.

From its first complete run-through, it was clear that *Violin Concerto* was a major work. Less frantic and less architecturally complicated than the *Symphony*, it used its eight corps de ballet couples in witty and innovative ways, framing the heart of the ballet, which was its two contrasting *pas de deux*. The first, for Karin von Aroldingen and Jean-Pierre Bonnefoux, showcased her muscular sensuality and acrobatic ability and his panther-like attack and grace. The second *pas de deux*, for Mazzo and Martins, was ultra-romantic and depended greatly on their physical contrast. She, delicate and dark-haired, and he, tall and blond and always there to support and catch her when she (purposely) fell off balance: the man continually manipulating the woman, but with her consent. Beautiful!

Symphony in Three Movements followed by the *Stravinsky Violin Concerto*—what on earth could follow that? *Firebird,* in the newly refurbished Marc Chagall décor and costumes, had been premiered three years earlier as a showcase for the then-seventeen-year-old Gelsey Kirkland. For this evening, Balanchine had replaced Gelsey with von Aroldingen, and the Firebird's costume had been changed from the hummingbird-styled mini-tutu worn by Gelsey into a huge-winged, all-white affair complete with a train and an enormous headpiece. This costume was based on the Chagall painted front drop. Poor Karin could barely move, let alone dance. Mr. B. wanted this ballet to be about Stravinsky and Chagall, and by reducing the Firebird to practically a mimed role, this was what he accomplished.

Gelsey Kirkland and Peter Martins in
the premiere of my *Symphony in E Flat*.
Photos by Martha Swope. Used with
permission of NYPL swope_781215 and
swope_781216.

If *Firebird* was a letdown, it didn't really matter. After all that had
gone before, the audience was exhausted but exhilarated. Mr. B. was
back! If he never choreographed another thing before or after *Symphony
in Three Movements* and the *Violin Concerto*, that night he had secured
himself an honored place in dance history.

We still had six nights to go, and program number two was my
night. That evening began with my *Symphony in E Flat*. It went over re-
spectably and Richard Buckle gave it a wonderful review in the *London
Times*. Gelsey and Peter danced well, although she was such a sourpuss
for all her rehearsals that I was pleased to replace her with Merrill Ashley for our appearances in Saratoga. Merrill really came out of herself
in this role (more on that later).

Next came *The Cage* by Robbins, followed by John Taras's all-male
Concerto for Piano and Winds. This tanked. Then came some real fun
for me as a dancer. Mr. B. had choreographed a completely new version of his Ballet Russe de Monte Carlo success *Danses Concertantes*,
which originally starred the legendary Alexandra Danilova and Frederic

Above: Me and Christine Redpath in *Danses Concertantes*. Photo by Martha Swope. Used with permission of NYPL swope_781696. Choreography by George Balanchine © The George Balanchine Trust.

Right: Me and Christine Redpath in *Danses Concertantes*. Photo by Martha Swope. Used with permission of NYPL swope_781696. Choreography by George Balanchine © The George Balanchine Trust.

Franklin. Lynda Yourth and I were the leads in this, with four *pas de trois* completing the cast. I believe the choreography was probably superior for the jazzy fourth *pas de trois,* but, according to Danilova, it was the same with the original production. The music for the *pas de deux* is less catchy and rhythmic than that for the fourth *pas de trois,* but the opening and especially the finale were my showcases.

Mr. B. used much of my flexibility, such as having my partner support me in a big attitude *penchée* or by having me rest in a fifth position grand *plié* for what seemed like forever. Lynda was soon replaced by Sara Leland, and then by a particular favorite of his, Christine Redpath. Both these girls were wittier dancers than Lynda, and Mr. B. wanted a very Commedia dell'Arte, almost Music Hall approach for this ballet. He kept me, and only me, in this until my departure, but he changed my partners quite a bit. Years later, it was revived successfully for Robert La Fosse and Darci Kistler, both very theatrical personalities. Mr. B. always told me "more Hollywood" for this ballet. He knew what worked.

The third night was a smörgåsbord. There were no major new works other than possibly the *Divertimento from "Le Baiser de la Fée"* with Patricia McBride and Helgi Tomasson. (After I left the company Mr. B. added a plaintive ending where the lovers are pulled apart, which gives it a pathos it didn't have at the 1972 premiere.) Mr. B. created a wonderful and very unusual solo for Helgi and a bright, technically difficult variation for Patty, which foreshadows some of the pointe work he would later refine and bring to a stunning culmination for Merrill Ashley in *Ballo della Regina.*

My duty for this third program was to dance the lead with Sara Leland in John Taras's *Ebony Concerto,* a reworking of his earlier version. We barely had any rehearsal time and it was over before I knew it. I scarcely remember dancing it at all.

Also on the program were Richard Tanner's *Octet* for four couples; *The Faun and the Shepherdess,* which was sung and not danced; and Balanchine's delightful romp for a female corps dressed like Russian peasants and led by Karin and Kay to *Scherzo à la Russe.* The program closed with Robbins's *Circus Polka,* danced by forty-eight children from the school, with Jerry himself as the Ringmaster. It finished with all the children forming the giant initials and periods I.S. This went over very well again when danced by the students of the Paris Opera Ballet in 1974, on a night when I had the honor of dancing *Rubies* with Patricia McBride as "étoiles invitées."

The fourth program began with John Taras's *Scènes de Ballet,* a lovely romantic work for McBride and Bonnefoux, and then another Balanchine masterpiece, *Duo Concertant.* I was sitting in my usual place out front in the last row of the First Ring, next to Mr. B (these were the ballet master's seats). He usually preferred watching from the first wing stage right, but on this night he was watching from the front. I had not seen *Duo Concertant* in rehearsal, although Ronnie Bates had told me it was one of Balanchine's most unusual and romantic works. I had no idea that this was a big understatement.

The curtain rose to reveal a piano downstage right, with our pianist Gordon Boelzner and concertmaster Lamar Alsop in place by its side. Standing next to the musicians were Kay and Peter in simple practice clothes. The first movement was played as an overture, with Kay and Peter just listening. After this section, they walked, hand in hand, to center stage and stood calmly side by side. The pianist began to play, and the dancers began by moving only their outside foot to the side and then quickly back, in exact time to the rhythm. Then, when the violin joined in, their arms began to move in a complicated counterpoint to their feet, to the music, and to each other's arms. As more of the melody emerged, they began to pantomime playing a violin, but still kept time with their feet. Peter also made motions with his arms as if they were the hands of a clock. So, in just a matter of seconds, rhythm, image of time, and the melody had been choreographically linked. Peter and Kay then backed up and began to dance. Nothing too complicated, just sweet and simple steps. The second dance movement (the third musically) was an adagio, very romantic. The following musical movement featured alternating solos for the dancers, and then the real magic of this work, the final section.

This movement began in total darkness, except for the music-stand lights for the musicians. The music started and a single spotlight focused on Kay's face, with her looking down as if in thought. She brought her right hand up to her lips, kissed her fingers, and reached out as if blowing a kiss. She then brought that hand back and covered her cheek, and turned her face away. All this took place on a blackened stage with only the follow-spot lighting her. The light faded out on Kay. Then a small follow-spot came up on center stage and Peter's hand reached into it. At first all we saw was his hand and arm up to his elbow. Then Kay's hand came into this light and took his hand. Peter lifted and turned her hand and kissed the back of it, and knelt at her feet, looking down. He was now fully lit in a follow-spot, but all we could see of Kay was her arm and hand above him, as if hanging in space. Another spotlight came up on Kay's feet and traveled up her body, fully revealing her. As this happened, Peter raised his gaze following this light. When she was fully seen, he stood and backed up, almost as if he was discovering her for the first time. He then ran to her and the dance began with them first twining their arms around each other as if two vines were growing together.

The ensuing adagio was one of longing, yearning, coming together, and separation. This movement was one of the most emotionally exposed of all Balanchine's oeuvre, somewhat similar to his *Meditation* for Suzanne Farrell and Jacques d'Amboise, but more subtle and obscure. At the end Peter knelt at Kay's feet, as if in prayer, after kissing the back of her upraised hand. All we saw was her hand suspended in mid-air and Peter at her feet. This was a repeat of that earlier image.

When the curtain descended, there was a moment of silence. The audience was that moved. It was the most emotional night of the festival. Then the ovation started and wouldn't end. Mr. B. just sat there. I said, "Go take a bow or they won't stop." He looked at me and said in the quietest voice, "I did it for her." Whom did he mean? Later, he told me it was for Kay, but I'd always imagined it really was for his lost love, Suzanne. When she returned to the company Suzanne did indeed dance it. I personally preferred Kay though.

With the *Stravinsky Violin Concerto* and *Duo Concertant*, he gave Kay and all the rest of us two wonderful gifts. No one has ever really been able to replace her, in my opinion. In both those ballets, *Violin Concerto* and *Duo Concertant*, Kay and Peter were so perfect together physically, and artistically, that they are almost impossible to equal. Mr. B. always said, "Only God creates; I assemble." He called himself just a craftsman. But after *Duo Concertant*, I wasn't so sure.

This masterpiece was followed by Taras's *Song of the Nightingale*, a disappointment even with Gelsey as the lead; coming after *Duo* was a certainly a challenge. The program ended with *Rubies*, wonderfully danced by McBride and Villella. I was glad I wasn't dancing it that night because I would have missed seeing *Duo* from the front.

The fifth program, on June 23, began with Tanner's *Concerto for Two Solo Pianos*.

Balanchine had given me this music to choreograph a few years earlier, but I found it too dry for my taste and I had learned by then not to tackle a score that Balanchine was thinking about possibly using himself. Tanner cast Gelsey and me as the leads with solo roles for

Colleen Neary and James Bogan. It didn't go over too well and was soon dropped from the repertoire, as were Tanner's other ballets.

I was really looking forward to the second ballet on that program, *Piano-Rag-Music,* which Todd Bolender had choreographed for me and Gloria Govrin. It was one huge joke. Just imagine the voluptuous Jane Russell or a black-haired Anna Nicole Smith *en pointe*! Gloria is about five feet nine, and has the same curves, and compared to my five feet eight, she absolutely towered over me when she was on full pointe.

Her costume was all bright day-glo orange. Orange tights, shoes, leotard, practice skirt, and a bright white-and-orange polka-dot bow on the top of her head completed this cartoon picture. I was dressed as a sort of Dead End Kid, all in purple, complete with a baseball cap. Gloria and I were put through every conceivable comic contortion. At one point, she picked me up by my sweatshirt and threw me across the stage! At another, I did a handspring over her shoulders while she was standing on toe. Our pianist was again Mme. Malraux, and as usual she did not use a score. Unfortunately, during the premiere she skipped a few bars of music, which luckily didn't throw "Glo" and me off too much. It was such a comedy anyway, no one would have noticed.

This joke *pas de deux* went over extremely well both in New York and later on tour. I think the audience needed a little comic relief, and we were glad to give it to them.

Robbins's *Dumbarton Oaks* followed. It was charmingly danced by Allegra Kent and Anthony Blum, took place on a tennis-court set, and was very "Great Gatsby." The finale had all the boys in tap shoes and even though Jerry changed this ballet numerous times, I personally prefer his original version.

The closing ballet was for some reason not as big a success as we had all thought it would be. Balanchine's *Pulcinella,* led by Villella and Violette Verdy, was an all-out slapstick comedy. Why it didn't work is beyond me. It had a mock-funeral, crossdressing prostitutes, a wily Devil danced by Francisco Moncion, and a knockdown spaghetti fight. I thought it was a hoot. The tour de force was the appearance of Robbins with Balanchine himself: they played two beggars dancing an "Anything you can do I can do better" contest to the famous "Vivo" part of the score. (Balanchine won the contest.) The ballet ended with the entire cast begging the audience for food, or if not that, at least for applause! The audience loved it, but the critics were cool. Perhaps

Above: *Piano-Rag-Music* with me and Gloria Govrin. Photo by Martha Swope. Used with permission of NYPL swope_781006.

Left: *Piano-Rag-Music* with me and Gloria Govrin in Saratoga performance. Photo by Martha Swope. Used with permission of NYPL swope_781006.

it's time for a revival; Balanchine and Robbins wore big masks so you couldn't tell who they were, and they didn't dance those roles in the filming in Berlin the following year.

The final program of the festival began with the great Bach *Chorale Variations on Von Himmel Hoch* as orchestrated by Stravinsky. This beautiful ballet was performed only once for the festival and unfortunately was never revived. It had a huge cast led by Melissa Hayden, Violette Verdy, Sara Leland, Anthony Blum, and Peter Martins. It was simple, elegant, and unlike anything else Balanchine choreographed for the festival. It had some similarities to his *Monumentum pro Gesualdo* in that it had gorgeous architectural formations for the large corps, but it also had solos for Hayden, Verdy, and Leland. The costumes were white leotards and short white practice skirts for all the women and white T-shirts, black tights, and white sox and ballet slippers for all the men. I was in it (nearly everyone was), so sadly I never got to see it from the front.

Jerome Robbins's properly austere and somber *Requiem Canticles* followed, and this ballet was later taken into the repertoire of The Royal Ballet with great success. It used a medium-sized corps de ballet but no soloists. Everyone wore black unitards. There was no bravura dancing, but the ballet made a dramatic if somewhat depressing impact, much like the music.

Mr. B. had earlier choreographed this score as tribute to Dr. Martin Luther King Jr. soon after his assassination. That version featured Arthur Mitchell as a sort of martyr figure and Suzanne Farrell was a weeping figure in white. That ended with the large corps de ballet placing lit candelabras on a slowly darkening stage. I was very moved when I saw it and have never forgotten the finality and sadness of that concluding image.

The last work of the festival was the *Symphony of Psalms*. For this, Balanchine requested that the entire company simply sit on the stage surrounding the chorus, who were placed on a raised platform. What a perfect way to close this unique, and, as time would prove, monumental creative achievement.

The choreographers, dancers, musicians, stagehands, and audiences knew this was a very personal moment for the man we all loved and respected. With this festival Balanchine was saying good-bye to his friend, peer, and in many ways his mentor. Now Stravinsky was with Mozart and Tchaikovsky, and Mr. B. would converse with him as he claimed he did with them. Mr. B. was a true mystic and believed in a very fundamental way that he was in contact with those who'd come before. I did not doubt him.

}}

The 1972 Soviet Tour

Kiev—St. Petersburg—Tbilisi—Moscow

After the excitement of the Stravinsky Festival, we had barely caught our breath when it was announced that we were going on a six-week tour of the Soviet Union. There would be four weeks in Russia and then two in Poland. We were told this right before our annual summer Saratoga season and we knew this was going to be very important, not only for Balanchine but for our company's international prestige.

The company had not toured Russia since 1962, a decade before, and at that time they had been a huge success. This tour would begin the following September, in two months, and Konstantin Sergeyev, then the artistic director of the Kirov Ballet, would soon be coming to Saratoga to discuss which ballets to bring. Mr. B. had many new dancers to show off and practically an entirely new repertory, what with all these new Stravinsky and Robbins ballets, so, clearly, we were all excited to strut our stuff.

I knew the only Stravinsky ballets that would be going were Balanchine's and Robbins's and that none of the other choreographers' works could be included, but I didn't mind as I was overjoyed that this would give me a chance to dance in Russia, and I hoped, in front of Plisetskaya. I didn't know what other ballets were scheduled but soon found that my dance card would be more than full. I was cast in my usual roles in Robbins's *Dances at a Gathering* and *Goldberg Variations*, the Scherzo in Balanchine's *Suite No. 3* (later called *Tschaikovsky Suite No. 3*), the third movement in *Symphony in C*, and, new for me, the *pas de trois* in *Emeralds*. I had never danced this before, but Mr. B. wanted me on the *Jewels* program, and since Villella was cast for all the

Rubies (he had been a major hit on their earlier Russian tour), dancing that *pas de trois* was the only way I'd be seen on that program. It seems Balanchine wanted me on for every single performance.

One morning during the Saratoga season before the Russian tour, Balanchine told us that Sergeyev would be giving us the company class that day. None of us were quite prepared for this surprise, and as usual, Gelsey wasn't there. I'm sure Balanchine would have wanted to show her off too.

Mr. B. stood in the doorway watching this class, and it was amusing to see that he was actually nervous. We tried our best, and it was eye-opening how alike the two men's classes were. Balanchine's was more musical and faster, but the underlying schooling was very similar. Worth noting is that Sergeyev reminded us always to stop in a tight fifth position when doing *battement tendus*. Balanchine looked annoyed, as that was precisely the way he wanted us to do it, and I guess we weren't doing it that well.

Later that afternoon some officials from the State Department lectured us as to how to conduct ourselves while in the Soviet Union. Things were much different then, and we were reminded that we were representatives of the U.S.A. and not just the New York City Ballet. We were told not to fraternize with the locals, as this could put them in serious jeopardy. We would be visiting, but they would have to face the consequences of being too friendly with us "decadent" Americans. The dancers who had been on the previous Russian tour filled our heads with horror stories of the bad food, lack of toilet paper, and inadequate heating. They advised us to bring cans of tuna, toilet paper, and extra vitamins as a precaution. Each New York City Ballet dancer could share a small trunk with another dancer, so Sally and I packed ours with nothing but canned tuna and toilet paper. It was a good thing we did. All those stories were true!

One special event that took place in Saratoga was Merrill Ashley's début in my new Stravinsky ballet. Gelsey had decided to stay in New York City to study with Maggie (she told Balanchine she was sick), which meant I needed a replacement. Merrill had gotten some nice roles by then but had not yet lived up to her potential. I kept telling Mr. B. that she was just insecure, especially dancing his ballets, so he just kept waiting patiently for her to blossom and get stronger. Well, she certainly changed his opinion the night she replaced Gelsey. She was a revelation. My ballet had a lot of Plisetskaya-style jumps, such as kicking the back of the head in a *grand jeté*, and other over-the-top Bolshoi theatrics. Gelsey had balked at these tricks as she was going through her "classical" ballerina phase. She did them all later in Baryshnikov's version of *Don Quixote* but at NYCB she didn't want to do anything unless Maggie gave it her blessing. Merrill had no qualms about doing what I asked, and since she wasn't dancing a Balanchine ballet, she wasn't at all nervous. Her partner was Peter, which gave her even more confidence because he was such a strong partner. By then, six years after he joined, he was mentally more committed to the company.

That night was a turning point for the way Balanchine saw Merrill. She danced extremely cleanly, doing the same allegro steps as fast as Gelsey, but with longer legs, and an even sharper attack. Balanchine told me later that night, after her amazing performance, "Now, she's finally awake." Later, when he choreographed *Ballo della Regina* for her, I recognized some of what was first displayed years before, especially that kick-your-head *jeté*, which was not typical at all for Balanchine's usual choreography.

In Gelsey's book she claims that Balanchine handed out some sort of amphetamines to get us "pumped up" before the performances. As

Merrill Ashley in *Symphony in E Flat* (in Saratoga performance). Courtesy of the author.

I was there, I can state categorically that this is false. What did happen was that our company doctor handed out vitamins because the quality of food in Russia was sub par. I had brought an over-the-counter food supplement called Energall that was mostly vitamin E and some caffeine, I believe. This did give one a slight kick—like drinking a few cups of coffee. Balanchine was always totally against drugs, even tobacco. The assertion that he supplied uppers to the dancers is ridiculous.

Our first city on the Russian tour was Kiev. It was late September, and the place was dreary, cold, and depressing. At that time you couldn't even get a Coke or a decent green salad. The people, however, were great. Warm, generous, fair-haired, and extremely attractive. (To me, looking out the windows of the bus that took us to the theater, the men looked like Vladimir Vasiliev and the women looked like his beautiful ballerina wife, and also Bolshoi Ballet star, Ekaterina Maximova.)

The maids in the hotel and some of security guards looked uncomfortable around us, however, and since we were all spoiled rotten Americans, I'm sure we must have gotten on their nerves. The lack of amenities was overwhelming for us pampered westerners, and when we asked the hotel staff for something simple, like more blankets, we were met with glares. On the rare occasions we weren't in the hotel or theater, the very friendly local teenagers constantly followed us around, asking for chewing gum or ballpoint pens. However, since our lives revolved around the theater, we really never saw much besides that. Still, Russia in 1972 was a shock.

The first theater we danced in was a 1950s Soviet-style convention hall and not the elegant opera house I had hoped for. Actually, for that whole Russian tour, we never played in a regular theater. To offset the expense of bringing our whole company, bigger venues were chosen over the more traditional smaller theaters where ballets were normally performed. This was a pity, because Russia has some lovely old opera houses that would have been perfect for Balanchine's ballets. As it was, the auditorium in Kiev was freezing (they wouldn't turn on the heat until late October) and the wooden stage was very uneven. We were thankful to have our own portable Marley (linoleum) floor covering, but unlike today, we did not have a fully portable "sprung" dance floor. So if the stages were rock hard, as they all turned out to be, that was our tough luck.

Balanchine had decided to cast Gelsey with me in the third movement of *Symphony in C*, which infuriated her, as she had been dancing the second movement adagio. That is really the "ballerina's" movement, whereas the third movement is considered the "man's" movement because of all the jumps. Gelsey was still seething about this when the time came for the bows. Normally, Balanchine would have all four principal couples go out in front of the curtain at the same time, but the first night in Kiev he told us to go out as individual couples.

I assumed Kay Mazzo (who replaced Gelsey in the second movement) and Conrad Ludlow would bow last. But Balanchine first sent out Lynda Yourth and her partner Frank Ohman (fourth movement leads), then Violette Verdy and Jean-Pierre Bonnefoux, (first movement leads), then Kay and Conrad (second movement leads) and then, surprise, surprise, he sent me and Gelsey out for the final bow. This was completely without precedent. I was ecstatic, knowing that this was a great honor, but when I turned to Gelsey she was still pouting.

She was miserable the whole time we were in Russia and never took Balanchine's class, even when he requested it, because the Russian teachers were usually watching his classes. Gelsey actually had the nerve to do her own barre onstage in the wings to a tape of Maggie's voice while Balanchine was giving the morning company class on the stage. We could all hear Maggie's voice, even Balanchine, but he just ignored it. Any other teacher would have thrown her out, or at the very least, out of ear-shot. He was amazingly patient with her.

Unfortunately, I had a disaster on the next-to-last night in Kiev. I was dancing both *Suite No. 3* and *Dances at a Gathering* on the same program, and waiting offstage during intermission in a freezing theater wasn't helpful. I evidently had not warmed up enough again for the second ballet and I badly pulled my groin muscle (on the inside of the thigh, the adductor magnus). I didn't feel it that night, but the next morning when I tried to get out of bed, I felt a shooting pain. I literally could not stand up. I hobbled to the bus waiting to take us to the theater and told Balanchine I didn't think I could dance that night. My timing couldn't have been worse. Villella had just told him five minutes earlier that he was leaving the tour after Kiev. This meant that I was the only one to dance *Rubies*! When we got to the Leningrad performances the following week I had to dance it, no matter what.

I was taken out of the Robbins ballets, since Ricky Weiss could do those, and Mr. B. also replaced me in the *pas de trois* in *Emeralds*. Deni Lamont replaced me in *Suite No. 3*, but I somehow had to manage to dance *Rubies* and *Symphony in C* at all costs. So, from then on, I was taken to a hospital at eight in the morning for electrical stimulation treatments on my leg. For the performances, I wore a very tight elastic bandage that helped a bit, and I was able to change a few steps that were impossible to do with my bad leg.

One positive thing about being injured was that I had a little more free time. In Leningrad (now St. Petersburg), I was able to accompany John Taras and Eugenia Ourossoff, the managing director of SAB, on a private tour of the Vaganova Choreographic Institute, the school for the Kirov Ballet. I found the training impeccable for the first three levels (years), but after that something seemed to go wrong. The older students' bodies were less sleek and the technique was hit or miss. Of course, they had some amazing dancers, but given the sheer number of students, more than three hundred, I was surprised at how low the percentage was for their top level. In New York we had far fewer students but the ratio was better. I believe it was because of the choreographic stagnation in Russian ballet at that time. This is something that has now changed, mainly because both the Kirov Ballet (now Mariinsky) and the Bolshoi have opened their doors to Western choreography, especially Balanchine's. Both companies now dance many Balanchine ballets (some staged by yours truly), and their dancers are on a much higher level in general.

I was thoroughly depressed because I so desperately wanted to dance my best in Russia. Mr. B. was sympathetic, but I had a job to do, and even though he never said anything, I knew I had let him down. One amusing side note is that at the Sports Hospital in Tbilisi, our third city on the tour, as I was having my usual fifteen-minute long treatment, the nurses forgot about me and I was left all alone, not knowing how to turn off the machine. After the fifteen minutes were up, I thought my leg was on fire. After that awful scare, I found that I had been bitten by fleas while in the bed! Not a good day.

Tbilisi itself was not like any other Russian city, nor were its people. Strictly speaking it is not even Russian, and this Georgian state is now a separate nation. At that time, though, it was still part of the Soviet

Union, and the home of Balanchine's ancestral family, even though Balanchine himself was born in St. Petersburg.

They are a handsome people with tan, almost Mediterranean complexions and jet-black hair. The men are exceedingly good looking and the women are exotically beautiful. Many great dancers have come from there, and Balanchine claimed he would live to be 130, based on the longevity typical among these people. A pity he was so wrong, and the disease that ended his life might actually have been contracted there.

Tbilisi was not an especially clean city, and many of the dancers contracted a stomach parasite. There had been a big dinner party after the closing night, featuring what is known as a "goat grab," where a roasted goat is served almost whole. The diners grab chunks of meat from it with their hands. The day after this party several dancers got violently ill and had to be sent back to America. Luckily, Peter and I skipped the party. I always wondered if that was where Mr. B. contracted the disease that would eventually kill him.

Our American girls were regularly accosted on the streets by the very aggressive Georgian men, who were unaccustomed to the fair skin and blonde hair of some of our beauties. Our hotel was walking distance from the theater but the girls could not walk safely alone, and some of our more muscular men had to accompany them everywhere. It was not just the girls who were popular. Poor Bryan Pitts, the handsomest, blondest boy in the company (he was only nineteen and had hair the color of corn silk) was constantly followed around and flirted with by the ardent Georgian men; he was actually groped on one occasion, which totally freaked him out. That was the last time he walked anywhere alone.

Balanchine's brother Andria, a noted composer, lived in Tbilisi, and Balanchine's return was something of a national event as well as a family reunion. The theater was literally mobbed for every performance, and on more than one occasion, the police were called to hold back the crowds. They were quite literally breaking down the doors to see the company and the works of their most famous export.

To my relief, by the time we got to Moscow my leg was almost back to normal. Those treatments had worked. In Moscow we had a special demonstration by the Bolshoi school, with their various levels doing a private performance for us in their little theater attached to the school. One boy really stood out. He had extensions as high as Victor Castelli's. Victor was very proud of his sky-high leg extensions and he wasn't too happy to see a youngster match his own.

Balanchine then scheduled a reciprocal demonstration class by us for these students and their teachers, after which the company performed the complete *Stravinsky Violin Concerto*. Most of the Russian students could not afford tickets to the performances, so this really was a special treat for them. Balanchine pointedly asked Gelsey to attend this class, but once again she didn't appear.

Balanchine pulled out all the stops for this class. He had our corps girls moving at a tempo unheard of in Russia, and the boys doing extremely difficult combinations, both musically and technically. The teachers were surprised that the corps de ballet dancers took the class along with principals and were equally good technically, as this wasn't expected in Russian companies of that time. In Russian companies the principals and solo-level dancers took a class separate from that of the corps de ballet.

Normally Balanchine didn't allow tricks in class, but not that day. He even gave a special adagio combination just so that Victor could show off his high leg extensions. The teachers all laughed, as it was clear that Victor was competing with the young boy from the previous day. Mr. B. asked me if I was up to doing my "tricks," as he called them, and I said, "I'll try."

For my specialty, split-split *grand jetés*, and double *en dedans saut de basques*, Balanchine let me loose. These steps are quite common for male Russian dancers but at that time were not done much in the West, and were never done at the faster tempos Balanchine wanted. Because of my prior classes with the Bolshoi and Plisetskaya and Messerer, I was able to learn these maneuvers.

When Balanchine had me do them in his class it caused quite a stir. By having me do a Russian male virtuoso step I think he was just showing them, "See, we can do this too!" He used my double *en dedans saut de basques* in *Symphony in C* when I was dancing the third movement lead, but no other NYCB dancer did this in that ballet. Later Peter Martins added them to his variation in *Tchaikovsky Pas de Deux*. At that time though, Balanchine never used these tricks in any of his other ballets.

The last night's performance in Moscow was at the huge Kremlin Palace of Congresses, and it was a triumph. During the entire tour the loudest applause and best reviews were for Balanchine's ballets, not Jerry's. Comments from the audience and press continually stressed the uniqueness of Balanchine's vision. Robbins's ballets were well liked but were considered less "revolutionary." The *Stravinsky Violin Concerto* and all of *Jewels* were the high points, choreographically speaking. Audiences just went wild for them every night. Balanchine had made it his habit to go in front of the curtain after the last performance in each city and invite the audience to come see us in the next town. For closing night in Moscow, he invited them all to come to New York! That got a loud and appreciative laugh from the Russian audience, but I couldn't help wondering what our KGB handlers thought of it. We knew they were always shadowing us everywhere we went.

After the curtain came down on our closing ballet, *Symphony in C,* and the bows were finally over, we dancers were asked to join Balanchine on the stage, where he was getting an award from the minister

Company bows of *Symphony in C* on our closing night in Moscow. *Left to right:* Verdy, Ludlow, Mazzo, Kirkland, Irving, Clifford, Yourth, and Ohman (not seen is Bonnefoux who is next to Verdy). Photographer unknown.

Me and Marnee Morris in *Suite No. 3* (later titled *Tschaikovsky Suite No. 3*). Photo by Martha Swope. Used with permission of NYPL swope_780265s. Choreography by George Balanchine © The George Balanchine Trust.

of culture. As the usual speeches were winding down, suddenly all the press people turned their backs to Balanchine and the minister and started taking pictures of a beautifully dressed woman with striking red-auburn hair who had just entered. It was Plisetskaya, with her tall and handsome husband Rodion Shchedrin in tow. She was wearing a bright aqua-colored satin ensemble that looked very haute couture and really showed off her hair. She smiled for the cameras, did a few curtsies for the press, then headed straight for me! She told me how much I had improved (she hadn't seen me since 1969) and that I did well in *Symphony in C*. She liked the double *en dedans saut de basques*. She then said that they had my picture on their piano! My dance idol had my picture on her piano? Wow!

After Russia we still had two more weeks to go in Poland—a week in Warsaw and a week in Lodz. Instead of being depressing, Poland was luxurious compared to what we experienced in Soviet Russia. The food was much better, they had real lettuce in the salads instead of just green beans and beets, and we were finally dancing in normal theaters. This was so much better. The audiences were great, and my leg was almost completely healed.

For Balanchine's first class there, we all expected he'd take it easy, but instead he gave us a killer class emphasizing speed and cleanliness. He evidently wanted us not to forget that class was about perfecting, and not showing off, as he had allowed us to do in Russia. That class was damn hard. On arriving at the theater the first day I was met with a shock. In front, on the huge poster and taking up the entire frame, was a picture of me doing an arabesque *sauté* from *Suite No. 3*. I wasn't even a principal dancer, and normally that poster would have been a group shot, or at least of one of the ballerinas, and definitely not of a male. I was so flattered! I'm not saying Balanchine chose that photo—probably the theater did—but it was still a nice surprise.

34

Back in New York

The Berlin Films

We returned to New York City in triumph. The national magazines *Time* and *Newsweek* had sent reporters to the USSR to cover some of the performances, so America knew we had succeeded in winning over the Soviet public and critics. There was no question now as to Balanchine's title as heir to Petipa and his prominence as the greatest living ballet choreographer. His dark days after Farrell's departure and Stravinsky's death were finally over. As for me, I scored a personal best when I was the only American-born male dancer singled out by *Newsweek*. Only four principal men were mentioned: Helgi, Peter, Jean-Pierre, and me. The first three were born and mostly trained in their native countries. I was the only 100 percent "made in America" man of the lot. Balanchine later told me how glad he was to have had at least one man recognized for his own training.

Our New York City opening program after this tour included *Symphony in C*, and with the same cast as for the tour. This meant that Gelsey danced with me again in the third movement and she was still angry about it. New Yorkers had previously only seen her in the second movement "ballerina" lead, and she regarded this as a demotion. In any event, I didn't worry anymore about what she was doing to herself, and on opening night I just went out there and gave it my all. I don't think I had ever danced better or jumped higher. My leg was fine, no more pain, and being back in New York, with that wonderful audience, our "family," was like an aphrodisiac. Heaven on earth!

Balanchine, too, was in high spirits. Such love from the audience for our Boss was a great thing to behold. (Only Farrell and I called him "Boss" to his face.) His new star dancers—Kay, Sally, Karin, and Gelsey—were more than making up for Farrell's absence. Allegra Kent,

Violette Verdy, Patricia McBride, and of course Melissa Hayden were in glorious form, too, and even though Villella was dancing less, and Jacques was dancing fewer performances, Helgi, Peter, Jean-Pierre, and I were taking up the slack. Balanchine now promoted me to principal dancer status, thus making me the youngest male principal in the company. He seemed very happy again, and now we were all going to Berlin for a massive film project. We were to be filmed in eighteen of his ballets over a six-week period in two television studios, which were across town from each other, and the ballets would be split between these two studios.

During our union discussions for this project, Villella tried to get the dancers to ask for more money, saying that the work would be harder than we thought and that we should be paid more than our normal salaries. This put the whole project in jeopardy. The dancers had to take a vote on whether to go or not. Balanchine was quite rightly furious. Right before the vote he addressed the whole company. He said (and I remember this precisely because it was so funny), "This is like tomatoes. No one likes tomatoes, but sometimes you have to eat them because they are good for you! If you don't want to come to Berlin, fine. I will just take students from the school."

After that outburst, needless to say, we all voted to go. We ate our tomatoes. Villella was right about one thing, though. We did work a lot, and on concrete TV sound stages, no less. But it was all worth it, at least to me.

Once we got into the filming process we saw that the German directors were taking great liberties with camera angles and editing. This dismayed Balanchine, who had so hoped for faithful renditions of his work. The final products, for the most part, were chopped up into fragmented distortions of what his ballets looked like onstage. Only a few escaped this carnage. *Symphony in C, Divertimento from "Le Baiser de la Fée," Valse Fantaisie,* and *La Valse* seemed to be relatively free of the editor's scissors. All the other ballets had wonderful performances but are almost unrecognizable because of the constant edits and ridiculous camera positions. Side angles and super-dark lighting completely ruined some ballets, especially *Episodes* and *Serenade.*

I wasn't too happy either because instead of dancing the solo boy in the first *pas de trois* of *Agon,* as I had been doing for several years, I was cast in the purely pantomime role of the Devil in *Pulcinella,* which was being filmed at the same time in the other crosstown studio. The originator of this role, Frank Moncion, had a friend who was seriously ill, and he had to fly back to New York to take care of him. With practically no rehearsal, I was thrown into his role. At first, I was upset, as I really wanted to dance *Agon,* but after speaking to Barbara Horgan, I realized that Balanchine had bigger problems of his own. At coffee that morning, he sat down with me and unburdened to me his frustration about all the problems with the German directors and how they were "ruining" his work. That was when he told me about his wish that these films could be a true record of "how I want my ballets danced by dancers I trained and rehearsed"; that is how he put it. How could I now bother him with my petty concerns?

He turned to me as if reading my mind (which he did quite often) and said how glad he was that I was able to dance the Devil and once again "save the day." Flattery will get you every time, and he knew it. When we returned to New York he gave me a check for a thousand dollars as a personal bonus. Now that's class!

Balanchine did finally get a record of how some of his ballets looked by dancers he trained when a number of his ballets were filmed in the late 1970s for the PBS Dance in America programs. I wish I had still been in the company at that time, but unfortunately I was extremely busy in Los Angeles, and Baryshnikov had joined the company, dancing most of my roles. Obviously Mr. B. did not need another allegro male principal.

With Christine Redpath in the premiere of Jerome Robbins's *An Evening's Waltzes.* Photo by Martha Swope. Used with permission of NYPL. swope_781555.

35

The Formation of My Los Angeles Ballet ("Baby Steps")

After the Berlin filming was over we had our normal four-week lay-off. I always went back to Los Angeles during this time to relax and teach some classes for Irina Kosmovska's school. After the demise of Balanchine's attempts to establish a resident company for Los Angeles (the Western Ballet Association had long since folded), Irina continued turning out splendid dancers who always found their way into NYCB. Actually, she was the only non–New York teacher Balanchine invited on a regular basis to teach at the summer sessions at SAB. He even invited her to teach some special summer classes that were held at the Casino (an abandoned casino) in Saratoga Springs during our summer seasons. These were the seeds that later became the NYSSSA (New York State Summer School for the Arts) programs. Some of her students in this first program were Gelsey Kirkland and Colleen Neary before they joined the company. Irina was so popular that many company dancers would skip Balanchine's class to take hers. One day Mr. B., noticing some missing faces, remarked, "Well, Kosmovska is *my* student, too!" Irina, not wanting to offend him, then forbade any company members from taking her class. I taught occasionally for these classes also and was always so happy that Balanchine had given her, my old teacher, this honor.

When I was back in LA in 1972 during our summer layoff and teaching some classes for Irina, Betty Empey, the manager of Irina's student company, Los Angeles Junior Ballet, asked if I would like to choreograph a work for the students. How could I refuse? Besides, Irina always had extraordinary young talent (Darci Kistler was one of her students when Irina was my school's head teacher). I said, "Better yet, why don't I bring out some City Ballet dancers and do a benefit gala program for your company?" She accepted happily. Little did I know that this program would plant the seeds for another Los Angeles classical ballet.

Our first LA shows took place during NYCB's annual February layoff in 1973. I brought Allegra Kent, Bryan Pitts, Marilee Stiles, Lilly Samuels (she later married NBC president Brandon Tartikoff and has become a leading fundraiser for women's cancer charities in Los Angeles), and Bonita and Elyse Borne, for three performances. The Borne sisters, Marilee, and Lilly were all former students of Kosmovska's, too, so I thought it would be nice to include them. The program was Balanchine's *Tchaikovsky Pas de Deux* and *Valse Fantaisie*; my new Bach company work for the students, *Bachiana* (to Bach's "Was mir behagt, ist nur die muntre Jagd"); my *pas de trois* to music by the Spanish composer Ruperto Chapí, *Chapí Pas De Trois*; and Kosmovska's *Classical Symphony* to the Prokofiev score of the same name, in which I danced the lead.

I was approached after these successful first shows by two arts patrons, the attorney Jack Kimberling and dance patron Mrs. Marvin "Marta" Holen. They asked about the possibility of my establishing a local Los Angeles company. I said that was something I had always hoped to do one day, and so another set of performances was scheduled for later that December.

For these I brought out Violette Verdy, Anthony Blum, Sara Leland, and, again, Allegra and Bryan. We gave the company premiere of Balanchine's *Concerto Barocco,* with Allegra and Tony, and *Raymonda Variations,* with Violette and me, and Irina's students as the corps de ballets in both works. I also choreographed a new piece to the *Brahms-Haydn Variations* featuring Kent, Blum, Leland, Pitts, myself, and Irene Cosgrove, who was an excellent advanced student of Kosmovska's. I also choreographed a strange but hysterical little electronic *pas de deux, Poème Électronique,* with music by Edgard Varèse, for myself and the drop-dead gorgeous former NYCB dancer Jennifer Nairn-Smith. She was quite tall, and I am short, so this comedy *pas* accentuated these differences. This was a surprise hit and even reviewed favorably in *Newsweek* and the *Los Angeles Times.*

Martin Bernheimer in the *Times* called me "a returning California hero" and wrote that *Poème Électronique* "[was] a highly engaging, slickly angular, gratefully virtuosic *pas de deux.* Our little hero danced it brilliantly, together with another welcome guest: the vivacious Jennifer Nairn-Smith."

You may be wondering how we were able to get time away from NYCB during our *Nutcracker* season. This amusing story illustrates how Balanchine was a master manipulator as well as a master choreographer.

It so happened that at that time our City Ballet orchestra was negotiating their new contract, and, as in the past, they were threatening to strike. Three years earlier, they did strike, putting us out of work and putting the financial well-being of the company at risk, something Mr. B. took to heart. At this new threat of a strike, and one we heard would be delayed until *Nutcracker* opened, thus costing us even more lost income since our biggest ticket sales were for *The Nutcracker,* Balanchine called a company meeting. Since our contracts were being negotiated at the same time, he asked us to strike *before Nutcracker,* so as to put the musicians out of work first! Clever man! The musicians were still able to delay *The Nutcracker* for one week, but because of Balanchine's tactic the strike was much shorter than it might have been, and only one week of the lucrative *Nutcracker* box office was lost. I was able to schedule the LA shows during our strike. The second set of Los Angeles performances was even more successful than the first, and another program was scheduled for the following spring.

When I told Mr. B. that I would be going back to Los Angeles during the next layoff between the winter and spring seasons, he said I couldn't go for the whole four weeks because I was needed for *Coppélia!* *Coppélia?* No one had heard a thing about Balanchine doing this old warhorse of a ballet. I asked him why he needed me, because I didn't think there was a role for me. He said I'd be dancing Fritz. Fritz? I knew that Franz was the male lead, so I thought maybe Fritz was the name of the boy who led the Mazurka and Czardas in some versions.

When I asked him, he said, "Franz, Fritz, whatever. No, dear, you are doing the lead with Gelsey." Balanchine is doing a full-length ballet for Gelsey and me? Wow! I blurted out that I was astonished he was giving this to me, because I would have thought Helgi would have been better for the role. After all, Helgi was a more "classical" dancer than I was. Balanchine laughed and said, "No, dear. This is for you." He went on to say that Alexandra Danilova (the most famous interpreter of the female lead, Swanilda) would be teaching Gelsey and me all the original pantomime and that he would be re-choreographing the whole ballet. This would be the first three-act ballet for the company since his *Don Quixote*! I was overjoyed, but he wasn't finished yet. He said that before these rehearsals were to start, he was taking Patty McBride and me to dance *Rubies* with the Paris Opera Ballet for their "Homage à Stravinsky" program, and this was why I couldn't be in Los Angeles as long as I had planned. This was just too much. He wasn't taking Villella, who was still dancing this role—he was taking me! I later found out that this event would make me the first American male dancer to ever be a guest artist with the Paris Opera Ballet. I didn't know this at the time, but I found out later when their publicity director told me she checked in their archives. American ballerinas, such as Maria Tallchief and Rosella Hightower (another ballerina with Native American ancestry) had danced there, but I was to be the first American man. I realized that I would need to arrange something for the next Los Angeles program, as now my time was limited, so I sent Bryan to start rehearsals with the Los Angeles dancers, and I headed off to Paris.

36

The Paris Opera Ballet

How could I not love this man! He was my teacher, my mentor, my boss, and my friend. More than all of these things, though, was the undisputable fact that he was treating me as if he were the father I never had. All these great gifts he was giving me: the most beautiful and talented company in the world to choreograph on, great ballets to dance, creating ballets just for me, and now this, taking me to Paris!

As I was checking in to Le Grand Hotel across the street from the Opera (now the InterContinental Paris Le Grand), I ran into Suzanne and Paul. They looked surprised to see me, but happy too. They greeted me like a dear old friend, which was strange since we never really got along that well in the company. However, now both were very warm. They asked what I was doing there, and when I told them I saw just a flicker of sadness. I sensed they were very lonely, which was my first impression. Seeing me must have brought up so many emotions and memories.

They had stayed far away from New York and Balanchine since they left the company. Suzanne had gone on to be a big success with Maurice Béjart's Ballet of the 20th Century company, and Paul had tried to keep busy dancing and choreographing but without much success. When I told them that Balanchine was due to arrive at any minute, they both looked a bit panicked and said they had better be going. It was clear they didn't want to see him. I felt really bad for them both. As they left by one door, Balanchine walked in another. I wonder what would have happened if they had met then. It would have been interesting, but he seemed to be finally over her, so I didn't bring up that she and Paul had just been there. He was in a great mood, so why spoil it?

The Paris Opera Ballet's program, entitled "Homage à Stravinsky," was drawn from the New York City Ballet's 1972 Stravinsky Festival.

This program consisted of *Orpheus* (danced by Jean-Pierre Bonnefoux), *Agon* (with Ghislaine Thesmar and Michael Dénard), *Rubies* (McBride and me), Jerome Robbins's *Scherzo Fantastique* (featuring Noëlla Pontois), and *Circus Polka,* using the children from the ballet school of the Paris Opera. What an honor to dance with these superb French dancers, although when I saw the way they were struggling with the speed, musicality, and stamina of Balanchine's choreography, I was even more in awe of what Balanchine had accomplished with his American dancers. This was a fact brought home over and over again when I saw other non-Balanchine-trained dancers trying to keep up. Even the best foreign-trained dancers who joined City Ballet had a period of adjustment.

Patricia Neary had staged *Agon* for the French dancers, but Balanchine was now overseeing the final rehearsals, and an amusing thing happened at one rehearsal. During the first *pas de trois,* some mix-up was happening with the dancers' hands. Balanchine asked me what the proper *port de bras* was since I had been dancing the man's part. I said, "The boy starts with his right hand." Pat said, "No, Johnny, he starts with his left hand." Mr. B. stood up and took over the boy's role.

First he started with his right hand, and then he tried it with his left. He changed back and forth several times, which made both Pat and me nervous because he was acting a bit like King Solomon deciding which mother would get the baby. I could tell Mr. B. was having a high ole time making us sweat! Finally, he said, "No, Pat, Cleeeford's right. I always start with my right. Right hand, right foot, it's always the same." I was relieved, but I also learned something so obvious. Mr. B. always *did* start on the right. He was so logical that the simplest solution was usually the one he chose.

This simple fact has made staging his ballets so much easier. Pat was a bit embarrassed, but after the rehearsal she asked me to come down to her dressing room. I thought she was upset, but instead she just wanted to go over all of her rehearsal notes and counts with me. Now that's a real professional!

The performances were a blast, once they finally started! Unfortunately, the first three performances were canceled due to a stagehands' strike. This meant a little extra free time, which Balanchine filled up by taking me to dinners and introducing me to people like the Baroness de Rothschild. I was certainly in heady company. Both Patty and I received wonderful reviews. The French newspaper *L'Express* said, "What a breath of fresh air, a shower of youth . . . McBride: the most spiritual legs on earth, and Clifford: a young, unleashed puma."

One night the Paris Opera Ballet was performing *Prodigal Son*. I asked Mr. B. if he was going, and he said, "No, of course not." I asked why not. Wasn't he curious to see what it looked like? He said, "I know what it looks like. It looks awful! Besides, I don't care. Let's eat!"

I asked if we could hold off on dinner until after *Prodigal* since it was first on the program and I was really curious to see how bad it could possibly be. He agreed, and off I went.

He was right. The French version, in those days at least, was extremely mannered, and the lead boy was a bit effeminate looking, especially when compared to Villella's rough-and-tumble portrayal. Years later in 1986, three years after Balanchine's death, when I restaged it for this company, I completely redid it from top to bottom. At first some of the dancers who were fond of their older version were horrified. But once they saw how powerful and immediate *Prodigal Son* could be, the whole company was won over, as were the critics. Even Jerome Robbins, who was there staging his *In the Night*, was impressed. He had danced the Son in the early 1950s.

I found out later from my dear friend Victor Castelli (who was in the room to witness) that Robbins told Peter Martins that "the definitive *Prodigal Son* was now being danced in Paris." Martins was not at all pleased to hear another company could do it better, but Jerry had made his point. The friction between them was coming to a boiling point at that time, and I guess Jerry wanted to dig in the knife.

After the Paris Opera Ballet's "Homage à Stravinsky," I had a few weeks available to go to Los Angeles and put on our third program for what was now called Los Angeles Dance Theater. The name Los Angeles Ballet was held by a school, but that soon changed.

For this run, I choreographed *Mandala* to a symphony (the Mandala Symphony) by Toshiro Mayazumi, who was the composer of Balanchine's *Bugaku*. I had had the honor of dancing *Bugaku* with Allegra Kent, and it was one of my fondest dance memories.

After having three very successful miniseasons with my own company, I was giving serious thought to moving to Los Angeles full-time and seeing this through. I could not expect the dancers in LA to commit to staying and working there if I couldn't. First, I needed to speak with Balanchine, and what about *Coppélia?*

Besides *Coppélia,* Balanchine had plans for a big new full-length ballet called *The Birds of America* (inspired by the album by John James Audubon), in which I was to be Johnny Appleseed, the leading character. I even had a costume fitting for this at Mme. Barbara Karinska's atelier. I know he was waiting for the full score from Morton Gould to be completed, but at this time the ballet seemed to be on the back burner, so I didn't much think about it.

It was another one of the big projects he was never able to realize, like *Beauty* at the State Theater, which couldn't be done in the lavish way he wanted because the theater had no trap doors. An old *New York Times* article once announced that this was to be an "epic," with Maria Tallchief as Pocahontas, so it was clear he had wanted to do this for many years.

Being the lead in that ballet, and *Coppélia,* certainly would have been a major career boost, but I'm not sure even that would have changed my mind about starting my own company in LA.

31

Coppélia, Variations pour une Porte et un Soupir, The Steadfast Tin Soldier, the New York Philharmonic Promenades, and My Aborted Broadway Début

On my return to New York, and still high from my successful Los Angeles program, I threw myself into the *Coppélia* rehearsals. Danilova started teaching the opening-act pantomime to Gelsey and me, and, for a change, Gelsey seemed happy. She really wanted to dance this role, and with the legendary Alexandra Danilova coaching her and teaching her the version Danilova had once danced herself, she couldn't complain that this was not a "classical" ballet. Balanchine choreographed the third-act male variation on me, which is not what is done today, and both Danilova and he were teaching us the first- and third-act *pas de deux*. All seemed right with the world.

Balanchine was using me in just about everything, and he had just choreographed a very taxing forty-minute *pas de deux* for Karin von Aroldingen and me, *Variations pour une Porte et un Soupir*. This was the most modern work Balanchine had done in several years. It was set to a screechy electronic score by French composer Pierre Henry, which had been previously used by Maurice Béjart. The "music" consisted of alternating sounds. One was a door, opening, squeaking, and slamming shut—the Porte—and the other sounded like a sigh, the Soupir. Karin was the Door, and I was the Sigh. This ballet was definitely strange but also grotesquely beautiful. Karin's costume consisted of a white unitard with some jewels at the bodice, and attached to her waist was a huge black China silk skirt that covered the entire stage, all fifty feet of it.

At the edges of this skirt were invisible wires that were attached to the stage's high battens, the pipes from which drops and lights are hung. The stagehands had musical cues for when to raise these, thus causing the edges of the skirt to fly up, sometimes twenty-seven feet or more. Then the battens would be lowered quickly, which caused the material to billow out, making fantastic patterns as the air under the skirt pushed up against it. I suppose this was more like a *pas de trois,* the skirt being the third dancer. Balanchine had a mock-up of the skirt made for rehearsals in the studio, and he was having a great time experimenting with ways to make the different shapes appear. My role was as an asexual creature all in gray, and my "look" was a gray unitard with black, wavy, vertical stripes, which slightly resembled veins. Silver/gray makeup, huge eyes, and silver hair completed this creature's look. The *pas* started with a solo for me, then Karin had one, then we took turns, for about forty minutes. It was only at the end that we had any interaction. He later cut the running time down to twenty minutes, but even that was exhausting for both of us.

Rehearsals were very different for this ballet than any others because a) there was no music, per se, and b) there seemed to be some kind of story developing, so it was clear that this was not just an abstract, "story-less" ballet (Balanchine's often-used word to describe his ballets). Pianist Gordon Boelzner sat with a tape recorder and referred to the "score." Yes, there was a score of sorts, in which Balanchine used to write quite a bit. I assumed he was making notes as to where various steps were happening, but one day he showed me what else he was doing. Along with his notes, he was drawing very pornographic cartoons! These were hysterically funny. I cannot give you the details for the sake of modesty, but he would take some of the composer's squiggles and add a few lines of his own, resulting in quite explicit X-rated images. He also had me doing what can only be described as *Kama Sutra*–influenced, very erotic sexual positions. It was kinky for sure.

Poor Karin had the worst of it. Since she was attached to this huge skirt, but still *en pointe,* she basically served as a kind of "mover" of this prop. Her actions were always static and jerky to correspond to the jagged sounds of the door creaking and slamming. Her sounds were harsh, and mine were soft. I also had the sound of a distant buoy, or bell, which was very sad, and gradually the "sighs" sounded like someone with asthma or some other respiratory problem. Karin not only had to deal with the skirt but also with every backbend, split, and contortion possible.

One day, knowing of my Martha Graham training, Mr. B. asked what kind of backbends I could do. I showed him a very controlled, slow-motion one, where as I leaned back I could actually control my descent until my shoulders touched the floor without my using my hands at all. He was amazed. The trick (actually this is a back hinged fall in Graham technique) doesn't depend so much on how flexible one's back is but how controlled the knee bends are and on holding on to one's balance. He loved it. Another trick that he wanted me to do was to hit the floor on my stomach and slide as far as I could. I could use my hands to control my forward fall and propel myself forward, but my momentum could continue as I arched my back. It was a total kamikaze stunt, and very me! Also, by that time I had perfected an *en dedans* turn *à la seconde*, where, after I finished the *à la seconde* part, I could immediately go into a backbend in attitude and do two or three more turns in that position, all without doing another *relevé*. Think of it as an ice skater's backbend spiral turn. I'm not sure if anyone who danced the role after me did this turn.

This ballet is totally dependent on the dancers coordinating their movements, matching the sounds exactly, and understanding the darker aspects of the story. The Door is a predatory monster that devours the Sigh in the end. She literally wraps him, and herself, up in that skirt. It's funny and horrific all at the same time. At the premiere the audience didn't know whether to laugh or be outraged at the strangeness of it all. During the bows there were some bravos but also some very loud boos! I had never heard any boos in that theater before, and I was worried that they were for Karin and me. After the final bow Lincoln came backstage all smiles. I said I couldn't believe all the boos. He laughed and said rather nonchalantly, "Oh, that was ME. It's about time we had a little controversy around here!" What a clever man. By doing that he got the audience going, and that ballet has been controversial ever since.

When Karin and I staged it for a small company in France, the Ballet du Nord, years later, the audience seemed completely mesmerized. The French reacted to it quite differently. They did nothing but bravo, and

Me and Karin von Aroldingen in *Variations pour une Porte et un Soupir*. Photos by Martha Swope. Used with permission of NYPL swope_781757, swope_793626. Choreography by George Balanchine © The George Balanchine Trust.

they took it very, very, seriously. I asked some of the French dancers in that company what they thought of it, and they said it was like "some beautiful nightmare." That it was.

For the 1974 spring season Balanchine needed another new ballet, and I suggested that Bartók's Piano Concerto No. 3 that I had just choreographed in LA for my fledgling company might work. He had seen a rehearsal there of the first movement and liked it. He agreed, but back then it was a novel idea. Not many ballets choreographed for other companies were taken into the repertory. *Bartók #3* proved to be a success and even made some history. Because of an injury to the first movement lead, Susan Hendl, I put in Debra Austin, an African American corps dancer of great talent, who was at that time the only Black female dancer in the company. According to the *New York Daily News,* this was the first time in history a Black classical ballerina had danced a lead in the company.

The reviews were uniformly good. Clive Barnes, in the *New York Times,* wrote, "Clifford's most mature work to date," and all would seem right with my world, except for one thing. Even though I had *Coppélia* waiting right around the corner, and Mr. B. had also started to choreograph *The Steadfast Tin Soldier* for Gelsey and me, and he had just brought me to Paris, I was unhappy.

My love of choreography was gradually beginning to burn out. Why? I asked myself this question over and over, and after all these years I'm still asking myself the same thing. What went wrong? I think maybe I was doing what all sons eventually do. I was competing with my father. All sons want to best their dads on some level. For me, it was choreography. This was impossible, of course. I knew that. Balanchine was a genius, and I was not. I was talented, energetic, and willing to learn, but at twenty-six, I honestly believed I had learned all I could

Debra Austin in my *Bartók #3* (the first time in history a Black ballerina danced a leading classical role with NYCB). Photo by Martha Swope. Used with permission of NYPL. swope_781890.

from him as a choreographer. I felt that if I stayed under his influence any longer I'd lose any spark of originality I still had.

Things were going very well in LA, and if that company were going to develop into something serious, I would need to be there full-time. Mr. B. was as healthy as an athlete, and there was no reason to believe that I would be needed to take over any of his duties in the near future.

I approached Mr. B. around May 1974 with the idea of my leaving and relocating to Los Angeles at the end of that season. At first he was quite against it. When I explained that I was feeling completely unproductive as a choreographer, he began to listen. I explained that since I so loved his choreography and that for me at least it was futile to even try to choreograph in his presence, my only recourse if I were to remain a viable choreographer was to leave. He understood at last and actually warmed to the idea of my having a Los Angeles company. Don't forget that he had tried in the past and that he had always had a soft spot for Los Angeles, and especially Hollywood. He even suggested I call it the "Hollywood Ballet" because, he said, "No one even knows where Los Angeles is, dear."

When I announced my imminent departure, everyone was truly shocked. How could I, the favored son and possible heir, leave? Merrill Ashley gave me a really strong talking-to and tried to get me to reconsider. However, once I made my mind up it was final. Some, like Violette Verdy, Barbara Horgan, and Betty Cage for example, understood. Others took Merrill's stance: Allegra Kent, Melissa Hayden, and Jacques d'Amboise really wanted me to stay. There were so many conflicting emotions hitting me at once that something had to give. It was my back.

The previous spring, in 1973, I had taken over Villella's duties as a guest artist with the New York Philharmonic's Promenades concerts. These were the "pops" programs produced each spring, where dance was featured. André Kostelanetz was the conductor, and whether Villella chose not to continue or the Philharmonic wanted a change, I don't know, but I was very happy to have this opportunity. I was already a bit stressed and definitely working too hard, and while rehearsing for this I strained my back. I spoke to Balanchine after a doctor told me nothing was wrong except that I was suffering from stress and overwork. Mr. B. then said to me, "Dear, the real problem is that you just need to be loved!" How did he know? I had kept a love affair that was sadly ending very discreet, and I hadn't let anyone know, but somehow he knew.

He knew everything.

For these Promenades, I choreographed a *pas de deux* to four Richard Rodgers songs for Gelsey and me as we had been getting along together a lot better because of the *Coppélia* rehearsals. We were still a great team onstage, no matter what our problems were offstage. Because of my back I couldn't dance these concerts, so I asked Peter Martins if he could fill in for me. He did, and he seemed to have a ball dancing to that music with Gelsey.

As time drew near for my last performances with the company, the question came up as to who would be dancing my roles. This was a real problem because, by that time, I had inherited most of Villella's repertoire as well as all the ballets Balanchine and Robbins had created for me. I had a very full load, and some ballets, like *Variations pour une Porte et un Soupir* and *Danses Concertantes,* were uniquely suited to my technique and temperament, and harder to recast. Other ballets, such as *Valse Fantaisie, Harlequinade, Rubies, Symphony in C, Symphony in Three Movements,* and *A Midsummer Night's Dream,* where I usually danced Oberon or Puck, I taught to Bonnefoux, Tomasson, Weiss, Frohlich, Castelli, and Cook.

My last performance (or so I thought) was as Oberon in *A Midsummer Night's Dream.* Gelsey and Kay were the leading ballerinas. Kay was my Titania and Gelsey was dancing the second-act Divertissement. During the front-of-curtain bows, they both handed me bouquets and the audience cheered. I was very moved by this and almost cried. Clive Barnes, writing for the *New York Post,* said, "I don't think this is the last we'll be seeing of John Clifford." How prescient of him.

Later that night I was going to what I thought was a little dinner at Christine Redpath's apartment, when who should I run into in the elevator but Mr. B! I later learned it was a surprise party for me, and was set up by Balanchine. He had asked Christine to throw this party for a small group who were my closest friends in the company. The next big surprise was Balanchine's gift to me of a German Shepherd puppy. I loved these dogs and had had one as a child (he knew this, of course). He had also already given it a name: Vinghoff! He told me when he lived in LA making films he owned a German Shepherd he named "Vinghoff." I said this was a pretty harsh-sounding name, and he said, "Well, you don't actually call him Vinghoff. You say, 'Here, Vingy, Vingy, Vingy!'" He was an absolutely beautiful puppy, and I was truly touched that Balanchine had given me this gift.

Before I could leave New York, one very tantalizing offer came my way. David Merrick, the legendary Broadway producer, was readying a new show for Broadway that would be a cross between a ballet and a play. *Dancers* would feature two ballets performed during the course of the show and was to be choreographed by Robert Joffrey. My agent at Ashley Famous Agency, Ed Limato (later copresident when Ashley Famous became International Creative Management, or ICM), gave me the script to read, and although I didn't see myself in the part, nonetheless it was worth considering. What I did like about it was that all the actors were to be real ballet dancers.

After finally deciding that I wasn't going to stay in New York under any circumstances, starring in a Broadway play notwithstanding, I went to the theater where auditions were taking place to return the script. I walked in the stage door and found myself on an empty stage facing a dark house, a cliché of all those old Broadway audition scenes in films. A disembodied voice called out from the dark and said, "John, why not start from page twelve?" I said, "Oh, so sorry, no. I just came to return the script." There was some muttering, then the voice said, "No, please just start at that scene." I repeated, "No, really, I just came to drop off the script. I'm not really interested, but thanks anyway." Later that day, I got a frantic call from Limato, asking, "Are you nuts? They wanted you for the part, the audition was only a formality." I said, "Ed, I'm leaving for LA. I didn't leave Balanchine to stay in New York. Sorry, but that's it." Limato had had it with me anyway because for some months his agency had been trying to get me to choreograph various Broadway musicals but I had turned them down. The only one I would have accepted was called *Smith,* which was being produced by Cheryl Crawford and directed by the great director of *Equus,* John Dexter. Dexter was adamant that I take on *Smith,* going so far as to say that if I didn't do it, he wouldn't either. That show like so many others fell by the wayside, but I made a good friend in John.

The next day the author of *Dancers* called and asked to take me to lunch. At this meeting he told me that he had written the script specifically for Allegra Kent, Edward Villella, Alexandra Danilova, and me. We were the prototypes for his characters and he wanted to know why I wasn't interested. I explained again that it had nothing to do with his script (although I really didn't think my character was at all believable). He said he would change whatever was bothering me. I was very flattered but again said, "No, thanks." I later heard that Villella, Kent, and eventually Peter Martins, and almost all of New York's other classical ballet dancers were offered roles in this, but no one wanted to spend the time away from the ballet stage to do it. It never got off the ground, but it was an intriguing idea. Later, the film *The Turning Point* mined a lot of this same territory, and to much better effect.

My last surprising new role in the company was as the partner for the legendary ballerina Melissa Hayden in *Cortège Hongrois*. She was fifty at this point and I was twenty-six. I had danced *Valse Fantaisie* with her for some concerts but nothing with the company. This grand classical divertissement using music (and some choreography) from Petipa's *Raymonda*, was Balanchine's farewell gift to his longest-lasting prima ballerina.

Born in Toronto, Canada, Hayden first danced in American Ballet Theatre before joining Balanchine. Clive Barnes, in the *New York Times*, had christened her America's true "Prima Ballerina Assoluta." The first two performances of *Cortège* were with her most frequent partner, Jacques d'Amboise, but as fate would have it he injured himself right before the third show, a Saturday matinee. So, guess what? I got a call that morning telling me Jacques was out, and Balanchine wanted me to replace him in two hours! Shades of what happened in Monte Carlo and *Rubies*. I rushed over to the theater, and there was Mr. B., Jacques, and Milly. They quickly taught me the role, and I was on. Luckily, Balanchine kept me in this with her until I left the company. I taught it to Helgi Tomasson and Peter Martins, but had I stayed I'd have continued dancing it with Patricia McBride, who was the first after Hayden to do it.

My day of departure finally came. Polly Shelton, an extraordinarily beautiful California girl, and Johnna Kirkland decided to leave City Ballet with me and become my first two principal dancers. Vingy (who went with me under my seat on the plane), Polly, Johnna, and I all

Me and the great Melissa Hayden in *Cortège Hongrois*. Photo by Martha Swope. Used with permission of NYPL. swope_792912. Choreography by George Balanchine © The George Balanchine Trust.

headed to our new futures with optimism, and of course a bit of fear at leaving the security of Balanchine and the New York City Ballet. He had told me that I could always come back if things didn't work out, but he had not made the same offer to the others. I'm sure he would have taken them back, though, if I had failed.

38

The Los Angeles Ballet

I began at once to teach daily classes when I arrived in LA and to meet with various Los Angeles arts patrons about joining our board of directors. Besides Jack Kimberling, Betty Empey (who was now acting as our general director), and Marta Holen, we added, in short order, Jean Stone (wife of the author Irving Stone, who wrote *The Agony and the Ecstasy*), educator Ruth March, Marjorie Fasman (the daughter of legendary producer/director Sol Lesser), Mrs. Stafford (Roberta) Grady, Victor M. Carter (a multimillionaire arts patron), Jim Jacobson (vice president of Prudential Life Insurance), Ruth Clayburgh (an arts patron from Seattle who was instrumental in the early days of Robert Joffrey's career), and several others. A young man from Saratoga, New York, Ned Waite Jr., whose family owned a bank there and who had just gone to work as Lincoln Kirstein's assistant, decided to join us as business manager, so I thought we were off to a good start.

Several interesting things happened almost immediately, which should have warned me about how different Los Angeles would be from New York. The former New York City Ballet and American Ballet Theatre star Nora Kaye, wife of the film director Herbert Ross, asked to meet me. When I went to their opulent Beverly Hills mansion, her maid told me to join her at the pool. She came off as a bit grand, but she got right to the point. She said she would consider helping us financially, and then she phoned her neighbor, the film producer Ray Stark, to come right over to meet me. He arrived quickly and was very enthusiastic about my ideas for my new company. I left that meeting feeling overjoyed that people of that importance were willing to be involved. Nora came by a few days later with Joanne Woodward to watch some rehearsals. Joanne had always been a ballet lover and was often at City Ballet, so she was much warmer to me than Nora. They both seemed excited about the talented dancers, and Nora especially couldn't believe their high level technically. My first soloists were Johnna Kirkland, Polly Shelton, Marilee Stiles (also from City Ballet and a Los Angeles native trained by Kosmovska), Nancy Davis (a tall, fashion-model-glamorous soloist from the National Ballet in Washington, DC, and a former SAB student), Colette Jeschke (who had also trained at SAB and was our own dramatic firebrand à la Melissa Hayden), and Kevyn O'Rourke from the Stuttgart Ballet (originally from LA and SAB). The men were headed by Victor Barbee, eighteen years old and fresh from SAB (now associate director of The Washington Ballet after a long career at ABT), Ken Mraz (a blond, Greek god type), Charles Flemmer (a very handsome and excellent partner, like Conrad Ludlow but with black hair), Reid Olson (a boyish all-American, red-headed charmer), and Kipling Houston (who later went on to many years as a soloist with the New York City Ballet).

A few days later, Nora had a meeting with several of my board members and Mrs. Empey. Nora told them she would use all of her considerable influence in Hollywood to help the company—but there was a catch. She wanted herself and former choreographer and ABT dancer James "Jimmy" Starbuck to be named as co-artistic directors along with me. Nora literally wanted to buy her way in. When Betty told me of this offer, of course I said, "No way. I didn't leave Balanchine to work for Nora Kaye and Jimmy Starbuck." That's what would have happened, because money always calls the shots. Betty declined Nora's offer as gracefully as possible, but Nora was furious at being turned down. For years after that she bad-mouthed me and my dancers. Only eight years later did I hear that she begrudgingly admitted I had developed a fine company. Joanne Woodward, on the other hand, was class all the way. She came to several more rehearsals, and when Nora pulled out she stepped in. Our first major grant (for $50,000) came from the No Such Foundation, which had been started by her husband, Paul Newman.

The second portent of doom happened when I met Dorothy "Buffy" Chandler, the self-appointed queen of Los Angeles culture. She was the mother of the publisher of the *Los Angeles Times*, Otis Chandler. This gave her incredible power over the social scene in Los Angeles, which in turn translated into fundraising clout. This formidable woman had single-handedly raised the funds for the beautiful Los Angeles Music

Center and its 3,300-seat opera house, the Dorothy Chandler Pavilion. I met her at the office of my optometrist Bernice Brown. She was Buffy's eye doctor, too, and Bernice thought a casual meeting between us would be a good thing. She meant well, but it backfired. Within minutes of our meeting Mrs. Chandler made it clear that a ballet company was not going to be something she would support, or even allow, in "her" city. Buffy said she had read all about me coming back to Los Angeles. I said that my decision was, in part, because of her.

Growing up in Los Angeles, I always knew we couldn't be a truly sophisticated city with real culture until we had an arts center and major live theaters. I told her that because of her work we now had a fine place for major opera and ballet. She then said, "Well, to tell you the truth, I don't much care for ballet." She then threw me a curve ball. "You don't have anything to do with that horrible Stanley Holden do you?" I said, "No, I don't really know him, but I'm sorry you don't like the ballet." (Stanley was a popular former Royal Ballet principal who was trying to start a school and company in town.) She then went on to say that some years earlier she had been persuaded by local ballet lovers to open the doors of "her" theater to help him and his wife, Judy, but that they were most "ungrateful" and that "all this ballet nonsense" had put her very "off" the ballet. She said, "Good luck!" But the way she said it was quite sarcastic.

The third, and worst, bad omen was when Martin Bernheimer, the notoriously acid-penned *Los Angeles Times* music editor and dance critic, asked to meet me for lunch. He had built his reputation on being vicious to various artists, and I was very wary of him. He wanted to know my plans and if I would be continuing to bring New York City Ballet stars to guest in our programs, as I had for the first three miniseasons. I said, "Probably not, since I want to develop our own talent." He didn't seem to like that answer and then said the oddest thing. He asked if I left City Ballet because of any problems with Balanchine. I said, "No, not at all." He then said that he couldn't believe I had just up and left that glorious city, New York, to come to culturally barren Los Angeles. Ah, ha! So that was it! He was a cultural snob. He went on to say that the arts could not survive in LA because the people were not interested in anything of quality. *How small-minded,* I thought. I told him I had grown up in LA, and that the New York City Ballet, the Royal Ballet, American Ballet Theater, the Royal Danish Ballet, and even the Bolshoi Ballet had all visited often and that the theaters were always sold out.

I expressed my belief that the audiences in LA were just like anywhere else. He looked down his nose at me and said, "Well, I doubt you're right, but no matter what I may write about you in the future, just go ahead and do what you think best." *Was he now giving me permission to work?* That's how it felt. A critic was telling an artist that he had his permission to work, even though he may be writing some negative things in the future? So odd. I came away from that meeting sure he was going to do his best to prove me wrong and himself right.

I could go on with more details about my Los Angeles Ballet, but that would be another book. The games played by the press, the dramas with the board of directors, the anxiety of the dancers' personal lives, and well-known show-business Hollywood personalities might make interesting reading someday, but this book is really about the great times and lessons learned at my master's feet. Balanchine was not through with me yet!

39

A "Guest Artist"
with the New York City Ballet

It was not Balanchine's habit to invite dancers back to the company as guests or take them back at all once they'd left, so I was extremely surprised when I received a call from Barbara Horgan barely four weeks after I left. She said the company was coming back to the Greek Theater in August for a two-week summer season, and Balanchine was wondering if I was available to dance. "Of course," I said. "Wow!" I asked what he wanted me to do, and she said she didn't know but to be ready for anything. When the company arrived, I showed up for the company class and looked on the cast list to see what I would be dancing. Turned out I was cast for every ballet I'd danced in the company that they brought to LA. *Stars and Stripes* (with Gelsey no less, who hadn't left the company yet), the third movement of *Symphony in C, Symphony in Three Movements, Capriccio (Rubies)*, and more. What a blast!

I would be dancing with the NYCB for my hometown LA audiences as an adult for the first time. My new company was just starting to be talked about, and Balanchine, by casting me in this extraordinary repertoire, was giving me a big boost of publicity. The audience was sold out, as usual, and my appearance was met with heightened expectations and warm support. I was Balanchine's golden boy and I was going to bring ballet back to Los Angeles . . . at least for a while (ten years to be exact). Back then, I just thought we were off to a fantastic start.

After those first Greek Theater guest performances I thought that that was probably the last time I'd be dancing for Mr. B. But I was so wrong. The very next NYCB fall season Barbara called me again and asked if I could come back to New York for a few weeks. Mr. B. evidently needed me again. So, once more I danced all my old roles. The other men who had started to take these prized parts were not too happy to see my face, which was perfectly understandable; but what could they do? Balanchine wanted me to dance and that was that. The same thing happened the following spring season. Barbara called to say that Helgi was injured and that Balanchine wanted me to dance *Harlequinade*. When I arrived and looked at the casting, I saw that I was dancing not only that ballet but was again cast for all my old roles. This went on for a couple years until Baryshnikov joined the company. Balanchine then had another virtuoso technician, and I was no longer needed—except for one last time in 1980.

I had a few weeks free time in July 1980, and I thought it would be fun to visit the company in Saratoga. I had always loved going there, and this time my most loyal patron, Marta Holen, would come with me. When we arrived, the company was getting ready for their opening-night ballet, *A Midsummer Night's Dream*. I was so looking forward to seeing it again—and Balanchine. He had been ill, and at that time no one knew exactly what was wrong. He had had a successful triple coronary bypass surgery a few months earlier, but now he was losing his balance quite often, and even his memory and eyesight were giving him problems. I didn't realize how serious this was until I saw him that summer. He was not himself, at least not the vibrant and energetic Balanchine I knew. He was no longer teaching class regularly, and he tired easily. He could no longer sit for any extended period or even spend a full day at the theater, as had been his habit.

The hints that something was more seriously wrong went undiagnosed until 1981. I had noticed in the late 1970s that his classes were very different from what they were in the late '60s and early '70s. He was giving steps and combinations that were too fast—and not the normal "fast" that was typical of Balanchine. He also began to ignore front and back positions at the barre. He would sometimes only have the dancers do all the exercises to the side. When I realized he was not going to be teaching in Saratoga I was sorely disappointed. So, that first day I took Peter Martins's class, as by that time he was starting to teach more company classes. I found his class to be all right, if maybe a bit too slavish to Stanley Williams's. He had also adopted some of Balanchine's more mannered exaggerations that had crept into his classes the last couple of years. Peter's approach was more like speaking a language phonetically but not really understanding the words' meanings.

After his class I stayed in the studio: because the Butterflies were going to rehearse the Scherzo, which was where Oberon dances his variation. Just for fun, I jumped up and danced my old role. I saw Peter peek his head in to watch but thought nothing of it. After this was over I headed to the stage to see Mr. B., but Rosemary Dunleavy, now the company's head ballet mistress, intercepted me and said Mr. B needed to see me immediately because there was an "emergency." She told me Helgi was injured and there was no one to dance Oberon that night. Ib Andersen was also dancing that role, but he wasn't coming to Saratoga until the next day. *Oh no! Not again,* I thought. *This can't be happening. I'm not ready for this!* I was then thirty-four years old and hadn't danced that killer role in six years. Evidently, Peter had told Balanchine I was still in good enough shape to dance it. I saw Mr. B. a few seconds later, and he said "Dear, I heard you can still dance! Do you think, maybe, you can do us a leeettle favor?" "Of course," I said. "Whatever you need." I could never say no to Balanchine. I said that first he should see me dance himself. If he thought I could still cut it then I'd do whatever he wished. There was a full-stage rehearsal later that day, and he could watch me then. I was so nervous at that rehearsal. What the hell was I getting myself into?

After this onstage run-through Balanchine said, "My dear, I'm surprised you can still dance. You can dance tonight? Yes?" "OK," I said. "If you really want me to." That was it—I was on. Because this opening night was a gala, and the governor of New York would be there, Mr. B. asked if I was okay with letting Helgi mime the Oberon role (so as not to let the press know that the company was caught off-guard), and I would just dance the Scherzo variation as a surprise guest. This is the only real dancing Oberon does in the ballet, so I said, "Sure, but what character will I be?" He said, "You can be our guest bug, from California." Ha!

The Scherzo has twenty-four children dressed as bugs, moths, and dragonflies, and it seemed now I was to be their leader. Ducky dressed me up in a green unitard with chiffon wings; I then covered myself in glitter. I did indeed look like some kind of big green insect.

As I was sitting in the dressing room before the show, frantically sewing elastics on some shoes I had borrowed (since I hadn't been expecting to dance and hadn't brought a new pair with me), I kept thinking, "Why am I doing this?" Okay, okay, I know I always say I never said no to Balanchine, but this was ridiculous. I hadn't danced anything this difficult for years, and this role was the hardest of them all. It used to take me two weeks of doing it full-out daily after class just to be able get through it. It was much harder than *Rubies* or *Tarantella*. Just then, Jacques came bursting through the door, and in his typical enthusiastic d'Amboise style he lifted me off my feet and gave me a huge bear hug. He then said he had just run into Balanchine, who told him I was dancing that night. According to Jacques, Mr. B. said I was "saving the day once again" and that everything was fine because "Cleeeford" was back. Well, after that, how could I not give it my all?

I did give it my all and then some. I went way over the top; and since I wasn't actually dancing the role of Oberon I decided to be very flamboyant and actually do a Plisetskaya-like, over-the-top approach. After all, I did look like a big dragonfly! On one of my three exits, but still during the dance, I ran up to Balanchine (who was standing in the wings watching) and, panting, blurted out, "I know I'm being a bit too much, but since I'm not actually dancing Oberon I thought maybe I should go all the way and really be some otherworldly creature." My adrenaline was running so high at that point that I was talking very fast, even for me, and I must have seemed as if I were on speed. Balanchine just laughed and said, "No, dear, it's all right, but you have another entrance." He thought I was losing count of the music and started pushing me toward the stage. I said, "No, I know where I am. I'll be back in a sec." With that, I jumped back onstage. What fun I had that night. I was told by some of the older dancers that many of the newer ones who had never seen me dance were shocked by my extroverted style. The others who knew me just said it was good to have "the old times back." Since Mr. B. wasn't teaching much by then, the company had already started to lose just a bit of its attack, and its sense of fun/danger. This wouldn't have been noticed by the typical ballet patron, but I was aware things were starting to change even then.

After my part was over I went back to the dressing room to change out of my costume. I heard a knock on the door as the first act finished. It was Ronnie telling me that Mr. B. wanted to see me in the green-room (the backstage lounge). When I got there, I found a big reception going on with the governor and other Saratoga bigwigs. I was still in my bathrobe, but Mr. B. ushered me in anyway and introduced me to the crowd. He told them that I had agreed to dance so that the show could go on. I was very embarrassed by all this but so pleased that I hadn't let him down. He then proceeded to present me with a magnum of Champagne (the second time he had done this; remember *Four Temperaments?*). Then he asked me if I could stay in Saratoga for two more weeks and dance *all* the remaining five performances of *Dream*, this time dancing the actual role of Oberon. I enthusiastically said, "Yes, boss."

The very next performance, scheduled for the following afternoon, was a children's matinee. When I woke up that morning I knew immediately that I was in big trouble. My legs felt like concrete, my muscles were totally cramped, and my back was in a spasm. Still, I thought after a long, slow warm-up I would be all right, and I still thought I could get through that matinee. Boy was I wrong.

During the last entrance in the Scherzo I badly tore my left calf muscle. I hopped offstage, doing a series of little *cabrioles* so as not to let the audience know anything had happened. Luckily, Ib was out front, and he immediately rushed backstage.

He changed into the costume and quickly took over. My first thought was that I was so glad that Mr. B. wasn't in the theater. He had stopped coming to most of the performances by then because his health wouldn't allow it. I didn't want to have his last impression of seeing me dancing to be of me limping offstage.

When I was in the doctor's office immediately after the show, two male soloists (who shall remain nameless) came in to sympathize and told me that they felt terrible about what had happened. I did look pretty bad. My ankle was swollen with the blood from my torn calf, and I was in a lot of pain. They said that they just didn't feel prepared to dance that role. "What?" I said. "You two are understudies? Why didn't you just dance anyway? God knows we never get enough rehearsals." They said that they were just afraid to look bad. I said, "What happened to 'the show must go on?'" One of the boys said that he thought it was "horrible" for Mr. B. to have forced me to dance. This really pissed me off. "He didn't force me to do anything, and if anyone's to blame, it's me for thinking I could pull this off. You both should have jumped at the chance to dance," I said. I was so mad that they would blame Balanchine for my problem. Later that day, Mr. B. called me at the hotel to say how sorry he was I had hurt myself, but I assured him it was my fault for not warming up (all right, I lied to him, I had warmed up thoroughly) and that it was nothing really.

It took six weeks to recover, and my calves have always been the first to go from that day forward, but it was worth it to dance for Balanchine that one last time. It was during this week that I overheard a conversation between Martins and two dancers that really bothered me. I was sitting in a restaurant booth directly next to them. There was only a thin partition between us, so voices could be heard, but you couldn't see who was speaking. Peter has a distinctive deep voice that is hard to miss. He and the dancers were making jokes about Balanchine's health and how "out of it" he was and guessing how long he'd "last." When I couldn't take it anymore, I stood up so they could see me and I just glared at them. They all looked embarrassed at being caught red-handed, as it were. I stormed out of the restaurant furiously.

This was the first time I really became aware of what was going on behind the scenes without Balanchine's knowledge. I had known for years, ever since Martins first joined the company, that there were problems between Mr. B. and him, but I thought they were long passed. Starting with the 1972 Stravinsky Festival, six years after Peter joined, he seemed more appreciative of Balanchine, and Balanchine started choreographing for him more and more. Then, when Balanchine's health was failing, he seemed to rely on Peter, having him teach classes and encouraging his choreographic ambitions. Balanchine was always encouraging young choreographers. Even though he knew full well that no one could replace him, I believed he did want the company to go on after his death. Lincoln later told me this might not have been so.

PART IV

40

The End of My Company, the Death of Balanchine, and the End of an Era

Even though things were always a struggle in Los Angeles to keep my company financially afloat, the work itself was good. We had five national tours and performed in Korea, the Philippines, Taiwan, Mexico, Canada, Guam, Hawaii, and even Saudi Arabia. The reviews were always great for these tours, and the only real negative press we ever received was from our own local *Los Angeles Times*. According to my board member Jean Stone, Dorothy "Buffy" Chandler saw me as stealing nonprofit funds away from the Los Angeles Music Center. She told me that Buffy had called her personally to ask her to resign from my board because, according to Buffy, "the Music Center needed her." Mrs. Stone said she told her, "Buffy, right now the ballet needs my help more than you do." Chandler didn't like this and continued harassing my various board members. I say "harassing," because what else could you call it? Suffice it to say that it made my life hell and caused numerous fundraising difficulties for us. The board held on until the final straw. That straw was Nancy Reagan.

In 1982, the Music Center was making plans to build a symphony hall for the Los Angeles Philharmonic, and the center had received a $50 million grant from Diane Disney, via the Disney Foundation, to name it Disney Hall. This meant that a lot of free time would now be available at the Chandler Pavilion, the usual home of the Philharmonic. (This was years before the Los Angeles Opera was born.) A search committee was formed by the Music Center to see what to do with the pavilion now that they would have so many open dates. Since my LA Ballet had performed our *Nutcrackers* there already for three holiday seasons, successfully selling more tickets than ABT's Baryshnikov version, and we had also done *Coppélia* there, both with full orchestra, we felt we were a shoo-in. Annually, we did over one hundred shows in Los Angeles and its environs, so we were the obvious choice to be a resident company. As a point of fact, we had the second largest budget of any Los Angeles performing arts group, behind the LA Philharmonic. Not too shabby for a company that was only eight years old.

The Music Center's search committee made the decision that a local ballet company would be the way to go, but would it be ours? They met with my board and said they had narrowed it down to three options: start a new ballet company from scratch; bring in an existing ballet company as a resident company; or take our Los Angeles Ballet . . . but without me as the artistic director. I was told by at least one potential donor that the years of Martin Bernheimer's negative reviews about my work had made me toxic to the powers that be. This was even after these New York City rave reviews:

> The Beethoven ballet was typical of the impressive attack and style of the company.
>
> Anna Kisselgoff, *New York Times*

> Clifford has created a fine company and a significant one in his own dance image—you can't do more. . . . A truly creative company of dancers who move in a totally clean, neo-classic stream-lined style.
>
> Clive Barnes, *New York Post*

> Clifford's "Symphony" involving the entire company in pure dance with rapid-fire footwork sent a message: "We're a force to be reckoned with." It seems to be true.
>
> Janice Berman Alexander, *Newsday*

> Clifford has his own style, which is fluent and spicy, peppered with ingenious steps and tricky acrobatics.
>
> Hubert Saal, *Newsweek*

Sadly, none of this was enough for the Music Center. They even called Balanchine for his advice. Barbara told me Mr. B. said to them, "You already have good company. Cleeeford's, I give them any ballets they want, and is very good company." That seemed to turn the tide (and my board said that they would not remove me under any circumstances anyway), so plans were being drawn up for my company to become the official resident ballet company of the Los Angeles Music Center. Then Nancy Reagan stepped in.

I received a call in early 1983 from Philip Semark, the president and general manager of The Joffrey Ballet. He told me that the Joffrey had just made a deal with the Music Center to be their resident ballet company. He told me he wanted to tell me personally because he and Bob Joffrey felt terrible since they knew this could ruin my company. This was a complete shock to me, but I later found out that several men on my board, who were also on the LA Philharmonic's board, knew about this but didn't want to tell me. Semark told me that the president's son Ron Jr. had just been hired by the always financially strapped company and that Mrs. Reagan has asked a friend, David Murdock (a real estate mogul originally from Arizona now living in Los Angeles), to offer the Music Center two million dollars as underwriting if they would name The Joffrey Ballet their resident company.

This has now been documented in the press, but at the time it wasn't known by the public. Ironically, the very day The Joffrey Ballet opened in Los Angeles, George Balanchine died. A visibly shaken Bob Joffrey had to go out in front of the curtain, right before their début, to announce this sad fact. My always witty and sardonic best friend and our company's music director, Clyde Allen, quipped, "Leave it to Balanchine to upstage the Joffrey!"

One of my biggest heartbreaks about closing my school and disbanding my wonderful dancers (all of whom landed on their feet with great careers in companies ranging from the San Francisco Ballet to the National Ballet of Canada, the Pacific Northwest Ballet, the Zurich Ballet, and even Les Ballets de Monte-Carlo) was the loss of some of my most promising students, most noticeably the eighteen-year-old Damian Woetzel.

Damian came to me at fourteen from Boston on the advice of Violette Verdy who was then the director of the Boston Ballet company and school. He was abundantly talented, albeit a tad unfinished, and he had a keen intelligence, and an ambitious streak that reminded me of myself at his age.

Actually he was even more focused than I was at fourteen. Almost immediately I invited him to take the morning company class as well as Kosmovska's very demanding evening classes. I'm not sure how he worked this out with his high school, but he later received an MBA from Harvard Business School, so I guess he managed! He progressed so quickly that within a few months I put him onstage in a solo role I made just for him, and by the time he turned fifteen I had choreographed *Young Apollo* for him to Benjamin Britten's music of the same name. This proved a hit with all the critics in New York City when we took it on tour.

Arlene Croce wrote in *The New Yorker* that Mr. Woetzel, the "star and obvious inspiration" of "The Young Apollo" was "15 years old, admirably placed and trained, and already a dancer of power and distinction." Now, after a stellar career with the New York City Ballet, Damian is the president of The Juilliard School. Teaching and coaching have always been a great joy for me, and Damian Woetzel's rise has always made me immensely proud.

Let me now give you some background on Balanchine's last days.

I knew Balanchine was near the end when I visited him in late January and again for the last time on April 4, 1983. He died on April 30th. Barbara had called me in early January and told me that Balanchine was very ill and that if I wanted to, in effect, say goodbye, I needed to come to New York as soon as possible. Of course, I took the next plane and brought with me one of my loveliest and most charming young ballerinas, Ellen Bauer. I knew that if anything would cheer him up, it would be a smart and beautiful nineteen-year-old California blond. I met with Barbara before I went to the hospital, and she said that his dementia had increased and that he might not even recognize me. He hadn't remembered other familiar people and I shouldn't be shocked if this happened to me. His fainting spells, dizziness, and sight issues had been going on since 1980, but now it was clear that this was not an inner-ear problem, as earlier surmised. My boss, my mentor, my . . . everything, was dying.

I had grown a short beard at that time, and when I walked into his room (I thought it prudent to see him alone first before bringing Ellen), I saw that he was with Marika Molnar, the ballet's physiotherapist.

At first, he looked at me as though I were a stranger. I thought, *Oh Christ, he really doesn't know who I am.* Marika didn't even recognize me with that beard. Thankfully after only seconds his face brightened up, and he said, "Dear, what are you doing here? Why aren't you in Caleeefornia." What a relief. He motioned me to sit down and we began chatting. After about ten minutes, Marika left and one of his senior ballerinas arrived. He then did the oddest thing: He pretended not to know who she was. She was obviously very thrown by this and I felt so sorry for her. She really respected and loved him, and it pained her greatly to see him so incapacitated. When she realized that he didn't recognize her she said, "Mr. Balanchine, it's me,————." He said something indecipherable. She blanched and said, "No, it's me," and she repeated her name. He just yawned and looked away. With that the confused ballerina excused herself and quickly hurried out of the room. He then looked at me, and with that old mischievous look in his eye, waived "bye, bye" to her back. I thought that maybe he was only feigning his dementia in order not to talk to some people. He then said to me, "Why are you hiding?" I said, "What? I'm not hiding." He then pantomimed the beard covering my face. I got the hint. I was having troubles with my board, so I had grown that beard thinking it would age me and that maybe that would help since I always looked much younger than my age. He then pantomimed shaving. I said, "Got it," and shaved it off that night.

When I went to the hospital the second time with Ellen in tow, he was in good form, charming, witty, and very polite. Ellen then did something for which I will forever love her, and which was totally uncalculated and natural for this loving young girl. As we walked in, and right after I introduced her, she just jumped up next to him, sat on his bed, and kissed his cheek! He was normally very reserved with strangers, but I could see by his face that this innocent act of affection greatly pleased him. She was nervous and began to talk a bit too much, but he loved it. At one point I pulled out the repertory list that I was preparing for our company's next performances. We were then dancing sixteen of his ballets. I had barely pulled this out of my pocket when Ellen grabbed it and said, "What am I dancing?" Balanchine laughed and said, "She's just like you!" "How so?" I asked. He said, "She's *greedy*, just like you! She wants to dance everything!" Ellen chimed in and said, "Of course! All my life all I've wanted to dance is Balanchine." Balanchine and I were both surprised by this spontaneous outburst. He asked her what she meant. She went on to say that since she began training with me at fourteen all she ever heard were stories about "Mr. B." She said her only goal was to dance *all* of his ballets—at least once. He got a strange sad look in his eye and said wistfully, "Well, next year it will be something else." Without missing a beat, and before he could barely finish his sentence, she said, "Oh no! It will *always* be Balanchine. Now, what am I dancing, John?" Those statements, as silly as they were, caused him to smile broadly and actually sigh. I went on to tell him that my version of *The Nutcracker* had been very hard to choreograph, especially the *pas de deux,* after dancing his for so many years. He said, "Why, the *pas de deux* is easy music!" "Easy for you," I said. "It just repeats the melody over and over, so it's kind of repetitive." "No!" he said sternly, "It is not!" He then proceeded to *sing* the entire *pas de deux* music. However, when he got to the climax, he sang out very loudly, thus demonstrating for me that, indeed, this music was a lot more than just repeats. He was still teaching me after all these years.

After about twenty minutes, Ellen and I excused ourselves and left. He was getting visibly tired, and we didn't want to tax him. We had had a great time and Ellen had behaved absolutely perfectly, as had he. I wondered why more City Ballet dancers didn't visit him. Later I understood why. For many in the company Balanchine's illness, and eventual death, was a form of abandonment. Some seemed actually angry at him for getting ill and leaving them.

I visited him every day for the next few days until I needed to get back to LA. He seemed coherent but tired, and he absolutely hated being in the hospital and away from his company. I felt so helpless that there was nothing I could do for him. I had a fantasy of kidnapping him and taking him back with me to Los Angeles. I would put him up at the Beverly Wilshire Hotel, a place he loved. At least he'd have the warm weather. Another thought I had was why couldn't a video monitor be set up in his room with a televised feed straight from his favorite spot in the downstage right wing? That way he could still feel he was a part of his company. I found out later that as his dementia grew, he would call the stage manager's stand during rehearsals, and even performances, to speak to Karin, his closest friend by then. This caused her unbearable anguish. She would be onstage performing and then need to talk with him immediately before or after her entrances. How terrible for her.

On the last day of that trip, Balanchine and I talked about many things, and he was glad I was holding firm in LA and that finally a city he loved had a ballet company. The most important thing he said was a surprise, "Don't forget, dear. You remember!" "What should I remember?" I asked. "Everything," he said. "Only you! Never forget!" He was emphatic and getting a bit worked up. I told him he knew if there was one thing I had it was a good memory.

I was practically famous for remembering his choreography, so I wondered if that was what he meant. I told him I'd remember all his steps. He looked annoyed and said even more forcefully, "Not steps, dear, EVERYTHING!" "Okay, okay," I said. "I will Mr. B." He meant it. And I have.

The last time I saw him was for one visit in early April, just a couple of weeks before he died. My company was in New York for some performances at the Joyce Theater. When I visited him this time he had completely changed. His hair was stark white. His face had a translucent glow, and his eyes were shining like two bright stars. The nurse asked if I could sit with him a minute while she went to have a cigarette. "Of course," I said. He couldn't speak, but when I came into the room, he acknowledged me by widening his eyes and nodding his head. He tried to smile but it was clear he was almost totally immobile and that he was not going to stay much longer in that ravaged body. He fell asleep after a few moments and I waited all alone with him until the nurse returned. He woke up just as I was leaving, and I said simply, "I love you, Mr. B. Now I'm going to the theater to see your ballets. See you soon." He nodded. And that was it.

On April 30th, around 6:00 a.m. Los Angeles time, Sara Leland called to tell me he had passed away. I was not surprised and was actually relieved his suffering was over. I didn't cry then, but a few days later the dam burst. I knew the world had changed. Even though I had been away from New York and the company for a few years, I still always considered myself his dancer and a member of his company. It was clearly my life's mission to have my company carry on the great tradition that he taught me.

I knew that life would go on and that somewhere his ballets would always be danced, so, in that way, he would live forever. And I was right. His ballets are, for the most part, being danced splendidly, from

Me and Balanchine in rehearsal. Photo by Martha Swope. Used with permission of NYPL swope_1211735. BALANCHINE is a Trademark of The George Balanchine Trust.

Paris to Moscow, and from San Francisco to Beijing. His works are now more seen and more admired than even during his lifetime. As Balanchine always said, "NOW IS ALL THERE IS!" *My* Balanchine will continue to live forever, and I continue to be his apprentice.

Epilogue

You may wonder why I did not immediately go back to the New York City Ballet, my artistic home, after my company officially closed in January 1985. Balanchine had always told me that if I ever wanted to return (he knew how difficult it could be starting a ballet company in Los Angeles), the doors would always be open. Unfortunately, at that point Mr. B. had been gone over two years, and the company's new co-ballet-master-in-chief, Peter Martins (Robbins was the other), had made it clear in a letter to me that he did not think it wise, as he put it, "for both of us to be working in the same house." This was even after both Robbins and Kirstein had written to me that I would be more than welcome to return. Martins's negative attitude surprised me as we had worked together very successfully before. I had choreographed two ballets for him, and I also had brought him, along with Kay Mazzo, to Los Angeles to be guests with my company in *Duo Concertant*. I thought Martins would understand that I wasn't looking in any way to challenge his position, but I guess he thought it would be politically unwise of him to have someone as close as I was to Balanchine working "in the same house." Barbara Horgan, who by this time had set up the Balanchine Trust, told me to just come back and let Peter get "used to you" and that gradually he might come around; so that's exactly what I did. After a few weeks, he did relax and asked if I'd like to teach company classes again. I was thrilled to be working in that theater with many of the same dancers I had taught years before, and I felt right at home. Unfortunately, this didn't last long.

Contrary to popular belief, Balanchine left no clear documented successor to take over his company, or so Lincoln Kirstein and Betty Cage both told me after I returned. Betty told me this over tea at her house, and then a few days later Lincoln told me the same thing when he invited me to his home for a meeting. He asked me how I thought the company was looking after I had been teaching them for a few weeks. I told him it looked fine, but I had noticed a few changes to some of Balanchine's ballets, which I chalked up to normal attrition. After all, Balanchine himself had said on numerous occasions that things would change after he was gone.

I assumed the changes were mostly those of Rosemary Dunleavy, "Rosey," the company's longtime ballet mistress. Several dancers had told me she had taken over all the rehearsals of Balanchine's ballets after his death and didn't allow any others to rehearse them. Victor Castelli, for one, was extremely distressed because she wouldn't let him coach the roles Balanchine had cast and rehearsed him in, like the Poet in *La Sonnambula*. I asked him if he had told Peter about this, and he told me he had, but Peter brushed him off, saying, "Take it up with Rosey." He told me Peter didn't care as much about the Balanchine repertory as he did about his own ballets, and to be fair he was busy choreographing a lot during this time. As for Robbins, he was only concerned about his own ballets too. It seemed everyone was just fine with allowing Rosey to carry the Balanchine load, as it were. This really bothered me because when she had come out to LA to stage a couple of Balanchine ballets for my company, Mr. B. told me to let her only set the corps, not the soloists. He wanted me to teach all the solo roles, including the women's. This was in character because for his company the ballet masters never taught the soloists or principals. Either he did this himself, or the dancer who had been dancing the role did. He felt only a principal artist should pass on a role to other principals. This is how it has always been done in the major European companies and how it's normally still done today in most companies, except the NYC Ballet.

It was because of this break with tradition that as early as 1987 there started to be a stylistic and choreographic diminishing of the Balanchine "look" in the company. Suzanne Farrell was still dancing occasionally, but I noticed she wasn't rehearsing or coaching, and neither was Violette Verdy, although they both were sometimes teaching the company class. When I asked dancers I knew who were there from Balanchine's day why certain steps were different, the answer invariably came back that it was Rosey who had made the changes. Time was always limited and her insistence that she take every rehearsal of

Balanchine's ballets meant she was terribly overworked, and by her own choice.

When Lincoln asked me why I thought these changes were happening, I told him what I had learned, that I thought Rosey needed to let more people rehearse the Balanchine rep, and that probably it would help if Suzanne and Violette did some coaching too. To be fair, Karin von Aroldingen was allowed to teach the roles that Balanchine had made on her, but that was because he had left them to her in his will, and even then she had to insist.

Lincoln said, "Bullshit, Johnny. It's Peter's responsibility and he's fucked up." (Lincoln could be quite blunt.) I said I really didn't want to get into the middle of this, but Lincoln was right. Peter was the director, and it was up to him as to what happened with the company. "Well, Mr. B. named him to be the director, so what can you do?" I said. That's when Lincoln told me the full sequence of events.

According to both Betty Cage and Lincoln, when it became clear that Balanchine would not recover his health (and no persuasive evidence has ever been brought forward that he had named a successor), Lincoln and a couple of board members decided that instead of opening a Pandora's box by having a search committee formed (which could take ages and possibly cause all kinds of political mischief), it would be better just to have Peter slide into the directorship. It did seem totally logical, since for over a year he had been assuming more and more of Balanchine's duties. Jerome Robbins would not allow this, of course, and demanded to be named "co-ballet-master-in-chief." (This arrangement lasted for approximately six turbulent years, until Robbins had had enough and left to spend more time with the Paris Opera Ballet.)

I was obviously surprised at the revelation that there was no definitively named successor. Lincoln then said, "George wanted his crown to be fought over." Well, that did sound true because Martins himself once said that Balanchine told him that he'd "have to fight for it." That sounded so very typically Balanchine.

I had no reason to doubt any of what Lincoln told me that night. Lincoln had brought Balanchine to America in the first place and in a way always considered the company "his." I do know, based on what Lincoln and Betty told me, that Lincoln was dreading board interference after Balanchine died, so setting up Peter as the successor, according to what was perceived to be Balanchine's wish, would eliminate that chance, and put Lincoln in total control.

In an article in *Ballet News* in 1979, four years before Mr. B's death, the newspaper and magazine interviewer Ken Sandler discussed with Balanchine his thoughts on a successor and retirement. He asked Mr. B. about Robbins taking over, and the answer was no. He asked about Peter Martins, and again the answer was a short no. Sandler then asked about Mikhail Baryshnikov, who was then dancing with the company. Balanchine's answer was, "Nice dancer . . . but director? No." Finally, Balanchine said, "You know, I'm not going to retire. I'm going to die." This was so like Balanchine that I actually laughed out loud when I read it. He professed over and over, in live interviews and in print, that he never cared about the future. "*Now* is all there is!" That was his mantra.

A few years before his death, Mr. B. had gone on record as saying, "Après moi, le board!" He meant NYCB's board of directors and was paraphrasing King Louis XV of France's famous quote, "Après moi, le déluge." Balanchine had said that he knew his ballets and company wouldn't be the same after he was gone, and he really didn't care about the future, so it is likely he didn't bother much about the question of succession. Eventually, Suzanne Farrell, Allegra Kent, and Violette Verdy, who all had invaluable ties to the Balanchine style and were still living in NYC, were not really welcome at City Ballet. Farrell and Verdy did teach the company class for a while, but after a few years they were eased out. (A man of Balanchine's era would not be likely to think of a woman as his successor or director. In Balanchine's world the man supported the woman, figuratively and literally.)

Once in 1977, when I was in New York at Balanchine's invitation to "guest" with the company, Balanchine's close personal friend Lucia Davidova, asked me if I would consider rejoining the company full-time. I asked her if Mr. B. had asked her to ask me, a typical Balanchine ploy. She smiled and said yes. I told her that things were still going well in Los Angeles with my own company and that I hoped he wouldn't actually ask me himself. I told her it would be extremely hard for me to say no to Mr. B. and it would put me in a terrible place emotionally to turn him down. By then my company had become my "family" and it would have torn me apart to leave them.

She said Mr. B. missed me and that I should seriously consider returning to New York. Martins had started choreographing by then, but I guess Balanchine wanted me back anyway. Later that night, sitting next to me at a performance of *Diamonds,* Balanchine turned and sang a ditty to the Russian folk tune of the Scherzo movement. He sang, "All roads lead to Rome, Johnny Cleeeford's going home." He put his hand on my shoulder and said, "If you must, but come back when you want." Mme. Davidova had evidently spoken with him.

Peter's decision to exclude me from the City Ballet family actually had very positive repercussions for me professionally and certainly made me a better man and choreographer. Being forced to be totally on my own enabled me to work with many international companies in a way that would have been impossible if I had been with City Ballet full-time. Thanks to Barbara, now the former executive director of The George Balanchine Trust, I was commissioned to stage Balanchine's ballets for virtually every major company in the world. I did nine for the Paris Opera Ballet alone, plus others for the Mariinsky Ballet, Bolshoi Ballet, Royal Ballet, and the major companies at La Scala, Rome, Berlin, Zurich, Budapest, and more.

Working and teaching (something I insist on when staging a Balanchine ballet for a company unfamiliar in his style) has given me a broader understanding of his genius and has always brought me great satisfaction. My own ballets have also been staged on an international scale, which would have been unlikely if I had stayed in New York. What's that saying? "When one door closes another one opens?" That seems to be true. Being on my own enabled me to choreograph and produce my full-length *Casablanca—The Dance,* which was entirely financed by Warner Bros. Theatre Ventures, Inc., to the tune of $4.6 million. I put together a brand-new company to dance this, and we premiered to sold-out audiences and standing ovations in Beijing at the Great Hall of the People.

Even though it took me a while to understand and appreciate some of Balanchine's more esoteric works, the beauty I found was in letting them wash over me without thinking about them too much. It's very Taoist in a way. I was looking for things instead of just experiencing them. His ballets such as *Agon, Movements for Piano and Orchestra, Ivesiana, Episodes,* and even *Concerto Barocco* are best experienced with no expectations. Of course, when they're danced (or taught) wrong, and without understanding their subtexts, they can look dry and sterile. That is a real pity. Balanchine had his own very personal meaning in each of these ballets. I was so lucky that I stuck to him like glue during my years in the company and got to hear little hints when he let them slip out. He didn't want the dancers to over-interpret his thoughts, so he rarely spoke about these things, but every so often he did.

Equally illuminating was watching the way he cast his ballets. For new ones he seemed to get to the soul of the dancers. For putting new people into roles, he was simultaneously stretching their technique and expanding their artistry, while also being keenly aware of how their innate personalities would be right for any particular ballet.

Yes, I missed being part of the New York City Ballet family, and seeing the state of the company in 2011, when I was again living in New York, it is clear that Martins and I had very different views of how to run a company and of what Balanchine's lessons (life and professional) were. But Peter was correct on one thing. We could not have coexisted in the same house; so, as fate would have it, he did me a favor, although I could not see it at that time.

It took me a while to understand why Balanchine had asked me to re-choreograph my first ballet several times and to give me music I wasn't attracted to. It was simply his way of teaching me to be disciplined and distance myself from my ego, as well as from my own work. It also, I believe, enabled me to see his works through a different prism than if I were just one of his dancers—to be more objective, if you will, but also to respect them more and truly understand how important they are. His ballets are life-affirming. That is the greatest compliment I can think of and why I feel it so important that they are preserved properly. They make the world a better place.

As for how I see the Balanchine repertoire now being performed? All one needs to do is to look at the many films and videos made during his lifetime to see the changes. Not just style, but actual choreography, costumes, lighting (crucial to the Balanchine aesthetic), and décor have been changed. In some instances, other companies now actually dance Balanchine better than his own, and according to Arlene Croce, who was the longtime dance critic for *The New Yorker*, so does his school. There is no need for me to list all the changes, but it breaks my heart that today's dancers and audiences are being shortchanged when there's no real need for that to happen.

Maybe someday in the future things will be different for NYCB. But for now, no matter how well or badly the ballets are danced, lit, and costumed, that company still has the largest repository of the greatest ballets ever made. It's an enormous responsibility to do them right.

Balanchine was only half right about one thing, though. He thought his ballets would be forgotten. I disagreed with him. I told him his works would never be forgotten . . . at least not while I'm still here. I will always be "Balanchine's Apprentice."

New York City Ballet: Principal and Soloist Roles Danced by John Clifford

BALLETS BY GEORGE BALANCHINE

1. *The Nutcracker*
   Grand Pas de Deux, Candy Cane (lead), Tea (lead), Toy Soldier, Nutcracker-Prince
2. *A Midsummer Night's Dream*
   Oberon, Puck
3. *Harlequinade*
   Harlequin, Cassandre
4. The *Rubies* section of *Jewels*
   Lead
5. *Stars and Stripes: Ballet in Five Campaigns*
   Fourth Campaign *Pas de Deux*; 3rd Campaign, 3rd Regiment lead
6. *Cortège Hongrois*
   Classical section lead
7. *Agon*
   First *pas de trois,* second *pas de trois*
8. *Variations pour une Porte et un Soupir**
   A *pas de deux*
9. *Glinkiana* (later called *Glinkaiana*)
   "Valse Fantaisie" section lead*
10. *Suite No. 3* (later called *Tschaikovsky Suite No. 3*)
    Third Movement Scherzo lead*
11. *Danses Concertantes* (1972)*
    Lead
12. *Stravinsky Piano Sonata**
    A *pas de deux* (opened the 1972 Stravinsky Festival; only performed once)

13. *Tarantella*
   A *pas de deux*
14. *La Source*
   Lead
15. *Brahms-Schoenberg Quartet*
   Third Movement Andante lead
16. *Symphony in C*
   Third Movement Allegro Vivace lead
17. *Ivesiana*
   "In the Inn" *pas de deux*
18. *Donizetti Variations*
   Lead
19. *Symphony in Three Movements*
   Second Movement *pas de deux*
20. *The Four Temperaments*
   "Melancholic"
21. *Don Quixote*
   Juggler solo, *Pas de Deux* Mauresque
22. *Bugaku*
   Lead
23. *La Sonnambula*
   Pastorale, Blackamoors' Dance
24. The *Emeralds* section of *Jewels*
   Pas de Trois
25. *Movements for Piano and Orchestra*
   Lead
26. *Firebird (I)*
   Kastchei the Wizard

BALLETS BY JEROME ROBBINS

1. *Dances at a Gathering*
   Boy in Brick*, Boy in Brown
2. *The Goldberg Variations**
   Second *pas de trois* (with Gelsey Kirkland and Robert Weiss)
3. *An Evening's Waltzes* (Sergei Prokofiev, Suite of Waltzes, Op. 110,
   1946)*
   Scherzo *pas de deux*

BY JACQUES D'AMBOISE

1. *Tchaikovsky Suite* (later called *Tchaikovsky Suite No. 2*)
   Third Movement lead*, First Movement lead
2. *Irish Fantasy*
   Lead

BY TODD BOLENDER

Piano-Rag-Music

BY JOHN CLIFFORD

1. *Prelude, Fugue, and Riffs**
   Lead
2. *Sarabande and Danse*
   Second *pas de deux**

BY RICHARD TANNER

Stravinsky Concerto for Two Solo Pianos*
Lead

BY JOHN TARAS

Ebony Concerto
Lead

* *Premiere*

John Clifford Stagings of Balanchine Ballets

PARIS OPERA BALLET

1. *Allegro Brillante*
2. *Concerto Barocco*
3. *Capriccio (Rubies)*
4. *Divertimento No. 15*
5. *The Four Temperaments*
6. *Prodigal Son*
7. *Serenade*
8. *Tchaikovsky Pas de Deux*
9. *Theme and Variations*

BOLSHOI BALLET

1. *Agon*
2. *Tarantella*
3. *Tchaikovsky Pas de Deux*

MARIINSKY BALLET

1. *The Four Temperaments*
2. *La Valse*

ROYAL BALLET

Bugaku

SAN FRANCISCO BALLET

1. *Bugaku*
2. *Stars and Stripes*
3. *Who Cares?*

HOUSTON BALLET

Western Symphony

BALLETS DE MONTE-CARLO

1. *Concerto Barocco*
2. *Theme and Variations*
3. *Stravinsky Violin Concerto* (with Karin Von Aroldingen)

DEUTSCHE OPER BALLET (BERLIN)

Who Cares?

ZURICH BALLET

Divertimento No. 15

BALLET COMPANY OF LA SCALA

1. *Apollo*
2. *The Four Temperaments*
3. *Prodigal Son*

HUNGARIAN NATIONAL BALLET

Theme and Variations

BALLET TEATRO DELL'OPERA DI ROMA

1. *Allegro Brillante*
2. *Tchaikovsky Pas de Deux*

BALLET TEATRO DI SAN CARLO (NAPLES, ITALY)

La Valse

BALLET OPÉRA NATIONAL DE BORDEAUX (BORDEAUX, FRANCE)

1. *Apollo*
2. *Serenade*
3. *The Four Temperaments*
4. *Prodigal Son*
5. *Who Cares?*

PENNSYLVANIA BALLET

Rubies

BALLET CHICAGO

1. *Apollo*
2. *Rubies*
3. *Valse Fantaisie*
4. *Concerto Barocco*

UNIVERSAL BALLET (SEOUL, KOREA)

Theme and Variations

NATIONAL BALLET OF KOREA

Allegro Brillante

BALLET TERESA CARREÑO (CARACAS, VENEZUELA)

1. *Apollo*
2. *Concerto Barocco*

MILWAUKEE BALLET

Serenade

SACRAMENTO BALLET

1. *Allegro Brillante*
2. *Apollo*
3. *Concerto Barocco*
4. *The Four Temperaments*
5. *Prodigal Son*
6. *La Sonnambula*
7. *Serenade*
8. *Scotch Symphony*
9. *Stars and Stripes*
10. *Tarantella*
11. *Valse Fantaisie*
12. *Western Symphony*
13. *Who Cares?*

14. *Donizetti Variations*
15. *Tchaikovsky Pas de Deux*
16. *Rubies*
17. *Theme and Variations*

And stagings of *Allegro Brillante—Raymonda Variations, Ivesiana, Square Dance, Swan Lake,* and *Variations pour une Porte et un Soupir* for the Los Angeles Ballet and various schools, companies, and universities.

APPENDIX 3

Ballet Companies That Have Produced Clifford Ballets

Company	Number of Ballets
New York City Ballet	8
The Portland Ballet	7
Les Ballets de Monte-Carlo	4
Ballet of Teatro Colón (Buenos Aires)	4
Ballet du Nord (France)	4
Dallas Ballet	4
Zurich Ballet	2
North Carolina Dance Theater	2
Ballet Teatro dell'Opera di Roma	2
Deutsche Oper Ballet (Berlin)	2
Pacific Northwest Ballet	2
Sacramento Ballet	2
Santa Fe Festival Ballet	2
Atlanta Ballet	1
Miami City Ballet	1
Royal Winnipeg Ballet	1
Ballet British Columbia	1
San Francisco Ballet	1
Oakland Ballet	1
Maggio Danza (Florence, Italy)	1
Ballet Arizona	1

(The Nutcracker)
And over sixty original ballets for the Los Angeles Ballet and Ballet of Los Angeles, including full-length productions of *The Nutcracker, Cinderella, Coppélia, Spartacus, A Midsummer Night's Dream, La Boutique Fantasque,* and *Casablanca—The Dance,* produced in association with and fully financed by Warner Bros. Theatre Ventures, Inc.

ACKNOWLEDGMENTS

When I began this memoir, I made a list of all the people with whom I had worked. To my surprise, it was not only long but was also made up of an intriguing mix of characters. I first taped my memories and then my lovely sister Anne spent hours typing them up. I would also like to thank the aforementioned Dr. Allen, Mrs. Marta Holen, Donna Gulotta, Mindy Aloff, and Alastair Macaulay for their encouragement, advice, and editing. However, these are my words, for better or worse. This is not intended to be a "tell-all," and I hope not to embarrass anyone, but I have been honest.

When I stated that I worked with many people, I was not exaggerating. My list includes, in more or less chronological order, Kathryn Etienne (born Charisse, aunt by marriage to Cyd Charisse), Tony Charmoli, Dinah Shore, Morgan Brittany (whose original name was Suzanne Cupito, and who was my first dancing partner), Donna Reed, David Lichine, Tatiana Riabouchinska, Maria Bekefi, Maria Tallchief, Nicholas Magallanes, Carmelita Maracci, Eugene Loring, George Zorich, Irina Kosmovska, Danny Kaye, Gwen Verdon, June Morris, Anton Dolin, Maya Plisetskaya, Asaf Messerer, Hermes Pan, Carol Channing, Tamara Toumanova, Olga Spessivtseva, Alexandra Danilova and Lincoln Kirstein (both of whom told me many fascinating stories of Balanchine's youth in Russia, his early days with Diaghilev's Ballets Russes, and the formation of the NYCB and School of American Ballet), Stanley Williams, André Eglevsky, Pierre Vladimiroff, Muriel Stuart, Antonina Tumkovsky, Diana Adams, Francisco Moncion, Jerome Robbins, Todd Bolender, John Taras, Jacques d'Amboise, Joanne Woodward, Peter Martins, Eva Evdokimova, Suzanne Farrell, Ib Andersen, Conrad Ludlow, Edward Villella, George Skibine, Mikhail Baryshnikov, André Kostelanetz, Alicia Alonso, Frederic Franklin, Peter Martins, Leonard Bernstein, Darci Kistler, Damian Woetzel,

Rudolph Nureyev, and some modern pop personalities such as Freddie Mercury, George Benson, David Bowie, and the rock group Chicago.

I have also been blessed to have partnered some of the major ballerinas of our time, including Allegra Kent, Violette Verdy, Melissa Hayden, Gelsey Kirkland, Patricia McBride, Sara Leland, Kay Mazzo, and Mimi Paul. Their influences on me were extremely important, and I can't stress enough the value to my professional and my personal lives the many lessons I learned from these ladies. I thank them all.

The major influence in my life, both professionally and personally, and the person who appears and reappears throughout the book, is George Balanchine. The longer I live and the more experiences I have in the worlds of dance and life have only deepened my awe and respect for his genius and ethics. To me he is still very much alive.

INDEX

Varèse, Edgard, 242
Variations for Four, 35–36
Variations on Von Himmel Hoch, 223
Variations pour une Porte et un Soupir,
    180, 249, 252, 255, 287, 294
Vasiliev, Vladimir, 34, 228
Verdon, Gwen, 21–22, 47, 297
Verdy, Violette, 11, 32, 50–51, 54, 56, 70,
    73, 83, 110, 126, 128–29, 134, 159, 164,
    171, 174, 222, 224, 229, 237, 242, 254,
    273, 280, 282, 298
Vienna Waltzes, 180
Villella, Edward, 45, 50, 52, 83, 94–96,
    127–30, 133–34, 140–41, 144–45, 166,
    214, 221–22, 225, 229, 237, 244, 254–55,
    257, 297
Vladimiroff, Pierre, 41, 44, 80, 297
Vollmar, Jocelyn, 196

Waite, Ned, Jr., 259
Wall, David, 37
Warner Bros. Theatre Ventures, Inc.,
    283, 295
Warsaw Opera, 27
Wechsler, Gil, 196
Weiss, Robert "Ricky," 25, 62, 90, 112,
    185, 214, 230, 255, 288
Wells, Doreen, 37

Wenta, Stefan, 27–28
Weslow, William "Billy," 50
Western Ballet, 27–29, 36, 43, 59, 241
Western Ballet Association, 27, 43, 241
Western Symphony, 56, 64, 83, 167,
    292–93
West Side Story, 14, 27, 49, 101
Wheeldon, Christopher, 210
Who Cares?, 55, 93, 168, 291–93
Williams, Ralph Vaughan, 116–17
Williams, Stanley, 41, 44–45, 60, 119,
    147, 160, 264, 297
Wizard of Oz, The, 97
Woetzel, Damian, 273–74, 297
Wolf Trap Performing Arts Center, 147
Woodward, Joanne, 259–60, 297

Xenakis, Iannis, 98

Young Apollo, 274
Yourth, Lynda, 214, 218, 229

Zall, Deborah, 16, 176
Zaraspe, Hector, 24, 86
Zoloty, Madame, 67
Zorina, Vera, 19
Zurich Ballet, 273, 292, 295

John Clifford was a principal dancer and choreographer with Balanchine and the New York City Ballet from 1966 to 1974, and later, until 1980 as a guest artist. He choreographed eight ballets for NYCB and seven for SAB.

As the artistic director of the original Los Angeles Ballet (creating over fifty ballets), the ballet master/repetiteur for The George Balanchine Trust, and now founder of the Los Angeles Dance Theater, for which he created *Casablanca—The Dance,* Clifford is in a unique position to shed light on the creative aspects of George Balanchine and the last golden years of the New York City Ballet.